RONALDINHO

RONALDINHO
FOOTBALL'S FLAMBOYANT MAESTRO

JETHRO SOUTAR

**ROBSON
BOOKS**

First published in Great Britain in 2006 by
Robson Books
151 Freston Road
London
W10 6TH

An imprint of Anova Books Company Ltd

ISBN 1 86105 978 7

10 9 8 7 6 5 4 3 2 1

Typeset by SX Composing DTP, Rayleigh, Essex
Printed and bound by MPG Books Ltd, Bodmin, Cornwall

Front cover photography courtesy of Corbis Images
Plate Section photography courtesy of Corbis Images, Agencia RBS,
Pete Wilde, Offside Agency and the author's private collection.

This book can be ordered direct from the publisher
Contact the marketing department, but try your bookshop first

www.anovabooks.com

Particular appreciation goes to all those who agreed to be interviewed; thanks to the press officers at Grêmio, Internacional, Botafogo, Fortaleza, Santos and São Paulo; thanks to Ema Coelho de Souza and her team at the Grêmio memorial archive; those at the Porto Alegre city museum; to Flavio in Porto Alegre; to Jorge and all at the Periquito who made me so welcome; to Zé Pereira and the regulars at his local; to all at Radio Eldorado, Criciuma; to Jordi Gil of Sport; to Oriol Domènech at El Mundo Deportivo; to John Watson at the Scottish Schools FA; to Maggie Lett for her tireless subediting and feedback and Geoff Rowe as our go-between; to Dan Wilde for his photography; for general help, Roger Matas, Paco and Jesús Muñoz, Cori Comajuncosas, Joe Mather and Dan Woolstone; to Ian and Quentin for assistance and advice; to the various friends and family – including Kathy & Alex, Richard & Lucy, Dani & Carla, Ben & Yoko - who put me up while I was writing; to Josie & Kriss for chapter reading and 'Where-are-they-now?' research; special thanks to Elisabeth Weise and Víctor Guerrero for their encouragement and suggestions.

CONTENTS

WINNING IT ALL

In early 2006, Ronaldinho was asked what he would do once he had won everything. He contemplated the question for a few seconds before replying: 'Win it all again.'

Just a few months later, Barcelona having been crowned champions of Europe, he found himself in just such a position: he may only have been 26 years old but he had won every top prize there was to win in the world of football. He was both the two-time World Footballer of the Year and reigning European Footballer of the Year; he had won back-to-back Spanish League titles and led Barcelona to the Champions League, the highest of club conquests; he had helped Brazil win the World Cup in 2002 and was preparing to repeat the trick in Germany later that year.

The 2006 World Cup didn't go to plan for Ronaldinho. In fact, it was disastrous. There were several reasons why, but the whole episode served as a timely reminder that he was only human, that everything he touched didn't automatically turn to gold. His record of achievements may read like one non-stop success story, but there have been plenty of ups and downs along the way.

As is evident to anyone who watches him play, he is a very gifted footballer, one naturally blessed with a skill of touch and vision to which very few players, past or present, bear comparison. Yet equally important is the strength of will that burns inside him. He may be famous for his bright smile and cheery disposition but there is a steely determination lurking inside him, without which he would not have reached the heights he has.

He was born into a family of humble means and grew up in a poor neighbourhood in southern Brazil. His childhood was happy but traumatic too. From a very young age, football was presented as the easiest means for him to make his way up in the world and few people have ever been groomed to become a star player to quite the degree Ronaldinho was.

These days he *is* that star player, arguably the starriest player in the world. *France Football* placed him top in their annual earnings table of 2006; *Forbes* ranked him as the highest Brazilian in its 'Top 100 Celebrities' list, citing as justification the fact that twelve million people had visited the Nike website just to see an advert featuring Ronaldinho.

His football ability has led him to be compared to Pelé, widely considered untouchable as the greatest of them all. Ronaldinho's style of play is a dazzling combination of flair and efficiency: pragmatic enough to be always effective and yet flamboyant in the extreme. He has invented tricks such as the 'no-look pass', when his eyes gaze one way as his feet steer the ball the other. Yet such tricks are not merely for show. They do help him gain the psychological upper hand but more often than not they serve a more practical purpose in aiding him or his team towards scoring a goal, towards winning a match. Ronaldinho plays at the highest level of a game that gets ever more tactical, indeed ever more negative and defensive in some quarters. His capacity to surprise and to improvise becomes accordingly more important and decisive in tipping the balance in his side's favour. In this sense, Ronaldinho is a maestro leading his team and he is frequently the difference in an evenly matched contest.

His popularity is based on his incredible football ability but his personality is equally important. In an age where greed rules in so many walks of life, not just football, it is hugely refreshing to see an athlete perform with a smile on his face and transmit a rare sense of humility. In playing football for a great team, Ronaldinho is living the dream of every fan and, unlike many other players, he seems to appreciate this. He plays with a sense of fun and continues to enjoy himself, conscious that he is fortunate in his lifestyle. Supporters are thus able to better identify with him.

However, his character is complex and not just in terms of the grit that hides behind the grin. How is it that he has flourished so much in some teams and flopped in others? Where did Barcelona go right, Paris Saint-Germain go wrong? Why did he thrive at the 2002 World Cup for Brazil but fail so badly in 2006?

He has an almost childlike need for attention on the football pitch yet is fiercely protective of his private life and shies away from the media glare. His image is all about imagination and instinct, yet nobody reaches his position, especially not in commercial terms, without a certain amount of calculation and know-how. Just like the country he hails from, he is a bundle of contradictions.

In Catalonia, they seem to instinctively know how to get the best out of Ronaldinho. He relies upon certain conditions in order to play at his best and Barcelona are prepared to create the environment he requires.

They think he is worth it. Brazil is a different matter and part of the problem at the 2006 World Cup was that Ronaldinho didn't feel as if he was the main man.

He may act footloose and fancy-free but he also revels in the role of responsibility. Perhaps his most remarkable achievement for Barcelona has been not the trophies he has won but rather the manner in which he has transformed the whole mental health of a club that was in a crisis of low esteem when he arrived.

While Brazil went to the 2006 World Cup as overwhelming favourites yet underperformed massively, Barcelona were a club going nowhere fast when Ronaldinho entered the scene and yet he helped to turn them into the best side in Europe in under three years. Two different teams making completely contrasting journeys and yet Ronaldinho was the key figure in both. Only by understanding how he came to be in each of them and what baggage he brought with him is it possible to understand quite why.

Ronaldinho's career reached a crossroads after the 2006 World Cup. Did he have the desire to prove himself once more or would he rest on his laurels? Would he 'win it all again' as he claimed? By looking at his life and achievements thus far and by analysing what makes him tick, we can begin to answer those questions.

BIG BROTHER

'Yes, he is good, but it is the young one at home who is going to be the best in the world.'

Speak to those who knew Ronaldinho as a young boy and they will recall the prophetic words of his father, João de Assis Moreira, when Ronaldinho was no older than seven. They were directed towards anyone heard lavishing praise on his eldest son, Ronaldinho's brother Assis, then a rising football star himself, and have taken on mythical proportions not just because of their accuracy but also because João died not long after, denied the chance to see just how right he would prove to be.

Many people claim to have heard the famous words – friends, family, coaches, colleagues – and who's to say they didn't: Ronaldinho's dad was fond of saying the same thing to anyone who'd listen.

Ronaldinho was given a football by his father for his first birthday and would rarely be seen without one for the rest of his childhood. João was a fanatical football fan: he was an amateur player and avid follower of top local side Grêmio, where he enrolled both his sons in the club's youth schemes. In effect, Ronaldinho grew up at the club; he joined Grêmio when he was seven and wouldn't leave until he was in his twenties. He barely knew a life without playing and training at a professional football club. That he would become a player seemed always to be his destiny.

However, in Ronaldinho's case it wasn't a matter of having the talent to realise every other Brazilian boy's dream – to become a footballer. Ronaldinho was motivated by different forces: he worked hard at developing his natural ability simply because he wanted to be like his big brother.

The early story of Ronaldinho is really the story of that big brother, Roberto de Assis Moreira.

Born 10 January 1971 in Porto Alegre, Roberto was the first of what would be João's and his wife Dona Miguelina's three children (sister Deise would arrive four years later, Ronaldinho another five after her) and joined Grêmio's youth set-up when he was eleven. He was soon the brightest promise coming through the junior ranks and became known to all as Assis. A left-footed dribbler, his playing style was compared respectfully with Maradona's.

In November 1987, Assis was playing for Grêmio Juniors in the inter-state championship final at the Estádio Olímpico, Grêmio's home stadium. He put in an inspired performance and led his team to victory and the title.

In Brazil, it is common for a junior match to precede a first-eleven fixture as a form of pre-match entertainment, though the damage done to the pitch immediately before the professionals play makes it one of many questionable quirks of the Brazilian game. This particular match was part of the build-up to Grêmio's encounter with traditional rivals Corinthians, of São Paulo. The main event being a high-profile contest, the stadium was already half full as the juniors slugged it out, so there were many fans present to witness the dazzling display from Assis.

Among the early arrivals were two scouts from Italian giants Torino; the career of popular Brazilian legend Júnior was coming to an end at Torino and they had been sent out to Brazil to look for a likely successor. They had come to cast an eye over Brazilian international Valdo, star of the Grêmio midfield (who would instead sign for Benfica at the end of the season and go on to play for Paris Saint-Germain). However, when the Italians filed their reports they were with glowing reviews for one man in particular: the young Assis. There then followed what is known in Porto Alegre as 'the Assis kidnap'.

Assis was just sixteen years old. In playing for the juniors he had actually been performing in the age group above his own; he had also led the youth team, his year group, to the state championship the week before. He had yet to sign a professional contract for Grêmio and, five days after his winning display for the juniors, he was whisked on to a plane by the Italians bound for Europe. Before he really knew what was going on, he was undergoing a two-week trial in Turin.

Grêmio were outraged at the Italians' behaviour. They demanded his return and set about preparing the most attractive contract they could muster for the young star.

Torino eventually offered Assis a deal worth around £26,000 per year, which roughly translated as 3.5 million Brazilian cruzados, the local currency at the time. (Due to rampant inflation, the currency frequently changed name: cruzados would become cruzeiros in 1990 before transforming into the real (reais in plural, or BR$), their current incarnation, in 1993. This also means that BR$ currency convertions in particular should be taken as aproximations.)

Grêmio countered with an offer that featured an annual wage of just under 1 million cruzados but threw in a house worth 4.6 million cruzados and further perks totalling a further 1.4 million. The package was worth 580,000 cruzados per month, just shy of the 600,000 that main man Valdo earned. Assis chose to sign with Grêmio and moved with his parents, brother and sister to the new home he had helped choose in Guarujá, an up-and-coming neighbourhood on the banks of Lake Guaíba.

The family had previously lived in the modest area of Vila Nova. They had been happy there, surrounded by relatives and friends: the relocation to a more prosperous part of town would have had a huge effect upon all of them, especially the young Ronaldinho. The transition from the poor working-class wooden bungalows of Vila Nova to the bricked two-storey detached houses of middle-class Guarujá must have been quite a leap for a seven-year-old.

It would also have shown the young Ronaldinho a very clear and practical example of just what could be achieved through playing football.

However, this moving up in the world had awful consequences. A year later, the family was preparing a joint celebration to honour João's and Dona Miguelina's wedding anniversary. Assis had been away with the Brazil squad in Rio, preparing for the upcoming Under-20 World Cup in Saudi Arabia, but had been sent home to rest after having his appendix removed. His unexpected return meant the family could celebrate his recent eighteenth birthday at the same time (he was born a year to the day of his parents tying the knot).

What was to be a happy family occasion turned to tragedy before it had even begun; João was found unconscious in the swimming pool and would lose his fight for life a few days later. Ronaldinho was two months shy of turning nine. There seemed a cruel irony in the fact that the swimming pool, the very symbol of their new-found riches, was central to the disaster. The family would have it filled in soon afterwards.

When documenting these events, it is generally considered good form to say that João had a heart attack that caused him either to fall and fatally bang his head or to drown in the water while swimming. Yet many people in Porto Alegre believe drink played its part. They say that João had something of a reputation for boozing, had perhaps got celebrations under way early and already had a few by the time he took his tumble. Officially, he suffered a cardiac arrest before drowning but it remains unclear if, and by how much, alcohol contributed to the accident. He died in hospital after spending several days in a coma, just 41 years of age.

The tragedy devastated the family but at the same time drew them closer, made them stronger.

Assis had been acquiring something of a reputation for leading a bit of a playboy lifestyle. It was threatening to become the all-too-familiar story of the successful young footballer who fails to deal with the sudden attention and riches thrust upon him, but Assis was suddenly forced to mature very quickly. He resolved to take on the responsibility not only of head of the family and principal breadwinner but also to replace João as the father-figure in Ronaldinho's life.

Ronaldinho had always loved his big brother with that sense of admiration commonly felt by younger family members towards an elder sibling or cousin when the age gap is significant. Assis had nine years on Ronaldinho and his little brother looked up to him in all he did. Ronaldinho used to go with João to watch every match Assis played (as long as it wasn't too far out of the city) and the will to emulate him was strong.

Assis knew the influence he could have on his young brother and he began to make sure the example he set was a good one, that the fraternal respect and sense of hero worship could be channelled to inspire Ronaldinho. The challenge for Assis was to juggle these new commitments while trying to make a success of his own career.

He had been progressing well, helping Grêmio to the senior state title in 1988, 1989 and again in 1990, the year following his father's death. He had scored the first goal in a 2–1 win in the Brazilian Cup final of 1989, too, but a serious injury in 1991 kept him sidelined for eight months and the rhythm of his progress was altered forever. By 1992, he should have been playing alongside Cafu and Roberto Carlos as part of Brazil's Under-23 Olympic qualifiers team (which failed to make it to Barcelona), on the brink of full international recognition and being courted by the likes of Torino once more. But he had failed to convince observers that his injury hadn't affected his ability and potential.

Assis did still manage to negotiate himself the coveted transfer abroad that would secure the family's short-term financial future when he signed for Sion of Switzerland.

While he made a success of his time there, winning the Swiss Cup in 1995 and 1997, in terms of his footballing profile he had dropped off the map. Nobody followed the Swiss league with great interest in Brazil, nor rated achievements there too highly. Assis has since claimed that he could have become as good as his brother eventually did, but that he took a wrong turn with his move to Switzerland.

Be that as it may, his move to Switzerland did bring other benefits. Financially it was good business for Assis, his family and Grêmio. It can be viewed as the first of a number of sacrifices in which the welfare of the family took precedence over his own career development.

From abroad, Assis very much remained Ronaldinho's mentor and guardian and would advise him when negotiating new contracts (a role he still performs today as Ronaldinho's agent).

As for their mother, Dona Miguelina had her own way of coping after the death of her husband. She determined that, through sheer strength of character, she would fill the role of both parents for her children, particularly for her youngest, Ronaldinho. She was also more determined than ever to make the most of Ronaldinho's potential. João's demise had shown them all how quickly life could change, how an idyllic family situation could be wrecked in a matter of moments. Their opportunity in life had come in the form of the footballing ability of her two sons: the achievements of the eldest had enabled them to make the leap into a grand new home with a lifestyle way beyond their expectations. But fate had dealt them a cruel blow and events were conspiring to ensure that neither Assis nor the family were benefiting as they might have done from his natural gift.

Assis was doing well enough but, for somebody likened to Maradona in his early days, he wasn't quite fulfilling his potential. Dona Miguelina would make sure the family didn't miss out again on the opportunity presented by the ability of Ronaldinho.

It was almost as if Assis had allowed them the luxury of a dummy run. They could all learn from his mistakes and make sure that Ronaldinho was offered the perfect conditions in which to maximise his (and therefore the family's) potential. Ronaldinho would be the real deal.

This thinking manifested itself in many ways. Ronaldinho never had to worry about anything: he never had to put his clothes in the wash, tidy his room, help prepare or clear up after a meal; all such chores were done for him. In short, he was spoiled.

Dona Miguelina allowed him his personal freedom but she was strict too. He had to report back regularly and let her know where he was, who with, for how long. In one famous episode, after winning his first major trophy with Grêmio as a nineteen-year-old, Ronaldinho's phone call to his mum to tell her not to expect him home for dinner that night 'as it was all a bit crazy with the celebrations' was broadcast live on Rádio Gaúcho. 'OK, son, but be sure to ring me when you are leaving,' was Dona Miguelina's reply, followed by a resigned, 'All right, Mum,' typical of any teenager anywhere despairing at his overprotective mother.

Dona Miguelina also discouraged serious girlfriends, telling Ronaldinho there would be plenty of time for that later in life. Assis had got involved with a local girl, Carla, whom he eventually married. Dona Miguelina was aware that a love affair (or unexpected child) would make it more difficult for Ronaldinho to up sticks and seek his footballing fortune elsewhere, possibly halting his progress, and she took care to ensure that no relationships developed too far.

All these measures were designed to ensure that Ronaldinho had no concerns other than his football – and they remain in place today. Assis is still Ronaldinho's agent while his sister, Deise, has been his PA since 1999. Between them they take care to organise contracts and co-ordinate all off-field responsibilities for their brother, leaving Ronaldinho to focus entirely on what he does best and what the family empire is founded on – playing football.

The clan is often united in Ronaldinho's villa outside Barcelona, where Deise and Ronaldinho live alongside Valdimar Garcia, their cousin and Ronaldinho's personal trainer. Dona Miguelina has remained resident in Porto Alegre since Ronaldinho moved abroad, but is such a regular and long-term guest of his that she spends as much time in Catalonia as she does in Brazil.

Similarly Assis, as Ronaldinho's agent, is back and forth between Barcelona and Porto Alegre where he lives with his wife (he and Carla are still together), their young son Diego and baby Roberta. Diego is already enrolled at Grêmio and is said to show promise: the family legacy may have yet another generation to run.

Assis has kept the home he was given by Grêmio, 215 Rua Murá, Guarujá, and converted it into office space, from where he manages his various business interests: as well as his work as an agent (he represents several players alongside Ronaldinho) he runs his own football club, Porto Alegre Futebol Clube, which competes in the second division of the state championship and has links with Greek team Aris. Their cousin Bárbara helps run the office.

Back in Porto Alegre, the family now owns a huge purpose-built property on Avenida de Cavalhada in Ipanema, a wealthy area of the city right next to Guarujá. In truth, theirs is more of a road than a simple property: they have had several adjoining houses built along a cul-de-sac behind an imposing and heavily patrolled security entrance. Alongside the homes, which cater for Ronaldinho, Assis, Deise and Dona Miguelina, are two swimming pools (one heated and complete with flume), two mini-football pitches, a foot-volley court, two tennis courts and an underground party room designed in the shape of a football.

Whenever Ronaldinho is asked to name the most important thing in his life, he always gives the same answer: his family.

Whenever pressed to name his heroes and inspirations, his brother is cited with the same conviction. Assis was a young football star himself and could (and possibly should) have gone on to reach greater heights. But he lacked the necessary guidance, especially after the death of João, and he would then largely forfeit his own career to ensure that Ronaldinho didn't suffer a similar fate.

Assis himself remains loyally at Ronaldinho's side, often doing the dirty work, cutting the deals, even playing the role of villain while Ronaldinho gets on with playing football and turning on the charm as the consummate sports and commercial superstar.

Many people who have witnessed Ronaldinho's level-headed rise are also quick to credit the kind yet strong and determined mother behind his success. Dona Miguelina provided Ronaldinho with all the parental support anyone could ask for and thrilled to his success, keeping scrapbooks, making tapes. No one can deny that she always had her children's best interests at heart, but the personal drive and ambition of one remarkable woman should not be underestimated in the overall evaluation of Ronaldinho's achievements. As a single mother, she returned to school as a mature student to complete her primary and secondary education and then trained as a nurse.

In May 1999 *Sports News* of Porto Alegre dedicated a double-page spread to high-profile athletes from the region and their mothers for a Mother's Day special (it being celebrated on a different date in Brazil to Britain). Participants included club colleagues of Ronaldinho's such as Rafael Scheidt as well as Dunga and Christian from cross-city rivals Internacional. Messages from the boys typically read: 'A big kiss from the son who loves you.' The mothers' standard reply was: 'He is a good boy, success hasn't changed him and he deserves to be where he is today.'

Ronaldinho's message read: 'I love her, a mother for whom words don't do justice. She has always been with me in the good and bad times.' Then Dona Miguelina's dedication caught the eye for its unique angle: 'It is great being the mother of someone famous. We feel important and it is very gratifying.'

And finally there is João. The death of his father was to have a huge impact on Ronaldinho's life, tightening the family bonds that supported him. Yet his father also influenced Ronaldinho more directly. He showed his boys a hard-working ethic, grafting in the city's shipyards until an injury at work forced him into early retirement (Grêmio then gave him a job as a car-park attendant when Assis signed his professional contract). Those who knew him describe him as a strict and serious man and believe that the steely resolve which lurks behind Ronaldinho's grin is a trait clearly passed from father to son. Ronaldinho told the *Observer* newspaper that his dad used to make him play with only two touches. 'This took all the fun out of it for me and, at that age, made me very angry. I cried. I didn't understand. But now I understand what he wanted.'

Ronaldinho has often spoken of a determination to honour his father's memory and realise João's dreams.

'Yes, he is good, but it is the young one at home who is going to be the best in the world.'

If not quite a self-fulfilling prophecy, the desire to make those predictions of future greatness come true certainly had an important motivational role in Ronaldinho's success story.

FUTSAL

From the age of seven Ronaldinho was enrolled in the Grêmio soccer school where the emphasis was on *futebol do campo*, meaning field football, eleven-a-side.

But Ronaldinho was young and full of energy and just couldn't play enough football: away from Grêmio he joined as many teams as possible. In the summer, when not turning heads with his foot-volley skills, this meant turning out for beach team New Kids (named after the 80s boy band New Kids on the Block), based in Capão Novo, a seaside town up the coast where his family had a holiday home. While in Porto Alegre, it usually involved a game of *futebol salão*, or *futsal* for short.

Futsal is a popular form of football in Brazil that involves two teams of five playing for twenty minutes each way on a small pitch with the dimensions of a basketball court and handball-sized goals. Unlike the five-a-side football popular in Britain, there are no walls off which to bounce the ball, while the ball itself is smaller than a regular one and weighted to encourage play along the ground. The cramped pitch means that players have to develop very quick feet and learn to protect the ball. Meanwhile, the rhythm is more akin to basketball and teaches players how to rapidly change tempo: from a slow and patient build-up to a lighting-fast execution. National-team legends Rivelino and Zico are products of *futsal* and Ronaldinho himself has claimed that it taught him how to dribble in tight spaces. These days, his use of the toe-poke is perhaps the most obvious example of adapting a *futsal* skill.

There are many subscribers to the theory that the popularity of *futsal* among the young in Brazil is a major factor behind the country's predominance in football generally. The skills nurtured on the small pitch ensure that most players are extremely accomplished technically by the time they enter the bigger arena.

Ronaldinho first played *futsal* at his local infant school in Guarujá: Escola Langendonck. Ponciano Erli da Silveira, an accountant, lived four doors down from Ronaldinho with his son, Gilson, who played in the same school team. Ponciano would regularly go along to watch their matches and, in a scene replicated on school pitches the world over, used to offer his advice. 'The team was fourth in the league but should have been top. The coach, the PE teacher, didn't know what he was doing and had the team arranged all wrong. I let him know as much,' recounts Ponciano all these years later through spurts of laughter. 'We had a row right there on the pitch and he said that if I thought I knew so much and could do better then why didn't I take over. And so I did.' Thus began an involvement that was to last throughout Gilson's and Ronaldinho's time at the school.

Langendonck went on to win the city championship, the Campeonato Intercolegial, in 1993. Ronaldinho played an attacking midfield role: 'He was much skinnier then than he is now,' explains Ponciano.

Ponciano, or Erli as he was more popularly known to the boys, also looked after Ronaldinho's street side, the Rua Murá team. Zé Pereira, a community leader with a voice on the city council, organised regular tournaments in neighbouring Esplanada which took the form of either *futsal* or *futebol-sete*, a seven-a-side game, and teams comprised residents of different streets. 'We would usually win,' recalls Ponciano. 'We were a much more athletic road!'

As well as Ronaldinho, Ponciano's son Gilson would go on to play professionally; after being on Internacional's books as a junior he eventually represented several teams in the state interior. Ponciano also cites Deise, Ronaldinho's sister, as an example of the street's sporting prowess; he used to coach her at volleyball.

Before Barcelona, before Paris Saint-Germain even, the first European team Ronaldinho represented was Italian. In another local district tournament the Rua Murá team, which was basically the Langendonck school team, competed under the name of Ascoli: all the boys teams were given Serie A club names, while the juniors were named after Spanish sides. There were also *futsal* tournaments down by the riverfront, at the end of Rua Murá. The pitches which exist there now are made of either sand or shale but there were grass ones back in Ronaldinho's day and Ponciano would take care of friendly knockout competitions called the *Campeonatos Gaiolas*, or Cage Championships, named so because of the boards and netting that enclosed the pitches.

A schoolfriend of Ronaldinho's once told reporters that he remembered a match in which Ronaldinho scored all the goals in a 23–0 victory. 'It's very possible,' admits Ponciano. 'I no longer recall all his extraordinary feats;

there were so many of them that you began to grow accustomed.' And did Ronaldinho sulk when he lost? 'Oh, we hardly ever lost.'

Aside from Grêmio, the first club side Ronaldinho joined was called Procergs, a boys team run by several football-loving fathers including a lawyer named Ronaldo Eli, who also lived on Ronaldinho's street in Guarujá. When he was looking for a sponsor for the team, in stepped Asprocergs, the Association of Workers of Procergs, the state data-processing agency for whom one of the other parents worked.

Eli remembers being called to the local pitch by his son, Tales, to watch the amazing skills of a new boy in the neighbourhood. It turned out to be Ronaldinho, not long moved into the new house. Tales had been right; Ronaldinho was already something very special.

Another Procergs coach, Cleon Espinoza, tells a similar story; his own son talked about Ronaldinho so much that Espinoza eventually went to one of Grêmio's training sessions to see what the fuss was about.

Ronaldinho was soon incorporated into what became an unbeatable team. He would win some games single-handedly but the side also starred Claiton, who would become a long-term friend and go on to play for Internacional. Ronaldinho would later line up against him in the Porto Alegre derby. Up front, Procergs could count upon Thiaguinho finding the net. He went on to play *futsal* professionally in Spain (or *futbol sala* as it is called there) for Marfil Santa Coloma.

It is doubtful that any of them had the slightest notion of the goings-on at the data-processing office, but they helped form an awesome side. Procergs were crowned state champions in 1990 with Ronaldinho scoring a great goal in a 4–2 victory in the final against Caixeral de Pelotas in the Ibiruba gymnasium to finish as top scorer and player of the tournament. They were his first trophies – though it was obvious to anyone watching him that they would not be his last.

That match (as well as the company's name and the white kit and sky-blue tracksuit their sponsorship brought) was immortalised in 2006 when Nike released an advert mixing contemporary action with archive footage of Ronaldinho scoring for Procergs.

As with other tapes of the era, the Nike clips show Ronaldinho to already possess the ball skills, speed of movement and improvisation we associate with him now.

In an interview with *The Times*, Espinoza talked of one of Procergs' simplest yet most effective tactics: called the 'L' move, it consisted of Ronaldinho's three outfield team-mates lining up on one side of the pitch while Ronaldinho himself stood deep on the other side, producing the L shape. As most teams played a man-to-man marking system, this would isolate Ronaldinho and his opponent: Ronaldinho could usually beat anybody one-on-one and so would score a few goals until the man-to-man system had to be abandoned by their rivals. Of course, this only resulted in a more open game and more space for Ronaldinho and his colleagues to exploit.

Another of the fathers, Augusto Badeira de Mello, a cardiologist, was involved in running both Procergs and the New Kids. He told *Jornal do Brasil* about a road trip that stuck in the mind: 'My sons were sharing a room with him and late at night I could tell they were still up. I went over to the door and I could see the light was still on and I could also hear them talking: "360, 361 . . ." When I went in, I saw my two boys sitting down watching Ronaldinho, who was lying on the bed doing kick-ups. I told them off (it was late) but I left the room laughing to myself.'

While many of his early coaches reveal that Ronaldinho was lazy when it came to practising with his left foot or head, they all agree that kick-ups were another thing entirely. Augusto again: 'Once, one boy managed to do five kick-ups on his shin and Ronaldinho couldn't match him. The next time we got together, Ronaldinho had mastered it: he only stopped doing them because we told him to.'

Ronaldinho played for *futsal* teams all across the city, accepting invitations from friends to join them in various tournaments. He regularly accompanied his Grêmio buddy Tinga and turned out for Monte Castelo, a club side in Restinga, a poor neighbourhood on the edge of Porto Alegre.

Dona Miguelina was often not privy to his participation in so many matches. When asked by local newspaper *Olá Botanico* if he was familiar with the Jardim Botanico district, he replied: 'Yes, I played the Copa Paqueta in the Parque Ararigboia when I was thirteen or fourteen. Though don't tell my mum, as she never knew.'

His mother wasn't the only one trying to restrict Ronaldinho's participation: Grêmio became alarmed about him playing too much football outside their supervision and worried about him picking up an injury. Eventually, they forbade him from playing for anyone but Grêmio, though it is said that he sneaked back to don the Procergs shirt a few times more.

FAMILY TREE

As a young boy, Ronaldinho used to dribble around any obstacle that lay in his path in the family home, be it the furniture, his dog, even his mum. His father would hang plastic bags full of water from the corner beams of the house and offer to buy Ronaldinho a lollypop for each one he could hit with a free-kick.

Home was the pink wooden bungalow at 73, Rua Jerólomo Minuzzo, which the family owned in Vila Nova before football began to move them up the social ladder. Born via caesarean in the nearby São Lucas University Hospital (3.20 a.m., 21 March 1980), Ronaldinho would spend the first seven years of his life there.

His Auntie Carmen, Dona Miguelina's sister, still lives in Vila Nova and remembers Ronaldinho's early years fondly. 'He was a good boy, thanks be to God. I don't recall him ever causing any trouble or crying; he was always such a happy child. He was a normal kid and liked to play games with his cousins and friends but he did usually play with his ball.'

Carmen is three years younger than Dona Miguelina while Dona Elurdes is an older sibling who now lives in Restinga: 'Ronaldinho was a good boy, a happy child and a bright one,' she says. 'As I recall, he was walking before he was one. He liked to play with his ball a lot but he also did other things; I remember he was very fond of watching television. Whatever he was doing, he always wanted company, always wanted to be around people.'

Miguelina Elói Assis dos Santos was born in 1949, one of thirteen siblings, eleven of them sisters. They were from Santa Cruz do Sul, a small town some 150km into the interior of Rio Grande do Sul state from its capital, Porto Alegre. Seasonal work in the tobacco factories provided just three months' annual employment at best and so the family, led by their father, Ervino Assis, decided to up sticks and follow in the footsteps of relatives who had already migrated to Porto Alegre, the big city full of hope.

They settled in the Cristal area and times were very tough; putting food on the table was a daily struggle. The clan was eventually on the move again, this time no further than Vila Nova on the outskirts of Porto Alegre, a spacious and green area, though still poor and working class. They bought a plot of land on Rua Jerólomo Minuzzo, number 193, built a house and much of the family have remained there ever since (five of the siblings still live in the district). The original site of the house remains in the family, now owned by a cousin, though the building itself has changed.

In 1970, Dona Miguelina married João, a boy two years her elder and one of five siblings himself, and they moved into a house further down the same road from her parents' home in Vila Nova (again, the original building no longer exists).

The houses may have been humble and made of wood but João was a hard worker, a welder in the shipyards, and determined to provide for his wife and children. Dona Miguelina also worked, intermittently as an Avon lady, a cook and a cleaner. By the time Ronaldinho came along, the family wanted for nothing.

The extended clan would regularly convene at Ervino's house for a party or weekend barbecue. At one such social gathering in 1976, the men decided to organise a football team. They subsequently began to play every month and the tradition grew until, twenty years later, they had thirty players, all family members, and were playing every week.

At the turn of the millennium, they decided to register as a proper club and, when deciding upon a name, chose to honour the man whose home had always welcomed them and where the team had first come together: Ervino Assis. The club's full name is Sociedade Esportiva Recreativo Cultural Ervino Assis (Ervino Assis Society of Sport Recreation and Culture) but goes by the moniker 'Sérvia'. The badge, in homage to family roots, is a tree.

Every Saturday, Sérvia play two games on the Periquito, Vila Nova's dusty pitch and the first place where Ronaldinho learned to kick a ball. The games are friendlies, with the opposition usually put together by acquaintances in the surrounding regions.

The first match involves the veterans, mostly over the age of 35. Up front is Hilton, a cousin of Ronaldinho, who played professionally in China, Greece and Portugal. Of those who established the original team, Cebola, or 'Onion', is one of a select few who still plays today. A number 10, he appears to have taken on the shape of his nickname all the more over the years.

The original team also featured João, a very competent attacking midfielder by all accounts. He played amateur football to a high standard throughout the region, including for respected local side Cruzeiro.

And then there was João Ademar, better known as Miquimba.

Miquimba is Ronaldinho's uncle, the youngest of Dona Miguelina's brothers and sisters, and some say he was a better player than his nephew. He turned professional and played in various parts of the country but never really fulfilled his potential; a fondness for the drink is said to have always held him back.

In Brazil, it is commonly believed that you gain your genes not from your parents but from their siblings, and so it goes with Miquimba and Ronaldinho. Approaching fifty, Miquimba's game remains the same as Ronaldinho's and he still shines among the veterans, some of them fifteen years his junior.

If Ronaldinho still lived in his old neighbourhood he would play in the Força Livre, the Free Force, a kind of first team. Most of the players are cousins of his and he used to play *futsal* with two of them when he was younger: Andre and Zair. Watching Andre play today, it is not hard to tell he is a relative of Ronaldinho.

Ronaldinho never played for Sérvia; joining Grêmio Juniors at such a young age, he barely played eleven-a-side for anyone else. Assis, though, has lined up for Sérvia as recently as 2005 when he called down to join in a game.

It was on the Periquito where Ronaldinho first began to kick a ball around. João used to bring his boys down to play, Assis in the *peladas*, or kickabouts, on the pitch itself, Ronaldinho with his ball on his own at the side. João would lay down his *Zero Hora* newspaper to sit on and pour himself a drink, sit back and keep an eye on the elder boy, making sure he didn't injure himself, while encouraging the younger.

The Perequito, said to be named after the parakeets that sing in the surrounding woodland, doesn't particularly facilitate skilful football. Where there is grass, on the wings, it is too long, while the penalty areas and the strip in between is just an eroded patch of dry soil. Dust clouds kick up into the sky whenever the ball is struck. The changing rooms, meanwhile, are improvised huts thrown together using scrap wood and corrugated iron. The social area, a bar and a small stall where Carmen sells pasties and cakes, have been fabricated in the same crude fashion.

Sérvia want to move to a proper pitch where they can set up a proper headquarters. The club these days has evolved into more of a community project and the intention is to develop further. They have already located a suitable site on Rua Ne de Sousa and Dona Miguelina has donated the money for a five-year lease. They are still fighting for planning permission to build the clubhouse but their goal was to have the matter resolved and be up and running by early 2007.

Gilberto Machado is Ronaldinho's uncle, husband to Dona Miguelina's sister, Nelcinda. He grew up in the same neighbourhood as João and was a friend and co-worker of his as well as one of the original members of Sérvia. He now dedicates all his time to the club: 'Six years ago we registered as a social club and now we also do community work. This includes running a soccer school for eighty kids, needy kids from our community, Vila Nova, and the surrounding area. At the moment, this is just for football but we are organising a base and once we have that up and running we are going to develop further services including school help, computers for kids, *capoeira* (a Brazilian martial art) classes, a stationery office, theatre workshops, a dentist, a doctor and a clinic. This is our plan.'

The expansion of the club into a community project seems like the natural next step in its evolution. Sérvia already organise regular dances and a Christmas party with toys for the kids. In fact, every Saturday is party time as the players, their family and friends and any local residents who care to join in gather for beers, barbecue and samba in the club hut at the Perequito. Everyone is welcome.

Of course, such a grand scheme requires funding. 'We have no financial backing at all, neither private nor public,' explains Gilberto. 'At the moment, the senior players (the veterans) pay a monthly membership fee of 15 reais (roughly £3.50) and this pays for the pitch, with what is left over going on equipment for the youngsters. We are volunteers, me and three other coaches in the soccer school, and we have to beg and borrow in order to get balls and the like. Once we have a proper base and begin to expand the project, get all the community involved, maybe then, when the government understands the proposal, we might get some support.' It is certainly to be hoped so.

While Dona Miguelina stumped up the cash for the new pitch, Ronaldinho has no involvement at all with the club. 'This is a family club but, besides the fact that Ronaldinho belongs to the family, it has nothing at all to do with him. He plays his football, we admire him, cheer for him, will him on, but we have no links to him or his (immediate) family.'

According to reports in the Porto Alegre business newspaper, *Jornal do Comércio*, the city council is studying a proposal from Ronaldinho to donate land in order to establish a foundation dedicated to providing assistance to the homeless children of the city. Nevertheless it does seem strange that neither Ronaldinho nor his brother plays any real active role in their own family's social project, neither financial nor symbolic, even though it is organised in their grandfather's name.

In fact, despite the warmth of affection the mere mention of Ronaldinho's name brings, there is something of a sense of estrangement in the family with regard to their famous relative. Ronaldinho was apparently last in Vila Nova following the 2002 World Cup triumph, when crowds were so vast the situation became impossible. But Carmen and Dona Elurdes last saw Ronaldinho in September 1999 at Dona Miguelina's fiftieth birthday party when they were among the 400 guests invited to a *churrasquaria* meat restaurant for a surprise party laid on by her sons. 'He was already worth twenty million dollars by then,' recalls Carmen, the figure fixed in her mind, though based on what is unclear. 'I speak to her (Dona Miguelina) very occasionally. We rarely know where she is.'

They are too proud to admit as much but there is, perhaps inevitably, a feeling of having been left behind among those of the family still in Vila Nova. They repeat that they understand that Ronaldinho, Roberto (Assis) and Dona Miguelina had to move on in order to achieve what they have done, that the future is what matters, not the past. But such comments do seem to be as much for their own comfort and peace of mind as for the listener's. They really don't want to begrudge him his success or feel any sense of resentment towards the boy they remember so fondly. But it is no doubt hard not to.

Free of the duty of family loyalty, local resident Jorge is more vocal about the star family: 'I don't want anything from them, I'm not interested in their money, I don't want a loan or anything like that, nothing at all. I would just like them to recognise the friendships they used to have.'

Jorge was Dona Miguelina's neighbour and still lives on the road where Ronaldinho was born. He used to help her out: 'I would always buy things off her to help her sell her lingerie and jewellery and things, helped them with the house. Only they don't recognise that now. She only knew me when she was low and now she is high and a woman with money. She doesn't remember her old friends. It would be easy to just pass by, say hello, but no, not even this.'

His gaze fixes on Carmen with her baskets and plastic Tupperware, struggling along, selling her snacks by the pitch. 'I mean,' he says, 'I don't think it would be asking much to say, "Hey, Auntie, I am going to make you an offer and you pay me back whenever you can – I'm going to give you a hot-dog stand and away you go." But not even this. They just concern themselves with their own lives.'

A happy-go-lucky character, Jorge too tries to understand and see the best in a situation. 'Look, she (Dona Miguelina) was a warrior, she deserves it, and the important thing for them is to look to the future. Other members of the family had opportunities too and didn't make the most of them, so good for them, they deserve it.'

Vila Nova and the Periquito is a world away from the metropolitan capitals of Europe and Champions League arenas in which Ronaldinho now struts his stuff. Yet the community spirit, family values and positive outlook that he grew up amongst live with him and remain an important part of his being. For this the people of his original neighbourhood can be truly proud.

BASE FORM

Grêmio invest a lot of time and money in their youth academy. As a club that traditionally relies on collective teamwork and aggression, selecting local players who have grown up at Grêmio ensures fielding a line-up prepared to sweat for the shirt. The club has a proud history of forging successful sides based on players who have come through their junior system. National team linchpin and Juventus star Émerson is one such product. Rafael Scheidt, now of Botafogo but formerly (and infamously – a very expensive signing, he barely played a game) of Celtic, and Eduardo Costa, ex-Olympique Marseille and latterly of Espanyol, are others. Ronaldinho is its most distinguished graduate.

The youth setup is split into two sections: the *Escolinha*, or School, and the *Categorias de Base*, the Junior Ranks.

Boys can, as Ronaldinho did, join from the age of seven. They enter the *Escolinha*, which is a recreational soccer school. When it was originally set up, more than thirty years ago, it solely served the sons of *sociós* (members) of the club but it is now open to anyone for the price of a modest monthly subscription fee. The emphasis in the *Escolinha* is on fun; the boys are coached in basic skills but the idea is really to provide a place at the club for a kickabout.

Sérgio Vasques took over as co-ordinator of the *Categorias de Base* in 1993 but he had been at Grêmio for over ten years by then, working in public relations, and already knew Ronaldinho. 'Ronaldinho joined Grêmio when he was seven and already stood out from the others. Therefore nobody can really claim to have discovered him. Perhaps his father was the first to recognise his true potential when he said Ronaldinho was going to be better than Assis.'

Celso Roth would eventually become manager of the senior side but back in the late 80s he was a fitness coach at Grêmio working under Luiz

Felipe Scolari (later to coach the Brazil team), who was in charge when Assis was in the first team. 'I remember Assis bringing his young brother down to a training session at the Olímpico and we watched Ronaldinho kicking the ball around afterwards,' says Roth. 'Assis turned to us, me and Felipe, and said: "He is going to be a lot better than me".'

Roth could only agree. 'Ronaldinho wasn't particularly thin, fat, tall or small. He didn't stand out physically then but what did stand out was his technical level. He could control the ball with both feet and on his chest, he already had a sense of co-ordination very evolved for someone of his age; that is what drew your attention.' All those hours practising kick-ups was paying off.

Once the Grêmio boys reach ten, they are eligible for the *Categorias de Base* and this is when the serious business begins. It is an elite soccer school with the best players from the *Escolinha* being joined by those scouted from other teams around the state and those able to shine in a series of open trials.

There are several sections to the *Categorias de Base*: the *Pré-Mirim* and *Mirim* (Small and Very-Small classes) for ages ten to fourteen; the *Infantil* (Infant) for ages fourteen to fifteen; the *Juvenil* (Youth) for ages fifteen to sixteen; and the *Junior* (Junior) for ages seventeen to twenty. Age groups are decided on the year of birth, as if everyone were born on 1 January.

Most of the time, Ronaldinho was playing above his natural age group. 'When Ronaldinho was fourteen he was in the *Infantil* but was so good we moved him up to the *Juvenil*,' recalls Vasques. 'But, because of the way the ages were worked out, he could be playing with people almost three years older than him. Yet he was soon in the first team.'

Ronaldinho spent two years in the *Juvenil* and was then promoted to the *Juniores* aged still only sixteen. After a year there he was introduced to the professionals. One of the consequences of always playing against older boys was that Ronaldinho would easily be pushed off the ball. He learned to release the ball before the contact came and some people believe this is why today he plays with his head up, looking who he can pass to before he has even received the ball, and has such great vision. It is also possibly why he is so rarely injured.

Ronaldinho may have been the star of the academy, earning a call-up for Brazil Under-15s, but he was also part of a wave of talent coming through at the same time. In July 1996, Grêmio Juvenils were crowned national champions. This was the climax to a series of achievements that earned the team the nickname of *Supertime* (Superteam). They had not lost a tournament in three years, collecting three state championships and lifting the prestigious Copa Santiago (a tournament held in Rio Grande do Sul but open only to the best teams in Brazil and those invited from abroad) three times in a row.

Vasques remembers the 1996 national conquest well. The 32-team tournament was held in Curitiba in the state of Paraná. Grêmio were contesting the final against Rio-giants Flamengo, the favourites. 'It was 1–1 with five minutes to go and we were two players down. Then Ronaldinho got hold of the ball and won it for us.' He had already scored the winner in extra-time in the semifinal against Internacional.

'Another time, at Santiago, we were losing 1–0 and I remember someone from the radio came up and asked me how I thought things would turn out,' continues Vasques. 'I told him not to worry: "We'll bring Ronaldinho on and he'll resolve the game." In fact, he came on and made it 2–1, scored both.'

Carlos Gavião was the same age as Ronaldinho and they had played together in the youth ranks since 1994. Gavião would later be called up to Brazil Under-17s with Ronaldinho but he still recalls his friend as being on another level: 'Ronaldinho always was a different player, the one who stood out. We had very good teams back then but he was always the outstanding one.'

Paraná was again the setting for a Ronaldinho goal which sticks in the mind. 'We were playing in a tournament in Cascavel and Ronaldinho scored a beautiful goal, one of his classic dribbles,' says Gavião. 'Anyway, it was very unusual for a goal from a *Categorias de Base* game to get shown on the television back then, but it was so good that soon *Sportv* (Brazil's Sky Sports) were broadcasting it.'

Ronaldinho lined up as what is known in Brazil as a *meia* back then, a position just behind the strikers, more or less as he would end up playing for Barcelona. Luís Fernando Siqueira, better known by his nickname 'Pelotinha', was a radio sports journalist at the time: 'Ronaldinho was a class apart in the *base* but what often happens with such a player is that they get kicked off the park. But Ronaldinho was so well liked, even among his opponents, that I don't remember anyone being violent with him.'

Ronaldinho himself can recall having his lip split in a *Juvenil* game when a disgruntled defender punched him in the face after being dribbled past. But this seems to stick in the memory for being exceptional and Ronaldinho, for the most part, managed to avoid trouble. The fact that, even then, he never deliberately humiliated people must have helped. 'It is one thing to dribble going forward, heading to goal, quite another to dribble to the side, just for the sake of it. Ronaldinho was never disrespectful,' adds Pelotinha.

It probably also helped to have tough-tackling Gavião playing behind him, working the midfield engine room and keeping an eye out for his mate.

Once the boys join the *Categorias de Base* they are treated like professional players. Each age level has its own full team of coaching staff based on the first-team set-up. There is a director of football, a coach, a fitness trainer, a goalkeeper coach, a masseur, a kitman and a medic. All academy members are also provided with psychological and social care.

'Ronaldinho always worked very hard,' recalls Sérgio Vasques. 'He always stayed behind after training practising free-kicks to the point that one trainer had had enough and told him to go home. Ronaldinho came to complain to me and I talked to the trainer and he was then allowed to stay as long as he wanted taking free-kicks. So, as well as ability, he always had lots of will.'

'We were always careful with Ronaldinho; we knew he was a special player,' continues Vasques. 'We paid particular attention to his physical development. It was a balance between developing his physique without taking away his football ability. We used to do special fitness training with him, away from the other athletes. He was thin so we had to do special muscle work. Again, we had to manage the balance between bulking him up without affecting his natural ability.

'Whenever he was away with the *Seleção* (the Selection – Brazil's national team, in this case the Juniors), they didn't do any physical work, only ball skills, so when he came back to us he never had a good physical aspect. We never let him play directly with the ball when he got back, we did fitness work with him. But Ronaldinho had a good head; character as well as ability. He always liked talking to us (the coaches) and he always listened and accepted what we said. He liked training and he understood that he needed to do the physical work; that we were working for his own good.'

Gavião perhaps saw a different side to Ronaldinho. 'He liked training because he loved football but he was never a super athlete. He liked to play, to have the ball, do tricks, ball skills, take free-kicks, but not doing the running. The physical training was never that important to him, not something he ever got into. I don't know what he is like (in training) now but I doubt that he has changed too much,' he laughs.

It seems that Gavião is probably right. In an interview with *Playboy* magazine during his time at Paris Saint-Germain he was asked if he ever went running in the park next to his house. 'No, I do not. What is this? I don't want to run in my spare time,' was his incredulous response.

In conversation with Brazilian football magazine *Placar* a few years later, and by then a Barcelona player, he recalled his Grêmio training days: 'I was very skinny and in Brazil some said I wouldn't make it in football. But thanks to that (being skinny) I never lost my agility and I grew strong naturally. I grew ten centimetres between ages twenty and twenty-one.'

Though nature undoubtedly played its part, Grêmio's fitness training was clearly a big help. Club statistics show that Ronaldinho gained 4cm and 5.5kg in four years of monitoring, leaving him to stand 1.82m and weigh

74.5kg in 2000. In the same period, his muscular mass went up from 33.8kg to 36.3kg while body fat remained steady at 9.2 to 9.3 per cent.

Ronaldinho may have benefited from personalised training programmes but he certainly didn't receive preferential treatment. Sérgio Vasques made sure of that: 'He was the best but he had no privileges. To give you an idea, when I was in charge, earrings were not permitted. Ronaldinho wore one outside of the stadium but always took it out when he arrived at the ground.

'They are small details but important in his development, not in a football sense but in terms of discipline. And he was obedient. If he needed to be fined, he was fined. Not that I recall that he was but just to give a sense of how it was. He used to catch the bus to the stadium like the others, no privileges. Well, he did earn a little more than the others; quite a lot more in fact.'

As players enter the *Categorias de Base* the fees applicable in the *Escolinha* no longer apply and they begin to earn a modest wage. 'When we drew up his first contract he was fourteen and he earned what would be today US$700 (£370) per month. At the time, the other fourteen- or fifteen-year-olds used to be paid their travel expenses to and from the stadium, nothing more. When sixteen, Ronaldinho's salary rose to US$2,500 (£1,300) per month plus a bonus on signing the contract of US$45,000 (£24,000), making an annual US$75,000 (£40,000). Not bad for a sixteen-year-old. The others got US$1,500 (£800) per year when sixteen. A major difference, but he was that good and we believed a lot in him.'

To earn their wage the young apprentices would train every afternoon, Tuesday to Friday, and play matches at the weekends. Matches were played down on Grêmio's Parque Cristal, a series of pitches on a strip of land by the lake and behind the Jockey Club racetrack. Cristal was also the neighbourhood in which Ronaldinho's mother and father had grown up and met each other many years earlier.

As well as excelling on the football field and showing the required discipline off it, academy players were also obliged to attend primary school.

'In my teams I had a rule that all the boys must go to school. I used to look at their reports,' explains Vasques. 'I forced them all to study. I didn't succeed one hundred per cent, but maybe ninety-five per cent of the players from the *Categorias de Base* stayed in school. At pay time, I checked through their school reports.'

The Brazilian education system is split into three levels: primary, secondary and tertiary. Secondary and tertiary levels can be compared to Britain's A-level and university levels, respectively. The primary level, meanwhile, is called the *Primeiro Grau* (First Grade) and is divided into sub-grades 1 to 8. In theory, children pass through the *Primeiro Grau* beginning aged seven and completing aged fourteen. In practice, the repeating of years is very common and few children actually make it to the eighth grade at all.

Ronaldinho didn't care too much for studying. He started out at the Alberto Torres school in Vila Nova but moved to Escola Langendonck when the family moved to Guarujá. Grêmio then paid for Ronaldinho to go to the Santa Teresa de Jesus private school and sponsored Deise to head there too, perhaps hoping her more disciplined approach might rub off on him. While Deise excelled in her studies (she eventually graduated from university with a Business Administration degree), Ronaldinho continued to stall.

Grêmio eventually enrolled him at the ACM (Assosiação Cristã de Moços – The Association of Christ for Boys) where he received private tuition and a more flexible study scheme to better fit the demands on his time that football was making. This still failed to have the desired effect and he ended up repeating his 3rd and 4th grades, then dropping out at the 5th level. But it wasn't an entirely unrewarding time: ACM won the school league title and Ronaldinho met Tiago Oliveira, who would prove to be a lifelong friend (he lives with him and acts as his personal assistant in Barcelona to this very day).

By now Ronaldinho was approaching fourteen, the theoretical end of primary school. He was also entering the *Juvenils* at Grêmio and it was hard to argue that a football career didn't beckon. 'Ronaldinho wasn't a great student but he did go along to school. He may not have studied much but he was always going to be a footballer,' concludes Vasques.

Besides, he was gaining the kind of education many Brazilian kids don't get right there at Grêmio. A young Ronaldinho told *Olá Botanico* newspaper: 'If you join a football club, you make friends there and you end up dreaming of scoring goals. You don't have time to be thinking of drugs, smoking, alcohol. Your colleagues have the same objectives. They don't invite you to get into drugs; they invite you to play football.'

Ronaldinho was making some very good friends at the club. For those boys not from Porto Alegre, or from particularly poor backgrounds, there was a boarding house at the stadium, called the *concentração* (the concentration). Ronaldinho would make sure his friends didn't have to spend their weekends cooped up there.

'Ronaldinho was a good boy, he always looked after his friends. He used to take two or three or more to his home at the weekends,' recalls Vasques. 'In this way he became something of a leader. He had always been someone they looked up to, a sort of idol as regards football, but they were attracted to him as a person too. It would have been easy for someone like him to go around with a chauffeur and a chip on his shoulder but he was always modest. Off the pitch he was always a good colleague, a good friend,' says Vasques.

'When he was playing in the *Juniores*, he would come and ask me if he could play in tournaments with his mates in the age group below (for which he was eligible) and I always used to let him. Partly because of his football but also because of the sort of person he was and what he brought to the group.'

Gavião came from Itaqui in the Rio Grande do Sul interior (near the border with Argentina) and was one of those who boarded at the *concentração*. He was a regular guest at Ronaldinho's house. They would watch videos, play computer games, listen to CDs or have a kickabout; Ronaldinho's place had both a grass pitch and a sand pitch in the garden.

'By then we were already good friends,' Gavião declares. 'He used to live in a house and would invite some of us there, to stay with his family. So outside football, we also shared our lives. I have very fond memories of those times.'

However, Gavião is also able to reveal a few interesting character traits: 'Whatever we were doing, playing in the street or a game of cards, Ronaldinho was always very competitive. Despite being a fun person on the outside, he never liked losing. We would play video-game football tournaments and if he lost he would get very cross and argue and sulk until we agreed to play another tournament so that he might have another chance at winning.' Gavião recounts all this with a sense of nostalgia for the innocence of youth, but adopts a different tone to make a more serious point: 'I guess that is one reason why he has got to where he has. Behind the smile there was always a strong attitude. He is in a profession that depends upon a competitive edge and he has it, despite his appearance sometimes to the contrary, and it has been a benefit to him.'

One of Ronaldinho's best friends was Rodrigo Gral, who came from Chapecó in the neighbouring state of Santa Catarina and became another regular guest at the family home. The connection lives on today with Assis acting as Gral's agent.

Another close friend, indeed perhaps Ronaldinho's closest at Grêmio, was Tinga. Both Tinga and Rodrigo Gral were older than Ronaldinho but because Ronaldinho was always elevated to play in the year group above his own they were team-mates for a long time.

Tinga joined Grêmio at fifteen years. Ronaldinho was already there but they played *Juveniles* together and became professionals in the same era. Although from Porto Alegre, because of his poor background (his nickname being derived from his Restinga neighbourhood) Tinga lived at the *concentração*.

'Ronaldinho and I shared various important moments together,' recalls

Tinga. 'We did a lot of things together, went round his house, played, hung out, went out at night. When I had a few difficulties in life back then, he helped me out. We became very close.'

Both from humble origins, they seemed to form a strong bond based on common experiences.

'It was a special situation; we had nothing back then, but me and him got on great and our families became friends, to the point that my mother still speaks regularly with his mum.' Dona Miguelina and Nadir used to do many things together including going to handicraft classes in the Espalanada near Dona Miguelina's home in Guarujá.

'One special moment I'll never forget: we went to my house in Restinga and there was no light; my mother couldn't pay the bills. Ronaldinho took me to the bank – he earned more at that time despite being an amateur – and he took the money straight out to pay for the light.'

Pedrão, a security guard at Grêmio who was friendly with Ronaldinho, told *The Times* a similar story: after mentioning in passing that he needed to pay the builders, Ronaldinho showed up the next day and paid them himself.

According to Tinga, this is what makes Ronaldinho so special: 'I know the heart of him, the sort of person he is. He deserves all he has achieved because of his quality as a person, and he will achieve more still, I'm sure.'

ALEGRE

Ronaldinho is probably the most famous figure ever to have emerged from his home city, Porto Alegre. He is seen as something of an ambassador for the area and there are many who clamour for him to be recognised officially by the town council as such.

Porto Alegre began life in earnest in 1732 when families were shipped over from Portugal's Atlantic islands of the Azores. The Portuguese crown was keen to populate its northern and southern extremes to counter any advances and claims to land the Spanish might make, and the Azoreans had been encouraged to go over to Brazil and establish communities. The original group of Azorean immigrants comprised seventy couples and their children, and the settlement became known as Porto do Casais, meaning Port of the Couples.

Porto Alegre lies in Brazil's southernmost state, Rio Grande do Sul, and so the Spanish threat came from nearby Uruguay and Argentina, with borders then ill-defined. The state governor, José Marcelino de Figueiredo, resolved to establish a new capital and chose Porto do Casais for its geographical benefits with regard to communication and defence.

He renamed the town Nossa Senhora Madre de Deus de Porto Alegre – Our Lady Mother of God of the Happy Port. Our Lady was the patron saint of the governor himself while *alegre* means happy, gay and cheerful in Portuguese: the Azoreans had gained something of a reputation as fun-loving, happy people; despite their abject poverty (living conditions in the area were atrocious) and fierce religiosity, they were known for their dancing and general joyful nature.

Ironically, by naming the new capital after the cheerful disposition of the Azoreans, the governor was actually to earn their wrath; they themselves had christened the port São Francisco do Porto Casais (St Francis being the patron saint of the Azores) and resented the change forced upon them.

Nevertheless, the name stuck and it is entirely appropriate that Ronaldinho, a player as popular for his cheerful character as his football, should have become the Happy Port's most celebrated son.

The state of Rio Grande do Sul is often considered as different from the rest of Brazil. In a country as big as Brazil, it is inevitable that regional differences will be significant. Rio Grande do Sul has been just as heavily influenced by its Spanish-speaking neighbours as it has by Portugal and the rest of Brazil.

Natives of the state are referred to as Gaúchos. Ronaldinho himself is known as Ronaldinho Gaúcho to all Brazilians. The Gaúchos were products of mixed-breeding between Spaniards, Portuguese, native Indians and escaped African slaves. These cowboys originally roamed the pampas hunting wild cattle or protecting the land of a particular *caudilho* (chief) before becoming simple cattle hands once rearing became common practice. To this day, Rio Grande do Sul is known for producing the country's tastiest beef and best leather goods.

Porto Alegre has a population of 1.4 million people, making it Brazil's eleventh largest city. Locals like to say that Porto Alegre has the body of a metropolis, a cosmopolitan spirit and the soul of a province. It was named the Brazilian metropolis offering the best quality of life three times between 1996 and 2002, and is well above the national average in terms of personal wealth, education and literacy indicators. It is said to be one of the greenest cities anywhere and is located on the banks of the Lagoa Guaíba, a lagoon that flows into the Atlantic to its south and is so wide that Porto Alegre has a coastal feel.

It is a prosperous city in Brazilian terms with the economy traditionally built on the service sector and, as state capital, government business, while in the modern era it has developed a thriving conference circuit. A reputation for liberal politics is, in a contemporary sense, based on the fact that Porto Alegre pioneered the 'participatory budget', a scheme in which city residents and community leaders are consulted to discuss municipal spending. This led to the city playing host to the first World Social Forum in 2001, a gathering of social movements, NGOs (Non-Governmental Organisations) and other groups who oppose a world dominated by capitalism and imperialism. It has since held three more of the forums and remains its spiritual home.

In short, Porto Alegre is a bustling modern city. And yet, its more traditional cowboy heritage is never far from view.

Many of the city's poor scrape a living by sifting through rubbish and salvaging anything which might be sold as scrap or to the recycling plants. These unfortunates can be seen pulling makeshift wooden carts through the city's busiest streets. While this is nothing out of the usual – it's a common sight in any Brazilian city – what makes Porto Alegre unique among state capitals is that the job is done by horse and cart. If travelling through Porto Alegre, you will likely come across district football pitches with horses grazing on them.

You will also see locals enjoying a *chimarrao* in his or her doorway, a tea-like fusion of *mate* brewed in a gourd and drunk through a metal straw, also popular in Argentina. Ronaldinho is said to miss his *mate* when playing in Europe. Barbecues abound: all-you-can-eat meat restaurants, *churrascarias*, originated in Rio Grande do Sul and grilled meat kebabs are sold by street vendors on virtually every city-centre corner.

The legendary Gaúchos enjoyed a reputation as being brave and resolute as well as capable of the most callous violence. The legacy today is perhaps best expressed in the region's football: in contrast to the rest of Brazil, where flair and cunning are the qualities most appreciated, the footballers of the south are famed for their tough workmanlike style and ruthlessness in the tackle. Neighbouring Argentina, where the competitive spirit is similarly appreciated, is perhaps a better reference.

As Brazil's southernmost state, Rio Grande do Sul also has a more extreme climate than elsewhere in the country, temperatures occasionally even dipping below zero, and this is also said to have contributed to the more rugged style of play.

The Gaúcho state championship is thought to be one of the hardest of all to win: games in the interior usually take place on small pitches and the game is very physical indeed. Grêmio, even more so than city rivals Internacional, has built its reputation on organisation and teamwork in contrast to the skill and individualism that characterise Brazil's other top club sides.

For a player such as Ronaldinho, this can be both a curse and a blessing. He was not immediately taken to the hearts of the Grêmio fans, who prefer their young players to earn their blue, black and white stripes through sweat, blood and determination. Ronaldinho was signalled out for early criticism for his lack of commitment and participation in games.

On the other hand, in a team of triers playing against another team of triers, the skilful player will stand out all the more and one moment of magic can regularly prove decisive. This is eventually how Ronaldinho would prove his worth in the same way as Falcão, the elegant Brazil midfielder of the 70s and 80s, who began his career at Internacional before going on to earn the title of 'King of Rome' in Italy's Serie A.

Some people can still see the Gaúcho in Ronaldinho's game and claim that he is successful only because he has been able to marry his obvious natural skill with the determination and steel typical of the football in which he earned his spurs. Certainly, his bookings usually come from an ugly foul that would honour any match in the Rio Grande do Sul interior.

Some locals will tell you that what makes Rio Grande do Sul special is that it was settled entirely by European immigrants: after the Azoreans, Italians and Germans came in particularly large numbers. It is hard not to detect an element of racism in such a claim. In fact, the state received African slaves just as did the rest of the country; blacks arrived from southern Africa, Angola primarily, to work the *charqueadas*, farms producing a dried meat similar to jerked beef.

Slavery in Rio Grande do Sul is popularly believed to have been of a gentler form than in other parts of Brazil. This may be so, but it is nothing to be proud of: it was still a brutal practice.

The Brazilian south does have a reputation for being the most racist part of the country. Outbreaks of Nazism and a white-only separatist movement in Rio Grande do Sul and neighbouring Santa Catarina in the 1930s and 1940s is certainly an ugly chapter in the region's history. Brazil likes to think of itself as a nation of beautiful interracial mixing and harmony but, though certainly more advanced than many countries in the world, this is largely a fanciful notion. Most of the power and wealth remains in the hands of the white population. In this context, racism in Rio Grande do Sul is probably no different to anywhere else in the country; it is just more noticeable because of the small percentage of blacks.

A more obvious prejudice, and one that rears its ugly head more openly, is an inter-regional racism. The Gaúchos like to think of themselves as the best of Brazilians and this sense of local pride spills over a little too easily into regional antagonism.

Nevertheless, the region's minimal black population is an obvious distinguishing feature. It is worth considering that, once he had moved to the middle-class district of Guarujá or been enrolled in one of the private schools selected for him by Grêmio, Ronaldinho was usually one of, if not the only, black boy in his team or class. There is a theory that racial make-up explains why football played in the south is workmanlike, or 'European', compared to the more adventurous and less-disciplined approach favoured elsewhere in Brazil.

Football in Rio Grande do Sul certainly has a chequered history of racism. In October 2005, Juventude, a top-flight side from Caxias do Sul, the state's largest city after Pôrto Alegre, were ordered to play two games behind closed doors and away from its home stadium as a punishment for racist behaviour by its supporters: in a league game with Inter, monkey noises had been directed at Tinga, Ronaldinho's close friend, every time he touched the ball.

Several months later, the same team was in hot water again. This time ex-national team defender Antônio Carlos was seen making racist gestures towards Grêmio's black forward Jeovani. Grêmio lodged an official complaint.

Grêmio, however, has a murky reputation in this respect too. In April 2006, in the first leg of the state final against Internacional at the Estádio Olímpico, monkey chants from the Grêmio fans were directed at Inter players, Tinga once again coming in for abuse. In the return match, Grêmio fans (a significant minority) vandalised the Internacional stadium, including writing racist graffiti on the walls.

Gremistas, as Grêmio fans are known, have long called Inter supporters 'monkeys'; *macaco imundo* (filthy monkey) is a common taunt. Inter's nickname is the *colorados*, the coloureds, though this is in reference to their coloured shirts, a fierce red, rather than their racial make-up. However, it has developed racial connotations.

Grêmio Foot-Ball Porto Alegrense was founded in 1903 in a Porto Alegre restaurant by a group consisting primarily of German immigrants. It remained a club almost exclusively for players of German extraction for many years. Indeed, the incorporation of non-white players was only approved as late as 1952; Inter had been employing black players since the 1930s. This was also far from a liberal decision: in the previous twenty years Grêmio had won just two state championships compared to Inter's twelve.

Inter liked to portray itself as the team of the people as opposed to Grêmio, the team of the bourgeoisie. In the 1950s, in local newspaper *A Hora*, there appeared a cartoon character called Negrinho, a one-legged black man who smoked a pipe and supported Inter. He was supposed to symbolise Inter as the team of the people, but there was undoubtedly an attempt to mock Grêmio by creating the personification of its exact opposite. Negrinho proved popular: his name was eventually changed to Saci and he is the club's official mascot to this day. Grêmio are represented by a white moustachioed musketeer.

Still, Rio Grande do Sul is proud of its mixed heritage and does actively celebrate its black history. One of the state's most legendary figures is Negrinho do Pastoreio, a slave working on a cruel landowner's farm: he was tied to a plank, buried in an ant hill and left to die in punishment for losing an animal, but the next day he was found alive and well with the missing animal by his side; to this day he is the patron saint of lost things and asks only for a candle and some smoke as an offering.

The Negrinho do Pastoreio Medal was created in 1972 to honour natives of Rio Grande do Sul who distinguish themselves and become a source of pride to the state itself. It is considered the highest of local accolades and Luiz Felipe Scolari was a recipient in 2002 after leading Brazil to World Cup victory that year.

Ronaldinho

Ronaldinho himself had to wait a few more years but received the Negrinho do Pastoreio Medal in 2004 after being named the Fifa World Player of the Year for the first time. While the Fifa prize is easily the more widely recognised, Ronaldinho is proud of his background and the local honour would have been just as special to him in its own particular way.

SELEÇÃO

A chilly March Tuesday night in Glasgow is perhaps an unlikely setting for Ronaldinho's Brazil debut, but it was at Hampden Park, 7 March 1995, that he first pulled on *a canarinha*, as Brazil's canary-yellow jersey is known to its followers. He was a member of the Brazilian Under-15 team that travelled to Britain that year.

Scotland, who featured Paul Gallacher in goal (later of Norwich and a full international), James Paterson (a professional at Motherwell) in midfield and Robbie Neilson (a Scottish Cup-winner with Hearts) on the bench, beat Brazil 1–0 and the South American visitors lost their next fixture by the same score at Wembley. England's winning goal was scored by a certain Michael Owen, on his way to breaking the schoolboy's scoring record that year. Ronaldinho got little change out of a back line that featured Wes Brown (Manchester United), Michael Ball (Everton then Rangers) and Steve Haslam.

Latterly a non-league player with Halifax Town, Haslam played in the Premier League for Sheffield Wednesday. He remembers the Brazil match fondly: 'It was a warm day and the first time any of us had played at Wembley, so an amazing experience. A few of us had been at Lilleshall (England's elite soccer school) together but it was the first national squad at that level, the first chance to represent England.' Haslam played with Brown in the middle of the back four but nobody really marked Ronaldinho. 'He drifted out wide as he does today. I do remember him being good but my lasting impression was how very good they all were. They played in a formation we had never seen before and so they were very hard to mark.

'The game was played in good spirit and we got medals and pennants and stuff.' In fact, the plaque Ronaldinho received that day is still displayed, in pride of place, in Dona Miguelina's house. Nobody ended up with

Ronaldinho's shirt though. 'You had one shirt to last all season then, so there was no swapping,' recalls Haslam.

Brazil's touring party included a colleague from Grêmio called Maickel. When they were named in the squad, newspaper *Zero Hora* interviewed the boys and came across a quietly confident Ronaldinho: 'It is the first opportunity and I am not going to slip up.'

Maickel would not make it as a professional but there were four of that Brazilian squad who would. Júlio César, now of Inter Milan and reserve to Dida in the senior *Seleção*, kept goal in both matches. Jorginho Paulista enjoyed spells in Holland and Italy before returning to Brazil, last seen turning out for Vasco. Alexandre Negri has had a similar journeyman career: after a successful spell at Ponte Preta he now warms the bench as reserve keeper at Fortaleza in Brazil's top flight. He performed the same role on that tour of Britain: 'I was actually the Brazil Under-15 goalkeeper; Júlio César was too old but they wanted to give him some experience ahead of the South America Under-17 tournament later that year so he played. *Coisas do Brasil* (typical Brazil).'

Nevertheless, Negri nurses fond memories of the trip. 'I can remember staying in a hotel in Glasgow and I can remember going shopping in London, a bit of tourism; I must have a few photos somewhere.

'We were all very young, just starting out in the game. It was the first squad assembled so nobody imposed themselves particularly. But Ronaldinho was already different; he was playing *meia* then and was already the one who stood out. I remember him as a nice lad, humble yet cheerful, just as he seems to be today.'

Ronaldinho has played internationally at every possible level, something very few players in the world have achieved. This means Under-15, Under-17, Under-20, Under-23 and senior appearances.

In 1997, he and Grêmio team-mate Gavião were selected for the Under-17 Brazil team which would compete first in the South American qualifying tournament in Paraguay and then, if successful, in the world finals in Egypt.

'He started with Brazil before me, in the Under-15s,' recalls Gavião. 'By then, for Brazil too, he was always the stand-out player.

'I roomed with Ronaldinho in Paraguay and I remember he took a tambourine with him. He always loved music and used to have a drum kit at home. I asked him to teach me how to play the tambourine. He agreed, of course, but after three or four days of my hopeless practising in the room I was driving him mad. He began to despair; he said he wished he had never bothered bringing the thing in the first place.' Ronaldinho would always share a room with Gavião or, in later call-ups for the Under-20s, with Rodrigo Gral.

'I remember Ronaldinho used to hide stacks of chocolate bars and cans of pop in our room to have when the coaches weren't looking,' adds Gavião.

Despite such unconventional nutrition, the tournament ended in triumph, though it very nearly didn't turn out that way. Ronaldinho scored in a 4–0 victory over Bolivia but, after drawing with both Chile and Colombia in the group stages, Brazil needed to get something out of their final game with Uruguay. Brazil went a goal down, then Ronaldinho was presented with the opportunity to square things up from the penalty spot. He missed and as the clock ticked on Brazil looked to be on their way out. An incredible two goals in the final minute then rescued their tournament and saved Ronaldinho's blushes.

He sat the next game out, a 5–0 victory over Paraguay, and then came on only as a substitute in a 5–2 semifinal win versus Chile, but Ronaldinho was back in the team for the final against Argentina. The *Albiceleste* (literally, the albino-white-and-sky-blues, as Argentina are known in Brazil) scored first and took a 1–0 advantage into the interval. Then Ronaldinho rediscovered his touch and set up an equaliser for Matuzalem. As the ninety minutes wound down, Geovanni, who had been the last-gasp hero against Uruguay (and who would go on to play for Barcelona too, though just prior to Ronaldinho's arrival), scored another dramatic winner. Brazil were South American champions, Ronaldinho had won his first international trophy and they were off to Egypt for the Under-17 World Cup.

'We travelled to lots of places with the CBF (Brazilian Football Confederation). We went to Egypt, Holland, Australia. We were playing so it was work, but we also had free time which we made the most of to get to know the places. Everything was new to us,' recalls Gavião.

'But Brazil had never before won the Under-17 World Cup so the trip to Egypt was taken very seriously. We had a very good team. If we didn't all go on to play for the full Brazil team, most players became professionals, had successful careers, played abroad.'

Indeed, it was taken very seriously. The tournament began life as a youth competition for Under-16s in 1985 and had been played every two years since, adapting to become an Under-17 championship in 1991. Brazil's failure to win it in all that time was viewed as a major blemish in the record book of a country proud to be recognised as *the* football nation. The absence of an Olympic title is seen in much the same way today.

Sixteen countries gathered in September for the 1997 Under-17 event in Egypt. Brazil was based in the northern city of Alexandria, where they would play all their games until the semifinals.

In their opening game, the *Seleção* beat Austria 7–0, which included a Ronaldinho penalty. They went on to beat the USA and Oman too, to top their group. They then beat an Argentina side, which included future Real Zaragoza stopper Gabriel Milito, 2–0 in the quarterfinals.

The semifinal was against Sabastian Deisler's Germany in Ismailia. Ronaldinho scored the final goal, again from the spot, in a 4–0 win.

Ghana awaited in the final in Cairo. Ghana were the reigning champions and had reached the final at the last three tournaments, winning in 1991 too. There were rumours that Ghana were less than stringent when recording a player's true age, and so were considered formidable, if not always legitimate, opponents at this level.

The first half was nervy. A goal just before the break from Owusu Afriyie gave the Africans a half-time lead, but Brazil stepped up their game in the second half and ran out 2–1 winners. Matuzalem and Andrey got the goals, the last in the 87th minute.

In an impressive display, Brazil won all six games they played, scoring 21 and conceding just twice in the process. The only time they looked at all uncomfortable was in the first half of the final against Ghana.

Europe had traditionally been a poor performer at this level but Germany and Spain had done well (making the semifinals) this time. The Spanish side included Xavi, who would later become a team-mate of Ronaldinho's at Barcelona. Spain also featured a forward called Sergio Santamaria, who was voted player of the tournament ahead of Ronaldinho. He also ended up on the books of Barcelona and was even in the side when Ronaldinho made his home debut for the Catalans, though he soon moved on to Albacete.

For Brazilians, however, Ronaldinho had been the star and for Gavião and the rest of the team he had been the leader. 'The final was against Ghana; a great experience. Ronaldinho ended up standing out. He was a simple guy off the pitch but took on ever more responsibility when playing, which made him a leader on the pitch,' he says. 'He became the reference. He would start to shout on the pitch – criticism and encouragement – and we could see that he was a player who could win it for us and we responded to him. That is basically what happened in that Under-17 tournament.

'Brazil had never won it before and, for a country dedicated to football, this was important. Although it was only Under-17, the win had big repercussions for us. When we started doing well, we got the media's attention and Bandeirantes (Brazilian terrestrial television) picked up on the last few games and they were shown live in Brazil. We became national news. And it has to be said that the main headlines went to Ronaldinho. He stood out and was the biggest promise.'

Two years later, Gavião also played with Ronaldinho for the Under-20s *Seleção* in the South American qualifying tournament, this time held in Argentina. Rodrigo Gral was also in the squad. The competition was very tough with games being played every other day and players complaining of fatigue. Brazil safely negotiated the first round, including beating Paraguay 6–0 with Rodrigo Gral scoring four. But the second round was tougher:

four would qualify from six and, after losing to Chile and Argentina, the final match versus Uruguay seemed key for Brazil.

In the event, news of a draw between Peru and Chile filtered through before kickoff and took the pressure off (Brazil could now afford to lose and still qualify) but the game was fiercely competitive all the same. Brazil were losing until Ronaldinho got hold of the ball, did a quick step-over and set off at pace, tearing down the left flank. He cut into the area diagonally and, as the goalie came out, poked his shot past him with his right foot, subtle yet firm. The game was drawn and, not for the first or last time, Ronaldinho had come to the team's rescue.

One important observer that day was Vanderlei Luxemburgo, then the manager of the full national team. The goal stuck in the memory and Ronaldinho had made a strong impression that day. Only five months later Luxemburgo called him up to the senior squad.

(That goal would also come back to haunt Luxemburgo: several years later, Luxemburgo is the manager of Real Madrid and Ronaldinho is Barcelona's dangerman; Ronaldinho scored two close replicas of that goal in Uruguay to not only give the Catalans victory but even prompt some Madrid fans to get to their feet and applaud him.)

Brazil had qualified in third place; the hosts, Argentina, won the competition, with Uruguay finishing second and Paraguay going through in fourth spot. The Argentine press were impressed with Ronaldinho and compared him favourably to the other Ronaldo, then of Inter Milan. Influential newspaper *Clarín* selected Ronaldinho among its five players of the tournament along with Esteban Cambiasso, Aldo Duscher, Pablo Aimar (all future full internationals with Argentina and club players in Spain) and Roque Santa Cruz (of Paraguay and Bayern Munich).

Gavião had got himself suspended during the qualifiers after an altercation with the referee at the end of the Uruguay game, so didn't travel to the finals in Nigeria. But Rodrigo Gral was there to accompany Ronaldinho both off the pitch and in attack on it.

Brazil had a better pedigree at Under-20 level. They had last won the tournament in 1993 and, in total, had lifted the cup three times since the biennial competition began in 1977.

However, in Nigeria, Ronaldinho and Brazil found themselves with a tough opening game against Spain. The Iberians ran out comfortable 2–0 winners, and would go on to win the whole tournament with a side masterminded by Xavi, once again, and also starring Gabri, another later colleague of Ronaldinho's at Barcelona.

This early loss upped the pressure on Ronaldinho and the boys: no *Seleção* had ever before lost a tournament match and gone on to win the trophy; all conquests at all levels had come undefeated.

Brazil recovered to beat Honduras 3–0 in the next match with Ronaldinho bagging the last. A 5–1 win against Zambia followed, taking Brazil into the next round for a tie with Croatia. Ronaldinho scored twice in a 4–0 win with Edu, latterly of Arsenal, getting another.

In the quarterfinals Uruguay awaited in Lagos and, despite the problems they caused in qualifiers, weren't expected to prove problematic; they had only finished third in their group and had required a penalty shoot-out to eliminate Paraguay in the previous round.

Brazil played the better, brighter football and dominated but Uruguay scored on the counterattack and the sides were level 1–1 at half-time. A controversial penalty was awarded to Uruguay with five minutes to go, duly dispatched, and Brazil had lost 2–1 and were out.

The squad returned to face the criticism directed at any Brazil side going home without a cup. Yet Ronaldinho had again distinguished himself and is remembered as one of the tournament's star performers; Ashley Cole (England) and Damian Duff (Republic of Ireland) also left lasting impressions.

The Porto Alegre press were so taken by Ronaldinho's performances that they claimed him to be unrecognisable to the timid player who had struggled at Grêmio the previous year. If Grêmio could sign this Ronaldinho to replace the other one then he would be the star signing, they joked.

This was but the latest development in a club-versus-country debate that would plague Ronaldinho for many a year. At Grêmio, everyone watched him put in incredible authoritative performances for the national team at the various junior levels and then fail to recapture that form for his club.

Several years later, as Ronaldinho caught the eye of the world with his dominating performances for Barcelona, Brazil fans asked themselves why he never played like that for the national team.

Of course, comparisons of role and responsibility are impossible to make. In the case of his Grêmio days, he wasn't given the freedom on the pitch for his club that he enjoyed in the *canarinha*. For Brazil's junior sides he played as a *meia* out wide, much as he does now for Barcelona.

The other main problem was that his constant comings and goings meant he never had a serious run of games with Grêmio in the years he was trying to break into the team.

GRÊMIO

It would be untrue to say that Ronaldinho returned to Porto Alegre a star after winning the Under-17 World Cup in 1997, but his profile was raised considerably. He and the other players from the city involved in the conquest (as well as Carlos Gavião of Grêmio, Fábio Pinto and Diogo of Internacional had also been in the team) had their achievements recognised locally in various ways: the Gaúcho State Football Federation presented them with a diploma and they were awarded the João Saldanha medal (a respected sports prize named after a distinguished journalist and football coach – he guided the great Brazil team of 1970 through the World Cup qualifiers – and native of Rio Grande do Sul) along with civic honours at the city hall.

Perhaps more importantly for Ronaldinho, both he and Gavião were offered professional contracts at Grêmio. In fact, the club had tried to rush through the process before they had departed for Egypt but both were now able to command a contract well in excess of the typical BR$300 per month (roughly £75) offered to new professionals at the club. While Ronaldinho was viewed as the more likely future star, Gavião had already made the bench of the first team under previous coach Luiz Felipe Scolari.

Grêmio habitually spend pre-season at their base in the Serra Gaúcha mountain range, in the twin towns of Gramado e Canela. In 1998, a series of low-key friendlies for Grêmio were organised at Canela, including a match against local side Esporte Clube Serrano. Grêmio won 2–0 and Ronaldinho, aged seventeen, came off the bench to represent the senior side for the first time.

However, a game the following day, 18 January 1998, against Ortopé of Canela, is recognised as his official professional debut (the Serrano fixture must be considered more of a training match). Grêmio won 8–0 with Ronaldinho helping himself to a goal.

Ronaldinho was proving to be the main attraction at these friendlies, putting in several eye-catching displays and triggering debate among *gremistas* as to whether it was too early for him to be given a place in the starting eleven once the season proper got under way. Grêmio legend Tarciso, a forward who played at the club for over ten years and was a member of the 1983 World Club Cup winning side, was in the 'for' camp and was heard on local TV demanding that Ronaldinho be given his chance: 'I was a first-teamer aged seventeen. He who knows (how to play) knows and Ronaldinho has got it all to make it work.'

Grêmio's coach at the time was Sebastião Lazaroni, the former Brazil manager (still reviled by many in Brazil for his unsuccessful handling of the 1990 World Cup team) who had recently returned from a spell working in Turkey.

Lazaroni was forever being asked about Ronaldinho but, though clearly impressed, was keen to keep a sense of perspective: 'Some of the established players are still getting back up to speed and the youngsters are benefiting from working among them. Ronaldinho, for example, is only seventeen but he already displays great maturity. However, pre-season is not about evaluating individuals but creating a team harmony and that is what we are doing.' For many, Ronaldinho was still too wiry, so taking measures to gain more muscular mass was viewed as a priority. Tinga had turned professional the previous season and had suffered a similar stigma: he had worked a great deal to bulk himself up and was now being cited as an example to Ronaldinho.

In fact, Tinga was proving to be something of a mentor for Ronaldinho, guiding the young player through the process of entering the professional ranks. Initially shy, Ronaldinho would stick close to his friend while training. In that period, Ronaldinho was getting up at 6.30 a.m. to catch two buses to the stadium for training: Tinga would usually give him a lift home.

The Grêmio president, Luís Carlo Silveira Martins, better known as 'Cacalo', was clearly pleased with the progress of Ronaldinho and the other young professionals. When facing criticisms over the financial state of the club, he countered by claiming that in Ronaldinho, Tinga and Zé Alcino (a few years older than Ronaldinho, he would go on to play for city rivals Internacional as well as in France and China), the club had a trio of assets worth BR$16 million, or £3.7 million (Ronaldinho was valued at BR$10 million – £2.2 million).

To Cacalo's adversaries, this was pure fanciful thinking: how can a boy who has never played a serious game as a professional suddenly be valued so highly? However, it did highlight the club's belief in Ronaldinho's potential as well as (with the benefit of hindsight) serve as a warning of Grêmio's reliance upon him as their principal financial asset.

On 16 February 1998, Ronaldinho signed his first professional contract with the club. Represented by Jorge Machado, one of Brazil's major movers in the murky world of football agents, he put pen to paper on a three-year deal worth BR$20 million (£4.4 million) in his first year, BR$30 million (£6.6 million) in his second and BR$40 million (£8.8 million) in the third, which would ensure Grêmio of his services until the end of 2000.

No sooner had he signed as a professional with Grêmio than he was departing the club to join the Brazil Under-20 side, but he returned to Porto Alegre in time to come on as a substitute in a game against São Luiz on 22 February. Ronaldinho was already the fans' favourite but this game marked the beginning of serious debate about his contribution. He smashed a free-kick against the crossbar and then went on a mazy run past three defenders that nearly resulted in the winner. The fans went wild. However, coach Lazaroni was not so impressed: 'He played well but he must learn to participate more. A player can't just interest himself in attack. He has to get back and mark up so that his midfield colleagues are not overrun.' Local journalist Hiltor Mombach, writing in his column for *Correio do Povo*, agreed: 'Just like his brother, he needs to marry his great technique with a sense of the collective. It is not enough to just enter into the game when the ball is at his feet.' And so began a discussion that would mark Ronaldinho's early career at Grêmio.

It was not the easiest of times for a young player to be turning professional at Grêmio. It was early 1998 and the club was emerging from the most glorious period in its history: after a golden decade in the 1980s, including the pinnacle achievement of the World Club Cup, the 90s had seen Grêmio claim the Brazilian Cup in 1994 and 1997, the League in 1996 and the South American Libertadores Cup in 1995. The fans had grown used to success and were demanding more of it right away.

Gavião remembers the experience as a steep learning curve: 'It was a difficult period; Grêmio had won many recent titles, both national and continental, so there was a lot of pressure on what was a new team, one which we were trying to become a part of. There were lots of criticisms as the new team found its feet.

'Ronaldinho even came in for some criticism,' says Gavião. 'He had characteristics of ability and speed, while in our state football has different characteristics, so there were critics in this regard.'

The 'different characteristics' Gavião refers to are hard work and the team ethic, sources of local pride in Rio Grande do Sul, much more so than individual brilliance. This meant the unpredictable flair of Ronaldinho sat uncomfortably with the Grêmio fans. They sympathised much more easily with someone like Tinga and his all-action style. If a player is to become successful in the south, he has to pull his weight or, as one local commentator put it, Ronaldinho 'will have to learn that the other ten players won't carry the piano so that he can shine at concert time'.

Luiz Carlos Goiano, a midfield colleague of Ronaldinho, disagreed: 'All the coach asks is that Ronaldinho gets behind the ball when we are being attacked. But, if needs be, I'll carry the piano, the table and everything else for him. We all win together.'

For Gavião, Ronaldinho proving himself was only a matter of time. 'Bit by bit, the team began to improve and Ronaldinho began to show his qualities. He is a genius and he began to showcase his amazing skills and people began to go to the stadium just to watch him.'

He was soon winning Lazaroni over too, who commented, 'He always was very good technically, now he has become more participative. He is a player who doesn't need to improve any of the fundamentals, he has them all.'

Sérgio Vasques recalls a conversation with Lazaroni in the club's boardroom: 'Somebody said to him that it must be a difficult job, managing the team. Lazaroni replied that it wasn't as hard as you might think: you just pick Ronaldinho and ten others.'

But football is a fickle business and a disastrous result in Mexico, losing 1–0 to Guadalajara in the Libertadores Cup (it was the first year Mexican clubs had been invited to partake in South America's premier club tournament and so they were something of an unknown quantity), saw Ronaldinho made the scapegoat. Heavy marking ensured the game passed him by and he was substituted.

Most people were suddenly calling for Ronaldinho to be dropped but Lazaroni was advised to keep him in by the president himself, Cacalo. The decision paid off: Ronaldinho was instrumental as Grêmio defeated América, also of Mexico, in the next game of the Libertadores and drew the loudest cheers from the four hundred fans awaiting the team's return at Porto Alegre airport.

Further tribulations were soon to follow: a slump in form by the team in general saw Ronaldinho's contribution once again questioned. For many observers, he didn't quite merit the hysterical response he was inspiring in the fans: he was seen as something of an incognito; he liked to burst forward and not track back and yet rarely scored. In fact, he had even stated in the press that scoring goals really wasn't his thing. For some commentators this was too much: 'he does little and wants pampering too'.

Another question was where to play Ronaldinho. In Brazil, the standard formation is 4–2–2–2. This means a traditional back four featuring two *zagueiros* (centre-halves) and two *laterais* (full-backs), though in truth Brazilian full-backs are really wing-backs and expected to cover the entire flank, defence and attack. Two *volantes* (holding midfielders) sit in front of the defence and two *meias* (attacking midfielders) play just behind the *atacantes* (forwards). Guilherme was the only established *atacante* and Ronaldinho had been tried alongside him, as had Tinga, Zé Alcino and Beto, a Brazil international and recent signing from Napoli, Italy. All had also occupied the *meia* positions and generally been shuffled around, with every combination tried at some point.

For the next game in the Libertadores, at home to Guadalajara, Ronaldinho had a new role; he was given free rein to be responsible for the creative drive of the team. The change of tactic paid off – eventually. In the first half he was asked to cover too deep but, once freed of such chores, he led Grêmio to victory in the second half, scoring his first goal in official competition as a professional and then setting up the second. He was evidently relieved: 'That is how I know how to play. Thanks be to God, tonight I can finally sleep at ease.'

There followed a two-leg victory over Nacional of Uruguay and, against the odds, Grêmio had made it to the Libertadores quarterfinals.

But as Ronaldinho's reputation spread, so came extra attention on the field; it was widely believed that he had no answer to close marking. São Paulo hosted Grêmio in the Brazilian Cup and Zé Carlos, a member of Brazil's 1998 World Cup squad, ensured victory for the *saopaulinos* by barely allowing Ronaldinho a kick.

Grêmio soon exited the state championship too; defeat at the hands of Brasil de Pelotas was the end of the team's campaign and also the end of coach Lazaroni's time in charge. The manager who had given Ronaldinho his professional debut was sacked.

The new man at the helm was Edinho, a Brazil international at the 1986 World Cup who had gone on to play for Grêmio and who had been managing Rio club Fluminense earlier in the year. Edinho took over in time for the key Libertadores quarterfinal tie with Vasco. Despite a perceived improvement in the team's play, Grêmio were knocked out.

In June 1998, as the team prepared for the Brazilian championship, transfer rumours made the usual rounds. Most alarming of all the possible comings and goings for *gremistas* was the proposed sale of both Tinga and Ronaldinho in a combined BR$10 million package (£2.2 million) offered by an undisclosed Italian club. Meanwhile, Uruguayan agent Juan Figer, one of seven Fifa-recognised agents operating in Brazil at the time and perhaps the biggest of the lot, proposed paying Grêmio half such a fee for the pair and finding a club in Europe to stump up the other half. It might sound like a strange scheme but Grêmio had already sold two of its stars of the mid-90s, Paulo Nunes and Mário Jardel, in this manner. The agent and new club would then be joint-owners of the player, the agent treating his share as an investment to be sold in the future.

Yet, as the season got under way, at Grêmio they both remained.

The fixture list had thrown up a tasty start to the campaign with a local derby against Internacional in the opening match. Grêmio versus Internacional is known as the *Gre-Nal* and this was to be Ronaldinho's first. It would prove to be one for him to forget. Having been reduced to ten men, the team needed defensive cover and Ronaldinho was sacrificed, substituted after just half an hour as Grêmio slumped to a 1–0 defeat.

In fact, he had not been expected to play in the first place but rather start on the bench, with new signing Rodrigo Mendes taking his spot. In the typical hysteria that accompanies any derby defeat anywhere, the last-minute change of heart was heavily criticised as commentators questioned coach Edinho's logic. The choice of Ronaldinho and Tinga alongside one another was seen as an act of suicide as neither of them covered defensively. Ronaldinho was dropped for the next two games: both were lost and Edinho was on his way.

Celso Roth had worked under Scolari at Grêmio as a fitness coach in the late 80s before moving into management. He had recently enjoyed a successful spell at Internacional but had parted company from them early that year, 1998. He had since been in charge at Vitória in the northern state of Bahia but Grêmio made him a strong offer and he elected to return to Porto Alegre and to his native Rio Grande do Sul.

Roth managed to stop the rot with two goalless draws, but victories remained hard to come by. Soon, following poor performances in both the league and the Mercosul, Grêmio found itself having failed to win in ten successive attempts. Ronaldinho was in and out of the team as Roth searched for the winning formula.

The Mercosul was an intercontinental competition involving teams from the South American common market – Brazil, Argentina, Paraguay and Uruguay – plus Chile, which made up for lack of traditional prestige with generous prize money. Eventually, after fourteen games without a win, this competition brought an end to the streak, or fast (*jejum*) as Brazilians call it, with a decisive 5–1 win over Universidade Católica of Chile. Ronaldinho scored the fourth from the penalty spot. This was followed by league wins over Vitória and Paraná. The turnaround seemed complete when they beat the previously undefeated Santos in the league, but Grêmio's form remained mixed for the remainder of the season. A poor performance against Ponte Preta provoked major discord in their own supporters; Ronaldinho, copping the blame for the team's lack of forward fluidity, left the field to a chorus of boos when substituted. He responded in style, scoring the only goal of a 1–0 win over Vasco in the next game.

In a narrow league, Grêmio thus bounced between fears of relegation and dreams of sneaking into the play-offs (in those days, the Brazilian

Championship was decided by a play-off series involving the top eight league finishers). This yo-yo scenario repeated itself for the rest of the season until, somehow, Grêmio stumbled into eighth spot and a play-off contest against Corinthians, who had finished top.

By then, Ronaldinho had lost his place in the team. He had missed a couple of matches through injury and then been away with the Brazil Under-20 squad. By the time he returned, he was out of the loop and not involved as Grêmio lost the first game against Corinthians 1–0 in a sunny and packed Estádio Olímpico. To everyone's surprise, they recovered to win 2–0 away in the Pacaembu, Corinthians' preferred São Paulo home, meaning the series went to a third and final deciding match. Ronaldinho was recalled and took his place on the bench. Grêmio lost 1–0 and Ronaldinho's appearance as a substitute made little difference, but there was no disgrace in losing over three games to Corinthians, the highest placed team and the eventual champions – qualification for the play-offs had, in itself, been a minor miracle. A difficult season had ended with cause for optimism.

Celso Roth remembers the period well: 'Grêmio at that stage had recently won a great deal; Luiz Felipe Scolari had brought many titles. But when Ronaldinho joined the professionals, Grêmio were actually in a period of technical decadence.

'We had several problems when I came along. Grêmio were bottom of the Brazilian league and trying to incorporate various players from the academy – Tinga, Gavião, Rodrigo Gral, Anderson Polga and Ronaldinho himself. All were coming in at a time of transition as Grêmio moved from being champions to forming a new team.

'But that group (of players) was very important for Grêmio. They were strong friends and they had something special. I used to tell them that this was their time.'

Gavião agrees: 'We had all come through at the same time, so there was a family atmosphere among the five of us. We helped one another, going to watch and support each other all the time.'

Roth again: 'At the end of 1998, we moved from bottom to qualify for the play-offs. Ronaldinho played in some games but not all because of his comings and goings with the national squad. It was twenty days here, twenty days there, and that's why he didn't earn a starting spot straight away. Because he kept being called up for the *Seleção*, he had no sequence of games at Grêmio and it took him a little longer to establish himself as a starter.

'Ronaldinho also had physical problems around that time because he never got any rest, to recuperate, and yet he never did a proper pre-season, had proper preparation, either. This is one reason why many players don't make it when they step up from Under-17 to the professionals.

'It was hard on him. But he overcame it, demonstrating the star player he is.'

Rafael Scheidt was Grêmio's centre-back at the time. He was some four years older than Ronaldinho and had started at the club aged thirteen, so had been aware of him for a long time.

'I played with him in the professionals when he came through. People always expected a lot of him; Grêmio were grooming him, preparing him to be a great player. Physically and nutritionally he got different treatment. Everyone knew he could become a great player, because his brother had been one, and so everyone invested a lot in him and it came off.

'Really, he came through with Celso Roth. He wasn't an immediate starter, playing bit by bit in each game. He was very young. Everyone was careful with him and that is why he was often on the bench, to help him acclimatise and to take the pressure away. I think the coach helped his development a lot by doing this, to bring him in slowly and pick the right time to let him flourish.

'Which turned out to be the state championship of 1999.'

In Brazilian football, the first months of the year are traditionally dedicated to inter-state tournaments. Because of the country's huge size, a fully integrated national league was only begun in 1971, while state cups have been played since the early decades of the twentieth century. This means these have a longer tradition and are therefore respected and prestigious in their own right.

These days, the Brazilian national league, the Brasileirão, runs from April through to December and is seen as the most important domestic competition. There is also a Brazilian Cup, the Copa do Brasil, which is held in high regard because the winner qualifies for the Libertadores, South America's Champions League. The Copa do Brasil is only disputed by those teams who performed well in their respective state tournaments, but doesn't feature any of the teams playing in that year's Libertadores. This means that five or six of the best teams are not in it. The Copa do Brasil is, therefore, viewed as the easiest way to qualify for the Libertadores (the other spots go to the highest finishers in the Brasileirão).

The Libertadores, meanwhile, is the main focus for those teams competing in it. Usually getting under way in February, reserve players will often represent clubs in the state championships or Brasileirão ahead of key Libertadores fixtures, to rest the first-teamers.

But winning the Libertadores is not the be-all and end-all. This is the World Club Cup, the match traditionally disputed between the European Cup and Libertadores Cup winners in Tokyo but in 2005 expanded to include the club champions of other regions. Although not viewed as particularly important in Europe, in Brazil, winning this comes second in prestige only to winning the World Cup with your country. If a Brazilian side wins the Libertadores, the final typically being played towards the end of June, and is then to play the World Club Cup in December, they will likely play a reserve side in the league for the rest of the season. There is no real need to do well in the league because, as winners, they have already qualified for the Libertadores the following year. The risk of injury can be minimised and all energies can be directed to the World Club Cup, the pinnacle of club-football achievement.

For most teams, of course, such lofty ambitions are but a fantasy and the state tournament offers them the best chance of picking up some silverware. As for the fans, local rivalry often trumps the prestige of national or international tournaments and bragging rights for the next twelve months via the state title is seen as the priority. Therefore, although they do serve as something of a pre-season as teams integrate new players, these state tournaments are still keenly disputed.

For Ronaldinho, 1999 began with familiar problems presenting themselves; he was selected to play in the South American Under-20 qualifiers in Argentina in January, meaning he would miss much of Grêmio's training camp.

On a personal level, Ronaldinho was also sad to see his friend Tinga loaned out to play in Japan for a year.

But Ronaldinho was back with Grêmio for the start of the Rio Grande do Sul Championship, the Campeonato Gaúcho or, as it is popularly called, the *Gauchão*.

Celso Roth remembers the period thus: 'In 1999, in the first semester, Grêmio were in two competitions, the Gaúcho regional tournament and the Copa do Brasil, which is national. This is the more important as it provides a place in the Libertadores.

'We made it very clear to Ronaldinho that Grêmio would have two teams; the first-team squad which would dispute the Copa do Brasil and a mixed team of first-teamers and reserves which would play the Gaúcho.

'I presented Ronaldinho with a challenge: I told him that I would play him as a *meia* – more or less as he plays today for Barcelona – in the Gaúcho and we spoke carefully about this; if he was able to make himself a regular and play a long sequence of games in the Gaúcho championship, then he would be a first-teamer for Grêmio for a long time to come.

'Why? Because in Rio Grande do Sul we have certain particularities: the games in the interior are very difficult; the pitches are small, the air is terrible and the teams from the interior much prefer a physical approach to a technical one. Ronaldinho needed to overcome all this as part of a process of transition.'

In fact, it is usual procedure for the reserve players of Grêmio to negotiate the first round of the *Gauchão* with only occasional help from the odd first-teamer before the senior players take over in earnest in the second round. Ronaldinho duly took to the field to participate in the first match of that year's championship against Guarani. He scored two and created a good deal more in a 3–2 win.

However, Ronaldinho's much-needed run of games at Grêmio was again cut short as he and Rodrigo Gral joined up with the Brazil Under-20s to play the World Cup in Nigeria. In their absence, Grêmio struggled and the first-team suffered a first-leg loss to Flamengo in the Copa do Brasil.

Brazilian football never being shy to cash in on television money and clog up the fixture list, that year there was another cup to play for, the Copa Sul, a knockout tournament disputed by the leading teams from Rio Grande do Sul, Santa Catarina and Paraná, Brazil's three southernmost states. After disappointment in Nigeria, Ronaldinho was back in time for the Copa Sul's final in Curitiba, against Paraná Clube. Grêmio rose to the occasion and ran out 1–0 winners. Ronaldinho came on as a second-half substitute, as did Gavião, making the conquest their first senior trophy at the club.

This gave Grêmio a lift and improvement was subsequently shown with victories in the *Gauchão* and a spirited draw in the second leg of the Copa do Brasil versus Flamengo. Ronaldinho came off the bench to inspire a comeback but the game finished 2–2 and Grêmio were out. The *tricolor*, as Grêmio are known due to their three colours (blue, black and white), now had only the *Gauchão* to focus on.

Ronaldinho's influence was increasing by the game. He scored both goals in a 2–0 win against Lajeadense, including a classic slalom dribble which he would later pick out as his personal favourite of all the goals he scored that tournament. Playing as an out-and-out striker, he ran the show.

After the Flamengo game, Roth had admitted that Ronaldinho was now ready to claim a permanent place in the first team. His performance against Lajeadense confirmed his progress and Roth, noting how much Ronaldinho was benefiting from a prolonged run in the team, announced that Ronaldinho had made the right-side forward spot his own for the second round of the competition.

He was soon justifying such faith. Ronaldinho scored two, set up the third and even won and missed a penalty in a 3–0 victory over Pelotas. One of his goals would later be recalled by many as his best in a *tricolor* shirt: he dribbled through the whole Pelotas defence before entering the area from the left; as he approached the six-yard box, instead of shooting hard he applied a finish as cute as it was precise, poking it past the keeper into the opposite corner. He then jumped onto the running track at the side of the pitch, swivelled his shirt around so that the number nine was at the front and began beating his chest.

Ronaldinho later claimed that this gesture was directed towards his mum seated in the crowd and was merely a means of sharing with her a moment that to him symbolised that he had made it, that he was a first-team player for Grêmio. However, it was read by most observers as a snub to those who had said that he couldn't spearhead the attack.

A very dull 0–0 draw with Caxias followed but in the return fixture, this time at home, Ronaldinho orchestrated a 3–0 win; he scored one and set up the other two. The local press were not entirely satisfied and pointed out that Ronaldinho's by now routine match-winning displays were simply disguising the fact that Grêmio had no proper strikers.

Ronaldinho scored in a 3–2 win at home to Inter de Santa Maria next and soon Grêmio were through to the quarterfinals. The first leg proved disastrous; away to Avenida, Grêmio lost 1–0 and ended the game with ten men after no fewer than four players were forced off through injury. In the second leg, an eleven-man Grêmio won 3–0 to force extra-time (aggregate goals counted for nothing) in which a 1–0 win took them through to the semifinals. Ronaldinho was the best player on show and scored two while Gavião scored the winner with a long-range effort. Ronaldinho's brace took him to the top of the scoring charts with eleven, this despite not always being employed as an out-and-out striker.

Grêmio were drawn against Veranópolis in the semifinals, a side from the Serra who had made the last four for the second year in a row. In the away first leg, Ronaldinho bagged the second in a 2–0 win and in the return leg he scored with a penalty to make it 3–3. This took the tie to a deciding third game (the winning team must accumulate a theoretical five points) but, having picked up his third yellow card of the tournament, Ronaldinho was forced to sit out the decider. His colleagues did the business without him; Grêmio won 2–1 and headed to the final.

In most Latin countries, the term 'classic' is applied to any big match involving two popular, traditional rivals. Grêmio versus Internacional is the classic of the south – the *Gre-Nal*. The final match – in this case final three as the final was a 'best-of-three' series – is known as the 'decision'. A *Gre-Nal* classic as the decision was the dream ticket.

The *Gre-Nal* is a derby of sufficient standing to draw the attention of the rest of Brazil. But it is in the state of Rio Grande do Sul where it really matters. Everybody, whether from Porto Alegre or a town in the interior, favours either Grêmio or Inter. Even fans of other top teams in other cities will still have an allegiance to one or the other of the Porto Alegre giants.

Grêmio and Internacional are by far the two biggest teams in Rio Grande do Sul and, since the 60s, had met each other in the final of the *Gauchão* nearly every single year until the 90s. Juventude had then begun to break the hegemony and a *Gre-Nal* decision was now only coming around, on average, every other year, which had only served to ratchet up the tension and increase the rivalry. (In fact, after the 1999 decision, fans would have to wait until the *Gauchão* of 2006 for the next *Gre-Nal* final, won, despite major underdog status, by Grêmio).

The *Gauchão* was first played in 1921 and, by 2006, Grêmio had won the trophy 34 times Inter 37; in 1999 the balance stood 33 wins to 31 in favour of Inter. No other team has won it more than twice.

Back then, Grêmio had last won it in 1996 (against Juventude in the final) and had lost to Inter (then managed by Celso Roth) in 1997. Juventude had beaten Inter in the final the previous year.

The first game in the 1999 series would be the 339th *Gre-Nal* in history and it was generating all the excitement such a traditional fixture had earned over the years. Perform well in a classic such as this and you would be immortalised in the memory of the club and its supporters; choke and you would be forever marked as a loser, associated with fiasco. The stage was set for somebody to make a hero of themselves.

The pre-decision build-up focused on the attack duos of the two teams. At Internacional, Fabiano and Christian had been terrorising defences for quite some time. Christian had already played in Europe (in Portugal) and been capped by Brazil. His recent good form meant he was being linked with big-money moves abroad again (Paris Saint-Germain eventually snapped him up later that year).

In the opposite corner, Ronaldinho and Rodrigo Gral were just starting out in their careers but had been generating headlines. They were an atypical partnership: they didn't play side by side in the target-man and creator mould but, in fact, often played quite distant from one another. Yet they had made it work and had been able to transform their great friendship off the pitch into a brilliant understanding on it.

Adding spice to the occasion, Christian went into the *Gre-Nal* decisive series as the tournament's top scorer with fourteen, while Ronaldinho was a goal behind on thirteen.

Such hype had not been lost on the respective managers and the resulting first match, at Internacional's Beira-Rio stadium, was a very tight affair, dominated by defensive man-marking. Grêmio played three *zagueiros* with one, Rafael Scheidt, shadowing Christian. Inter's *volantes*, Dunga and Régis, dropped deep and kept very close tabs on Ronaldinho, preventing him from embarking on any trademark dribbles. He escaped on one occasion in the second half and, bursting in from the right, nearly scored. He also took a free-kick from the arc on the edge of the box which hit the crossbar and bounced down upon the line. There was a major dispute about whether or not the ball actually crossed the line (it probably did) but no goal was given and Inter, who scored through Gonçalves, took a 1–0 advantage into the next leg.

In the second game, at the Estádio Olímpico, Grêmio attacked from the off and generally put in a performance of tremendous spirit and determination – the Grêmio way. Some tactical fine-tuning saw Ronaldinho drop back as a *meia*. He was heavily marked again – in one memorable run down the left he was surrounded by four opponents who still couldn't stop him and had to resort to bringing him down, but he was able to find the space denied him in the first leg. He scored a great free-kick and was named man of the match as Grêmio ran out 2–0 winners, Agnaldo also finding the net. This meant Grêmio needed only to draw in the third game, also at home, to seal the title.

All the accolades were for Ronaldinho and he was exhilarated. 'This time the ball definitely went in,' he told reporters. 'I want a tape of the radio commentary to keep as it was my first goal in a *Gre-Nal*. Since childhood, my dream has always been to score a goal in the *Gre-Nal*.'

Yet he was also trying to keep his feet on the ground. 'I am pleased that my performance has been praised but it is not the time for this. We have to be focused for the game on Sunday as we have not won anything yet.'

Internacional's players were less pleased with the balance of play and began to protest in the local press. Dunga had been a high-profile signing by Inter in the close season. A living legend of Brazilian football, captain of the 1994 World Cup winning team, he was a native of Rio Grande do Sul and had begun his career with Internacional in the 80s, winning the *Gauchão* in 1982, 1983 and 1984. Since then he had enjoyed successful spells in Italy, Germany and Japan. His return to Inter had been a major coup for the club but an expensive one; he had arrived on a free but his wages were high. So far, he had not really been proving his worth and was under pressure.

After losing the second game he came up with a surprising excuse: 'The defeat shows that whoever commits the most fouls in the decision wins.' It was a curious analysis, especially from a player famed for his tough tackling and competitiveness.

However, several other Inter players joined the chorus, many condemning Ronaldinho's supposed dirty tackling in particular. 'Twice against me he went in with his studs showing. You don't do that,' stated Régis.

'Ronaldinho's challenges were malicious. He could have broken someone's bones,' added Gonçalves, Inter's centre-back. 'The consequences could be dangerous for him; he has his career ahead of him, I'm ending mine. If he continues tackling like this, sooner or later someone is going to chop him.'

Ronaldinho, while reluctant to enter into a war of words, denied any bad intentions. 'I always go in hard but if I injured him (Dunga) it was accidental. He is an example to us all and I admire him as a player.'

In fact, Ronaldinho was keeping fairly relaxed as the final game approached. He and Rodrigo Gral planned a celebration dance to perform if either of them scored. Inter rival Christian was already renowned for his fancy celebrations and it had been noted that Ronaldinho had picked the ball up and kissed it before taking the free-kick from which he scored. This was something that Marcelinho Carioca, a player for Corinthians and possibly the biggest star in Brazil at the time, was famous for.

That free-kick had also brought Ronaldinho level in the scoring charts with Christian. So, it was one victory apiece in the classic *Gre-Nal* decision with one game to go: Christian and Ronaldinho on fourteen goals each. Expectations were full to bursting.

The third game kicked off and Christian made the first impression, hitting the post with an early attempt. But the match was destined to be Ronaldinho's. On 44 minutes, he got hold of the ball and headed towards goal, beginning with a nutmeg (called a *janelinha* in Brazil – a little window) on Anderson, who had come to join Dunga in closing him down. He then laid it off to team-mate Capitão for a one-two and continued his run into the box, received the return pass and slid the ball with his left foot past goalkeeper Andre's left hand. It was the only goal of the game.

Ronaldinho had earned his place forever among the *tricolor* icons and left the pitch a venerated figure; the fans who had poured on to the pitch at the final whistle carried him to the tunnel, figure borne aloft, legs held together, arms akimbo.

It wasn't just the goal; he had been a constant danger, launching wave after wave of attack thanks to his dribbling ability. Local paper *Correio do Povo*, in its post-game analysis, awarded him 10 out of 10.

As for the subplot, his battle with Dunga, there was one very clear winner. First, Ronaldinho performed a *chapéu* or 'put a hat' on Dunga, as the Brazilians say, meaning he flicked the ball over Dunga's head, dodged round and collected it on the other side. Later, entering the area from the right-hand side, he conjured a dribble which had 'never been seen before', as *Zero Hora* declared. He dragged the ball around the back of his left leg using his right foot, in the manner of a Cruyff turn. He then shaped to perform a *chaleira*, which involves chipping the ball with one leg tucked behind the other and is usually associated with a flamboyant cross – but Ronaldinho produced a subtle chip to dink the ball over Dunga's left thigh. (The term *chaleira* is said to be a homage to Charles Miller, the son of a British railwayman and the man credited with introducing football to Brazil on returning from his studies in Southampton.) The dribble had all been done in one motion, on the run, and Dunga, who had been trying to jockey Ronaldinho away from goal, was left wrong-footed, unsure as to what had even happened. Ronaldinho skipped past him to follow the ball and whipped in a dangerous cross.

Dunga had warned Ronaldinho to expect some rough treatment and now the young man was humiliating him. However, Dunga never kicked Ronaldinho and then, as the half-time whistle blew, the old master won back his respect with a gallant gesture for all to see. He put his arm round Ronaldinho and praised his performance: 'That's it, that's how to play the game.'

For his part, Ronaldinho had also acted impeccably. He had sought Dunga out and asked for forgiveness for any late challenges in the second game. 'I told him it wasn't intentional, that I would never try foul play with someone who is an idol of mine.'

The moment was viewed as symbolic: a Brazilian legend who had seen it all looked on knowingly as a young pretender set off on the journey he himself had just completed. Dunga had once been in Ronaldinho's shoes and had proved himself to have the strength of character to fulfil his dreams, to go all the way. He had played in three World Cups, captaining his country to victory in one, to the final in another.

But Ronaldinho's nonchalant flick over Dunga's head had smacked of youthful exuberance and confidence, highlighting the fifteen-year age gap between them. It was time for the next generation to take over. Dunga was passing on the baton but doing so by providing an example of the dignity required to become a true great.

Grêmio's triumph had the orchestration of a maestro and would forever be remembered as the *Gauchão* in which Ronaldinho came of age. He finished the tournament as top scorer, with fifteen goals from sixteen games.

Celso Roth has won titles throughout his career as a coach but reserves a special place in the memory for that *Gauchão* of 1999. 'Ronaldinho said some things to us after the game, personal, important things, in tears, arms around us. These are the moments that mark the career of any professional. Now, when you see him winning prizes you look back with pride at those earlier times.'

Carlos Gavião agrees: 'That title was the start of it all for him really and he played a great match in the *Gre-Nal*, the sort I had become used to see him playing. It was our first real professional title and it affected me a lot at the time, but it does so even more these days, as back then I could never know just how great a player I was playing with and also living with outside football.'

One of the major factors of the triumph of 1999 was the number of home-produced players involved. As well as Gavião and Ronaldinho himself, Rafael Scheidt, Roger and Rodrigo Gral had all come through the club's junior ranks and had all represented Brazil at one level or other.

Rafael Scheidt played in the first two matches of the decision but was booked in the second match and suspended for the final game. Nevertheless, he too recalls that conquest as a special time: 'I played a bit in previous years' conquests (1995 and 1996) but '99 was the first thing I won as a regular. Great, great memories. Ronaldinho was an incredible person, always calm, humble, happy in his work, yet striving to succeed. In the dressing room he was always relaxed and friends with everybody, as he appears to still be these days. He was born to win and he has taken his opportunities and grown.'

Scheidt insists Ronaldinho's tendency to opt out of defensive duties never bothered him. 'I used to say, "Oh Ronaldo, don't you bother with marking – you just stay down there, score the goals and leave us to do the running for you."'

'He didn't do so many fancy tricks back then. He had the ability but he was more objective, trying to develop his game first in order to be able to do those things later. He was a bit more direct in his play, more forceful. Then in the final of the *Gauchão*, when he did the tricks on Dunga, that's when he began to reveal the moves that all the world has grown to love.'

Perhaps Celso Roth can best sum up the progress Ronaldinho had made in just a few short months. 'I had presented Ronaldinho with a challenge at the start of the year: to force himself into the starting eleven which played the Gaúcho. He didn't just pass that test, he became a regular in Grêmio's first-team proper, top scorer and voted best player in the Gaúcho, he scored the winning goal in the final and performed some amazing moves, including a *chapéu* on nobody less than Dunga, which will be remembered forever. And the next day he was called up for Brazil and so began his stardom.'

Indeed, the very next day Ronaldinho found himself named in the full Brazil squad set to dispute the Copa América. Life would never be the same again.

LITTLE RONALD THE COWBOY

If you speak of 'Ronaldinho' to a Brazilian, they assume that you are referring to Ronaldinho the 'Phenomenon', better known to us as Ronaldo of Real Madrid fame. Ronaldinho of Barcelona is, to Brazilians, Ronaldinho Gaúcho.

The confusion provides an introduction into the intricacies of Brazilian name-calling. Very few people use their full names. This is partly because they tend to be very long: but Luiz Inácio da Silva became president of Brazil in 2002 but was known to everyone by his nickname 'Lula' (which actually means squid but is also an affectionate alternative to Luiz), while the aforementioned Ronaldo (of Real Madrid) is really Ronaldo Luís Nazário de Lima.

Low levels of literacy and a corresponding disregard for the written word have undoubtedly played a role in the process but the real reason for the use of simplified names is that Brazil is generally an informal society and its people much prefer the familiarity of using a person's first name or alias. Some commentators would charge this peculiarity as another symptom of Brazil's fear of seriousness.

Ronaldo Assis de Moreira (Ronaldinho as we know him) was known at first to most within Grêmio as just Ronaldo as he made his way through the junior and amateur ranks. Yet soon, as his ability led him to progress faster than the other boys, he began to acquire the '-inho' extension. In Portuguese, the ending '-inho' acts as a diminutive, in effect turning Ronaldo into 'little Ronaldo'. (By the same token, Juninho means little Júnior, Serginho little Sérgio, Robinho little Robin.)

Having joined Grêmio at the age of seven, it is not hard to imagine how those working at the club and who had known Ronaldo Assis de Moreira from the beginning might come to affectionately refer to him as little Ronaldo, especially as he was always playing in the age group above his own with larger boys.

The Ronaldinho moniker was also convenient in that a full-back called Ronaldo had played at Grêmio for several years in the 1980s and a certain Ronaldo Alves was a first-teamer at the time Ronaldinho turned professional.

By the time Ronaldinho made the grade at Grêmio, the other Ronaldinho (he of Real Madrid) was no longer in Brazil, having moved to PSV Eindhoven of Holland in 1994, so there was never any need to distinguish between the two. There was some confusion at the Under-20 World Cup in Nigeria in April 1999, though, when foreign journalists thought this new Ronaldinho so similar to the other – in name, football ability and buckteeth – that they must be brothers. Their Brazilian colleagues had to put them right. But only when Ronaldinho was called up to join Brazil's senior Copa América squad in June 1999 did the problem really present itself.

Ronaldo the 'Phenomenon' had been given the '-inho' ending for similar reasons to Ronaldinho: when establishing himself, he was the young pretender with more established Ronaldos ahead of him. The Corinthians goalkeeper throughout the 1990s was called Ronaldo and, though he only made one appearance for the national team, was a high-profile player. Meanwhile, Ronaldão was busy winning everything in sight for São Paulo (Brazilian league, Libertadores, World Club Cup) and was a Brazil regular between 1992 and 1995. In the same way that '-inho' is diminutive in Portuguese, the '-ao' suffix is superlative, making Ronaldão 'big Ronaldo' – appropriate for the centre-half he was.

By 1999, both these other Ronaldos had departed the scene, but Ronaldinho (the Phenomenon) had become so successful and fans so accustomed to his name that it was difficult for them to adjust and allow him to graduate to full Ronaldo status. And so, as Brazil lined up for a friendly with Latvia, there was a real fear that two Ronaldinhos would appear on the team sheet.

Of course, it might seem logical to the outsider that all this confusion could easily be avoided by simply using one of the players' surnames: Ronaldinho Assis, perhaps. However, logic is little respected in Brazil when a creative way round a problem, *um jeito* as they say, can be found.

Manager Vanderlei Luxemburgo tried to exert some authority and told the press: 'I think that the more experienced Ronaldinho can lose the "-inho" and be just Ronaldo, like he is known elsewhere on the planet. The other, as he is just starting and is younger, can carry on as Ronaldinho.'

Left-back Roberto Carlos, meanwhile, had a more creative solution, announcing: 'I always just call Ronaldo "ugly" so Ronaldinho I'll simply call "hideous".'

The Porto Alegre newspaper *Correio do Povo* distinguished the two players by referring to Ronaldinho *o Nosso* (our one) and Ronaldinho *o Outro* (the other). Another attempt was to call the 'elder one' Ronaldinho of Inter (he played for Inter Milan at the time). The problem here was that as Grêmio's city rivals were also called Inter, it didn't quite sit right.

In the end, it was the fans themselves who solved the conundrum. After impressing in his first few games for the national team, Ronaldinho was sitting on the bench as Brazil cruised to an unimpressive victory over Mexico. Keen to get a glimpse of the hero of the hour, the terraces began to demand his introduction with a chorus of 'Gaúcho, Gaúcho, Gaúcho'.

It proved to be a successful chant; not only did Luxemburgo succumb to their demands and bring him on, but the Gaúcho label stuck. Ronaldinho would henceforth be known via the nickname affectionately given to the people of his state: Ronaldinho Gaúcho – 'little Ronald the cowboy', if you will.

It is perhaps hard to imagine John Motson describing an interchange of passes in the England midfield between 'Little Scouse Steve' and 'Big Cockney Dave' as Gerrard and Beckham combine, but that is what happens in Brazil when, say, Ronaldinho Gaúcho passes to Juninho Pernambucano (the Lyon player is from the state of Pernambuco whereas Juninho Paulista, ex-Middlesbrough, is from São Paulo state).

To this day, if there is a Barcelona game on television in Brazil – and virtually every Barcelona game is on television in Brazil – the commentators still yell Ronaldinho Gaúcho each time he touches the ball. And yet the other Ronaldinho, the 'Phenomenon', is now more or less universally known simply as Ronaldo.

Curiously, Ronaldinho's brother Roberto was, as a footballer, known simply as Assis. When he first started in Grêmio's juniors, there was already a Roberto so he became known by the family name.

At home, Ronaldinho's mum will usually refer to her 'Naldo', while typical schoolboy teasing also earned Ronaldinho the accolade *comedor do raton* (ratface) thanks to his goofy teeth. Some friends still call him *Dente* (tooth or fang), others, less obviously, 'Shock'. For a while, team-mates at Grêmio would label him *Lobão* (big wolf), after he began to celebrate goals by imitating the actions of an animal he had been impressed by in a documentary on the Discovery Channel. In Paris, the French, uncomfortable with the '-inho' pronunciation, labelled him Roni, a tradition carried on in Spain where he has become Ronnie, though much of the Barcelona faithful prefer 'Dinho'.

Elsewhere, Argentine television commentators for the ESPN sports channel like to give a nickname to every player and Ronaldinho has been burdened with the less-than-flattering pseudonym of Jah-Jah Binks, after the *Star Wars* creature.

However, when Argentina sports daily *Olé* challenged the validity of the original Ronaldinho Gaúcho name, they were really paying him the highest of compliments. After Argentina had fallen to their rivals Brazil in a high-profile international friendly, *Olé*'s headline proclaimed: 'This Ronaldinho is no Gaúcho'. In Argentina, the term Gaúcho means friendly and brotherly, and Brazil had won thanks to a dazzling display from Ronaldinho.

INTERNATIONAL WORTH, WEIGHT AND GOLD

While Ronaldinho was busy humiliating Dunga in the *Gauchão* final, a similar incident in the final of the *Paulista* (the São Paulo state championship) sparked scenes of mayhem.

Corinthians were cruising to victory over Palmeiras, their hated local rivals. The actual game was being drawn 2–2 so Corinthians' 3–0 first-leg advantage was in no danger of being challenged. After half an hour of the second half, the Corinthians players calmly stroked the ball to one another to run a few more minutes off the clock: Edílson, the centre-forward who had levelled the score just minutes earlier, even flicked the ball in the air and started doing kick-ups, going so far as to catch it and let it rest on his neck. This was viewed as a provocative gesture of absolute impudence by the Palmeiras players. Júnior, the Palmeiras left-back, was the closest player and threw himself at Edílson, closely followed by Paulo Nunes. Edílson, himself a former Palmeiras idol, kicked back and there followed an almighty brawl involving most of the players and members of the team benches.

So staggering was the on-pitch violence that the incident would gain notoriety in Britain a few years later as footage of the fighting did the rounds on email.

Vanderlei Luxemburgo had recently been Edílson's club manager at Corinthians – he combined the job of coach of club and country until the end of the 1998 league season when he left Corinthians to dedicate his time solely to the national team. He cut Edílson from Brazil's Copa América squad for inappropriate behaviour and replaced him with Ronaldinho.

Two pieces of outrageous ball trickery: one resulted in international isolation (it would take Edílson another year until he was called up again), the other opened the door to Ronaldinho. It is here we must recall journalist Pelotinha's description of Ronaldinho playing as a junior: 'It is one thing to dribble going forward, quite another to dribble to the side. Ronaldinho was never disrespectful.' Ronaldinho uses his skills to try to score goals, not simply to humiliate opponents.

As the news gradually spread and the press gathered to get Ronaldinho's reaction, he himself seemed dumbfounded. At first he couldn't believe what he was hearing and begged the gathered reporters: 'But is it really true?'

Ronaldinho was generally an unknown quantity outside of Rio Grande do Sul but Luxemburgo had been impressed by him back in the South American Under-20s tournament in Argentina and had monitored his progress ever since. He saw him as a potential wild card for the 2002 World Cup.

As the excitement grew in the build-up to the tournament, Ronaldinho provided the novelty value and was therefore the centre of attention. Indeed, he looked somewhat overwhelmed as the country's eyes fell upon him.

Ronaldo had been in the same position before and did his best to guide his namesake through the carnival of press coverage. A photo-shoot was hastily arranged with the two Ronnies and Ronaldo told the gathered throng that he knew how his fresh-faced team-mate felt: 'I also came into the *Seleção* very young. But we are a group of great players and he is here because he is one too.'

Ronaldinho, meanwhile, trying desperately to overcome his timidity, explained how Ronaldo, though now a colleague, had always been an idol of his. This was no simple diplomacy either. Pelotinha remembers a charity match down in Rio Grande do Sul when the two first met, though Ronaldo was less likely to recall the moment. 'At the end of every year there is what's called the Trianon, an all-star exhibition match organised for charity by an ex-player, Nei Oliveira. Assis always used to bring his family along. In 1993, in São Lourenço do Sul, Paulo Roberto (Grêmio star of the 1980s) arranged for Ronaldo the Phenomenon from Cruzeiro to play. Ronaldinho must have been thirteen and he knew of Ronaldo's fame. He was following him around, asking for autographs, getting in photos with him. Who would have thought that, a few years later . . .' Pelotinha tails off, needing to say no more.

In an attempt to help Ronaldinho integrate and feel at ease, he was assigned to room-share with Émerson, an established international whom he knew well from his Grêmio days. Émerson had graduated from the *Categorias de Base* and played for Grêmio in the mid-1990s, though he left just before Ronaldinho turned professional.

As a pre-tournament warm-up match with Latvia in Curitiba

approached, Ronaldinho seemed to be feeling more at home, both within the squad and in front of the media. It was expected that he would start the game against Latvia and he told reporters, 'I will not be intimidated. I know that I have to show up and play my own game. If I have a chance to run at someone, to try a dribble, I'll do it.'

And indeed he did: on 26 June 1999, Ronaldinho made his senior debut for Brazil as they beat Latvia 3–0. Ronaldinho played the full ninety minutes and performed very well; he supplied the cross for the first goal and was a generally busy presence all game, putting Ronaldo clean through late on (although he shot straight at the keeper).

Any Brazilian player still in his teens and about to partake in a major competition inevitably brings comparison to one legendary figure, and Pelé himself was impressed with what he saw. 'He was a surprise. He is a skilful player, smart and of quality. But let's try not to put too much responsibility on him just yet.'

In the Copa América, Brazil were drawn in Group B with Mexico, Chile and Venezuela. All games in the group were being played in Ciudad del Este, a city on the Paraguayan border with Brazil and Argentina.

In their first game, 30 June 1999, an ill-equipped Venezuela side let Brazil's attackers run riot and the *Seleção* were soon 4–0 up and heading for a routine victory. Ronaldinho was brought on in the second half to gain more experience at the highest level.

With fifteen minutes to go, and as practically his first contribution to the game, Ronaldinho controlled the ball on the edge of the area, flicked it over the approaching defender's head, ran round to collect it, touched it past another defender and moved in on goal. He then fired an angled shot into the corner beyond goalkeeper Veja before running to the arms of his team-mates, who surrounded him to celebrate the youngster's goal and the arrival of a new genius on the scene.

It was his first international goal and remains, to this day, his personal favourite.

Brazil went on to win 7–0 but everyone was talking about just one thing afterwards – Ronaldinho's strike. The goal was played over and over again on Brazilian television and Ronaldinho was suddenly a national hero and household name. When Ronaldinho dedicated the goal to his mother, Dona Miguelina promptly burst into tears.

Luxemburgo enjoyed the goal as much as anyone, as it seemed to justify the risk he had taken in promoting Ronaldinho. 'It was a goal of real beauty and defined the art of playing football with responsibility,' Luxemburgo said somewhat puzzlingly afterwards – probably alluding to the contrasting ways in which Ronaldinho and Edílson demonstrated their skills.

The next game was versus Mexico, and Brazil were leading 2–1 when, with ten minutes remaining, Ronaldinho came on for Amoroso. Brazil held on but Ronaldinho's cameo this time saw him barely get a kick.

Ronaldo took the plaudits in the next match, a 1–0 win over Chile. The 'Phenomenon' scored the only goal from the spot in the first half and, although Ronaldinho came on for Amoroso at half-time, his impact was once again minimal.

Chief rivals Argentina awaited in the quarterfinals. Any match between these two proud footballing nations is always a fiery affair and, with the game being played in Ciudad del Este, on the doorstep to both countries, this one was no different. Sorín opened the scoring for Argentina after eleven minutes but Rivaldo replied just after the half-hour mark before Ronaldo claimed what would prove to be the winner in the first few minutes of the second half. Ronaldinho made no appearance and watched from the bench as Ayala missed a crucial penalty for Argentina, completing what was a miserable tournament of spot-kicks for the *Albiceleste* (Martin Palermo had failed from the spot an incredible three times in Argentina's 3–0 defeat to Colombia in the group stage).

A rematch with Mexico in the semifinals was Brazil's prize. As Brazil laboured to a fairly uninspiring 2–0 victory, the fans clamoured for a glimpse of their new hero and called for Ronaldinho from the terraces. Luxemburgo complied with their wishes in a move that raised more than a few eyebrows. Firstly, for a coach known for his strong personality, it was a curious sight to see Luxemburgo so easily succumb to the demands of the fans. Secondly, in order to introduce Ronaldinho he took off Ronaldo. In previous games, Ronaldinho had come on for Amoroso: replacing Ronaldo with Christian would have been a more like-for-like switch.

Ronaldo was visibly unhappy at being taken off and it was evident to most observers that Luxemburgo was trying to provoke him. The manager appeared to be attempting to demonstrate to his star player that even he wasn't untouchable, that there were newcomers only too eager to fill his boots.

Five years earlier, Ronaldo had been the new kid on the block. He had scored a goal and set up the other two in a 3–0 victory over Iceland as a seventeen-year-old. This had earned him a late call-up to the World Cup squad of 1994 and all the hype and headlines that come with being the new sensation. He lived up to his early promise and became the youngest ever winner of the World Footballer of the Year award in 1996, aged just twenty, and then the first player to win the award back-to-back in 1997. But then came the drama of the 1998 World Cup final, when Ronaldo was struck down with a mysterious fit hours before kickoff, and he had been blamed in some quarters for Brazil's failure to lift the trophy. A flash lifestyle of fast cars (a Ferrari endorsement had been a particular PR nightmare in Brazil) and faster women was also isolating him from his Brazilian fan base, the vast majority of whom were of very humble means.

Now, with a potential new match-winner being unveiled in Ronaldinho, many fans and commentators suddenly no longer saw Brazil's future as so dependent upon Ronaldo, and were taking the opportunity to transfer their allegiances and bring the phenomenon down a peg or two.

The substitution seemed to embody all these underlying emotions.

In any case, Ronaldinho was unable to add to his fame in the fifteen minutes he was on the pitch against Mexico and the game petered out to end 2–0.

Uruguay then provided Brazil's final opponents and Ronaldo would come good, though Rivaldo would steal the show from both Rons.

Uruguay were not expected to pose too much of a problem; they had won just one match in the tournament group stages and had reached the final courtesy of victories on penalties over Paraguay in the quarterfinals and Chile in the semis and had no Europe-based players. In contrast, hosts Paraguay (who bizarrely emerged from a group containing Japan, the first non-American team invited to play the Copa América tournament) had exited undefeated in normal time having conceded a solitary goal.

Yet Uruguay's game was based on tight marking, discipline and a will to win, a recipe that could upset Brazil. What's more, the match would take place in Asunción, the first time during the tournament that the Brazilians had been forced to play away from Ciudad del Este, where they enjoyed considerable support.

For twenty minutes, Uruguay succeeded in frustrating Brazil and coped well with the *Seleção*'s great ball circulation. But Rivaldo was in inspired form and would not be denied. He scored two first-half goals, and when Ronaldo added a third just after half-time the game was over as a contest. Luxemburgo made no substitutions this time so Ronaldinho witnessed the final from the bench, but he had won his first senior tournament in the *verde-amarelo*, the green and yellow.

Brazil had arrived as reigning champions and favourites and never once looked weighed down by the pressure of expectations. They won all six of their games and scored seventeen goals in the process, conceding just two. It was the sixth time they had won the Copa América but the first occasion on which they had defended their status as champions. Established stars Ronaldo and Rivaldo ended the tournament as joint top scorers but, in Ronaldinho, Brazil had shown they had bright young things waiting in the wings. Everyone was satisfied.

The final had been played on 18 July 1999 and Brazil's Confederations Cup campaign was scheduled to begin just six days later, in Mexico. Seen as providing an opportunity for fringe players to establish themselves,

Ronaldinho was named in the squad while more senior players such as Ronaldo and Rivaldo were rested.

Before that the victorious Copa América party were first invited to the capital Brasília to celebrate the Copa América victory with an audience with the president, Fernando Henrique Cardoso.

Ronaldinho's sudden rise to prominence had been noted in Europe and there were many scouts at the Confederations Cup specifically to see him perform. Grêmio were being inundated with offers and inquiries.

The Mexican fans had obviously also been impressed with his Copa América displays and came out in force to cheer him wherever he went, treating him as the star of the *Seleção*. There was also much excitement in Porto Alegre: local boys Ronaldinho and Christian were to start up front for Brazil together.

The Confederations Cup brings together the champions of each continent and Brazil were in a group with the USA, New Zealand and Germany. They met the latter in their first game and won 4–0 with Ronaldinho in devastating form. When brought down for a penalty, he grabbed hold of the ball to take it himself. Serginho was Brazil's designated penalty taker, so confused eyes turned to the bench for guidance. Luxemburgo waved Ronaldinho to carry on and he duly tucked it away.

His scoring form continued as he netted the only goal – a header no less – in a 1–0 win over the USA. However, the *Seleção*'s performance was uninspiring, or 'bureaucratic' as Brazil's journalists chose to denounce it.

Ronaldinho also upset many by changing his goal celebration. Instead of the pirouette and punch in the air he had performed after his goal against Venezuela and repeated against Germany, against the US he fired imaginary pistols. Observers accused him of endorsing the gun culture so emblematic of Brazil's social problems. Although Ronaldinho tried to explain that it was simply a reference to a film that he and colleague Beto had been watching before the game, the incident served as notice of how fickle support of both fans and media could be; hero one day, villain the next. He was dropped to the bench for the following game.

This proved just as flat as the US contest with Brazil labouring to a 2–0 win over New Zealand and playing a football condemned as 'unworthy of four-time world champions' by the unsatisfied press corps. Ronaldinho had managed to enliven proceedings, scoring with a free-kick when he came on as a substitute, and thus earned back his starting berth for the semifinal against Saudi Arabia.

Here he finally dismissed all the critics with a sublime display; he scored three and was instrumental in many of the other goals in an 8–2 thrashing of the Middle East side.

The final pitted hosts Mexico against the *Seleção*. Mexico had a full-strength team playing and had lit up the tournament with an adventurous and attacking style of football. The match lived up to expectations and Mexico ran out 4–3 winners in a classic end-to-end encounter. Despite a superb performance, Ronaldinho was unable to find the net and ended the competition as joint top scorer with six goals, equal with Cuauhtémoc Blanco of Mexico and Marzouk Al Otaibi of Saudi Arabia.

Exactly one month after the Confederations Cup final, Brazil took to the field against Argentina in Buenos Aires for the first of a double-header of friendlies. A lacklustre display saw Brazil lose 2–0. Though celebrated at the time as the first match in which Ronaldo and Ronaldinho started side by side, given that Rivaldo was playing too, it was actually the first occasion that the triple-R strike force – which would win Brazil the 2002 World Cup – lined up together.

The return fixture was held in Porto Alegre (Brazil rotate their games around the country) a few days later at Internacional's Beira-Rio stadium. In training sessions performed on the pitch outside the ground, Ronaldinho had been booed by the watching Inter fans as soon as he touched the ball. There were real fears that such antagonism might carry over into the game itself and that Brazil might be heckled due to its Grêmio contingent (as well as Ronaldinho, there was Rafael Scheidt and former player Émerson). Luxemburgo, who had played for Inter in the 1970s, appealed for support.

In the end, nobody needed to have worried: inspired by Rivaldo, who scored a hat-trick, Brazil produced their most fluid display so far under Luxemburgo and ran out 4–2 winners. The fans were superb and cheered the team from start to finish, especially moves by the *gremistas*. In fact, the only booing heard all game was directed at coach Luxemburgo when he had the temerity to substitute one of the local heroes, Ronaldinho making way for Èlber with twenty minutes to go.

Rafael Scheidt had missed the Copa América and Confederations Cup but had since got back in favour with Luxemburgo. 'That game will stay with me for the rest of my life,' he says. 'Ronaldinho has enjoyed other great moments for the *Seleção* but I would imagine it is the same for him too because we were at home,' he reminisces. 'It was a South American classic, the two strongest teams of America, played in our home town; all our friends were there and the local support was fantastic.

'I remember I trembled before the game, my body just taken over with emotion and it was the same for him. He had a great match too. The game was just magnificent.

'Yes, there were many Inter fans there but that day we were all Gaúchos, it was that kind of relationship, everyone cheering for us.'

By this time, Ronaldinho was spending as much time with the national team, in its various guises, as he was with Grêmio. At the start of 2000, his club calculated that, what with the Olympic qualifying tournament, the Games themselves, World Cup qualifiers and friendly matches, in total Ronaldinho could be away from Grêmio for seven of the upcoming twelve months.

The football event at the Olympics was an Under-23 affair and the Brazil Under-23s had already played several friendlies, with Ronaldinho involved in all of them.

The senior side at that time usually played at least one friendly each month, typically in far-flung places. A parliamentary enquiry launched a few years later would investigate irregularities in the contract the CBF – the Brazilian Football Association – had with shirt manufacturer Nike: it was alleged, among other things, that the sport's brand itself arranged several of the *canarinha*'s friendly fixtures and had a good degree of influence with regard to who played in them; basically, Nike was accused of forcing the CBF to send star-studded Brazil teams to show off their kit in corners of the world where Nike wished to strengthen its market share.

Grêmio bemoaned the fact that Ronaldinho was called up for every single Brazil match and demanded that the CBF decide to which *Seleção* he actually belonged.

It is worth noting that, unlike in Europe where domestic leagues pause when the national teams perform, in Brazil it is very much a case of carry on regardless. Only during a World Cup tournament itself does the Brazilian league take a break.

Given his many commitments with the *Seleção*, some *gremistas* began to speculate whether or not Ronaldinho was really worth the bother: perhaps the time had come when they would be wise to cash in on their principal asset. They also claimed it was pointless to keep him when they couldn't get the best out of him: he was only an outstanding player when surrounded with other good players; at Grêmio, with mediocre colleagues, he was merely reasonable. The club was in a state of constant limbo without their star man, never properly developing as a team either with or without him.

This was the climate Ronaldinho left behind with the first of his appointments with the national team in 2000, the Olympic qualifiers.

Brazil take the Olympic football tournament very seriously indeed. It is the one major footballing honour the country has yet to achieve and, in a land that likes to call itself 'the football country', the pressure to complete the set is tremendous.

In order to compete for gold at the games, South American countries must first negotiate a qualifying tournament, which produces two representatives from the continent. As a measure of just how much of a priority the Olympic project is in Brazil, it is interesting to note that, prior to the 2000 qualifiers for Sydney, Brazil had won six of the ten South American pre-Olympic tournaments. They always send the strongest side possible.

Chile threatened to boycott the competition in a dispute over the uninspiring prize money on offer, but Luxemburgo claimed that his players needed no further motivation or reward than a possible gold medal.

Brazil hosted the qualifying event in 2000 with games split between Londrina and Cascavel, both in Paraná state. Brazil played all their games in Londrina and the crowds were large and demanding.

A lame 1–1 draw with Chile in the opener brought a chorus of boos from the stands. Ronaldinho was responsible for Brazil's brightest moments, setting up Alex for their only goal, but he was replaced in the second half. Not for the first time, substituting Ronaldinho, the crowd's favourite, proved problematic. Commentators argued that it had been clear to all that Brazil's weak defence would inevitably be breached but that, when it eventually was, Ronaldinho was no longer on the pitch to sort out the mess.

Brazil went on to defeat Ecuador 2–0 in the next game, Ronaldinho notching up the first, and followed this with a 3–0 triumph over Venezuela, Ronaldinho bagging the first and last. However, overall performances were poor and the atmosphere at games tense. There were even calls for Luxemburgo to go.

The last group game was against Colombia and a draw would see both teams through. Chile, the other team in the group still in with a shout, were so convinced that an amicable draw would be played out that all the players not involved in their final match headed home. Colombia also seemed convinced that a tie was a given and fielded a reserve team.

Yet Brazil had not read the script and stormed to a 9–0 win. Ronaldinho netted the second and last and was instrumental in many more. Incredibly, Luxemburgo told the press that he was not entirely happy with his star man. 'He hasn't been as good as I hoped, way too inconsistent,' he complained.

The next round also took a group format and Brazil won their tricky opener versus Argentina 4–2, courtesy of Ronaldinho and an inspired hat-trick. The fans had begun to enjoy themselves and Ronaldinho's name was chanted repeatedly.

In the next match, Ronaldinho was excellent again as Brazil beat Chile 3–1: he scored a free-kick and a header. This guaranteed Brazil a place at the Olympics (Chile would end up qualifying too).

The final game was with Uruguay, who, despite having been the most impressive team in the opening round, no longer had hopes of qualifying. They were determined to regain some dignity, however, and were soon 2–1 up. But Ronaldinho landed a free-kick on Fábio Júnior's head to equalise and Brazil were crowned the tournament champions. With it, Ronaldinho earned player-of-the-tournament accolades and finished as top scorer with nine goals.

So far Ronaldinho's rise with Brazil had been an almost nonstop success story – but matters were about to get more complicated.

Brazil's attention now turned to the 2002 World Cup qualifiers. South America's means of qualification was (and remains) a marathon league of home and away fixtures among the ten nations. Four go through direct, the fifth into an extra round to face a challenger from a different continent. Brazil's first match was to be against Colombia, and Ronaldinho was in the squad.

The Colombia game finished 0–0 and Luxemburgo's tactics were heavily criticised: he had left Ronaldinho on the bench and started with two target-men strikers, then brought Ronaldinho on with another creative forward, removing the attack's spearheads. The universal opinion was that it would surely have been better to mix and match.

The next qualifier was at home to Ecuador in April 2000. Ronaldinho was named in the squad that was expected to convene on the Sunday in São Paulo. Grêmio had a match on the Sunday and asked for dispensation for Ronaldinho to play and join up late but ready to train on the Monday. Flamengo and Atlético Mineiro made similar requests.

Luxemburgo and the CBF stood firm: it was to be Sunday and that was that. Grêmio were furious in the face of what they saw as unnecessary inflexibility and called Luxemburgo a dictator.

When Ronaldinho finally did show up, on the Sunday but a little later than planned, he was accused of being overweight by Brazil's delegation. Grêmio saw this as a direct insult aimed at the club's administration and vehemently denied such suggestions. According to Luxemburgo, Ronaldinho was four kilos heavier than he was during the Copa América and, in his book, players who arrived out of shape didn't play. Ronaldinho would watch from the sidelines. Rumours circulated that Ronaldinho himself then threatened to abandon the camp, though he later denied this.

Grêmio were indignant and stated that the club monitored every player's weight every day; Ronaldinho had left them weighing 75 kilos, he always weighed between 74 and 76 and, if he had put on weight since then, it was the *Seleção*'s problem.

The following day he was weighed again by Brazil's trainer and was found to be back below 75 kilos: he had lost three kilos overnight. Grêmio accused the *Seleção* of incompetence and the *Seleção* attempted to explain the confusion away by blaming unusual levels of liquid retention due to Ronaldinho having eaten salty food.

In any case, the damage was done and Ronaldinho remained dropped from the playing squad. Brazil started the game with Amoruso and Edílson up front, with some observers appreciating a certain kind of irony in the manner in which Edílson was now getting a chance at Ronaldinho's expense.

Brazil stumbled to a 3–2 victory and the team was booed and Luxemburgo taunted with donkey cries (in Brazil, the donkey insult is used for managers seen not to know what they are doing rather than for uncultured centre-halves). Luxemburgo was heavily criticised in the press, with the poor showing being put down to the farce regarding Ronaldinho's supposed fatness.

At Grêmio's request, Ronaldinho was excused from Brazil's next two friendlies (versus Wales and England in Britain) but when he was then left out of the squad to face Peru in the next World Cup qualifier, there was bewilderment from all sides.

Conspiracy theories did the rounds: some observers claimed it was due to Ronaldinho being sponsored by Pepsi and the *Seleção* by Coca-Cola; some said it was because Ronaldinho had refused a transfer to Europe that Luxemburgo himself had brokered; Gaúchos thought it was because of regionalism and a Rio/São Paulo bias (it had been insinuated during the overweight affair that Ronaldinho was fat because of eating too much *churrasco* barbecue).

Ronaldinho himself told reporters that it must simply be a case of other players being in better form than he was. However, this was said slightly tongue-in-cheek in the full knowledge that everyone knew what kind of great form he was in – Ronaldinho was on his way to winning player-of-the-tournament honours in the *Gauchão*.

The most credible explanation was that Ronaldinho had made a quip directed at the coach to which Luxemburgo had taken exception. This had led to the whole fatness episode and Ronaldinho was still being punished. Most people recognised that Luxemburgo was a manager with a strong personality and, in his own eyes at least, a certain star quality. None of his players – or their clubs – were bigger or more important than the manager himself and he was teaching Ronaldinho this the hard way.

Sure enough, Ronaldinho was recalled for the next game against Uruguay (drawn 1–1) and then again for the following tie versus Argentina. But here the whole overweight charade threatened to repeat itself: after running their usual tests, the *Seleção's* medical department claimed that Ronaldinho was injured and had clearly been so for some time. Grêmio hit back, denouncing such challenges to its integrity and claiming Ronaldinho to be in perfect health.

In the end, Ronaldinho played and a terrific team performance – and a 3–1 win – put Ronaldinho's fitness to the back of everyone's mind. He also picked up a booking, ruling him out of the next qualifier (versus Chile), so the club-versus-country spat was stalled.

On the eve of the Sydney Olympics, the *Seleção* had a World Cup qualifier to play against Bolivia. Romário, the star of Brazil's 1994 World Cup win, was in the squad and hoping to be included in the Olympic contingent (though it is an Under-23 tournament, the rules dictate that each country may play with three players above the age limit) and thus have a chance of winning the one international honour that had eluded him with Brazil. Ronaldinho was thrilled to be playing with Romário, a boyhood idol of his of whom he had watched countless videos.

The duo lined up together against Bolivia and Brazil won 5–0, but the scoreline flattered the *Seleção* and the crowd booed them. A few days later, Luxemburgo named the Olympic squad and Romário was not in it. With fans clamouring for Romário's inclusion, it was a bold move by the coach, especially as Luxemburgo was already working on borrowed time. Under his guidance, the national team's performances had been uninspiring and his bravura had begun to rub people up the wrong way. Meanwhile, he was also being accused of tax evasion, involvement in cocaine trafficking, falsifying his own documents when a junior player, and participation in players' transfers abroad (it was said that he picked certain players for the national team not on merit but simply to increase their market value, for which he was later rewarded with a kickback when the player was sold at an inflated price).

The quantity and variety of allegations being directed at him served as an indication of just how unpopular he had become: the scramble to find an excuse to sack him was leaving no stone unturned. In leaving Romário out of the squad, he was providing his detractors with further ammunition: should the team perform poorly and the decision be seen to have backfired, tactical incompetence would be the next charge.

Nevertheless, there were high hopes that this Brazil team could break the hoodoo of Brazil never taking football gold. They had won silver in 1984 (when, curiously, the Internacional team represented Brazil) and 1988 (with Romário in the team) and bronze in 1996. Without Romário, much was riding on the abilities of Ronaldinho and Alex, then of Palmeiras but latterly employed in Turkey for Fernabahce. For his part, Ronaldinho was certainly raring to go and declared that playing in the Olympic Games had always been a dream of his. By the end of the tournament, he would more likely describe it as a nightmare.

Brazil failed to impress in a 3–1 opening victory over Slovakia, with Ronaldinho and Alex anonymous. Then defeat by the same margin in the following game versus South Africa prompted all the usual soul-searching that comes whenever Brazil lose to a country viewed as lacking in footballing pedigree.

Everyone was poor, but Ronaldinho bore the brunt of most of the criticism. With his tactics being questioned, even Luxemburgo fumed at reporters, 'It is Ronaldinho who has to react, not me. He had an awful match.' This was the first time anyone could remember Luxemburgo speaking so negatively and directly about one of his players in his two years in charge. 'I only kept him on just to see if he could do one thing right,' he added.

Stung by the attack, Ronaldinho countered by telling the media that he was simply complying with orders, which were to stay open on the wing (as opposed to playing his normal game and dropping deeper to get the ball and then run with it).

In their final group game, a very laboured 1–0 win over Japan was enough to qualify them for the next round, though Ronaldinho was subbed off after another lacklustre display.

Cameroon awaited in the quarterfinals and a chance of redemption: all would be forgotten if Brazil kept progressing.

The Indomitable Lions' captain, Patrick Mboma, opened the scoring and, despite being down to nine men after two sendings off, Cameroon held on until the very last minute. A free-kick presented itself to Brazil and, with twelve seconds left on the clock, Ronaldinho fired in the equaliser.

In extra-time, Brazil piled on the pressure and missed two glorious chances to score, but it wasn't to be. On the counterattack, Cameroon's Mbami received the ball on the right, burst forward and hit a fierce shot from outside the box that left goalkeeper Helton with no chance: the Africans went through on a golden goal.

Wild scenes of jubilation in the Cameroon camp contrasted sharply with the utter desolation sketched on the faces of the Brazilians. Ronaldinho's trademark smile was nowhere to be seen, replaced by a pained look of anguish and sorrow. 'There are no words: nothing went right,' was his only comment. Luxemburgo himself was in tears: he knew that defeat was the end of the line for him, and he was fired shortly afterwards.

Cameroon went on to win gold with Samuel Eto'o, who would become Ronaldinho's strike partner several years later at Barcelona, a key component. The Brazilians, meanwhile, had to satisfy themselves with the unwanted consolation prize of the Fair Play trophy.

AH, E, RONALDINHHÔÔÔ!

Having become the star of the Grêmio team and a local hero in the *Gauchão* earlier in the year, Ronaldinho returned from the Confederations Cup a world star and national idol too. And if Ronaldinho had converted himself into one of the brightest prospects of the world game, Grêmio had to make changes too: they had to adapt to having become a club with one of the brightest prospects of the world game on their books.

The speed of Ronaldinho's rise was surprising to most *gremistas* and alarming to others. Coach Celso Roth was heard bemoaning the fact that Ronaldinho had only begun to shine because he had been free of junior *Seleção* commitments for the first time in his career and had been able to get a run in the Grêmio team. Having been absent for so long (two months), this time with the senior *Seleção*, Roth feared they would have to start all over again.

Much speculation had begun to link Ronaldinho with several big-money moves abroad in the wake of his Copa América exploits and these rumours only increased in number following the Confederations Cup. He claimed to Brazilian reporters that he wished to stay but mixed reports suggested that he had confided to others that he was ready to move to Europe.

Grêmio had raised his salary following the *Gauchão* triumph and he was now said to be earning BR$90 million (£22,000) per month. Such a figure had not escaped the public's attention and becoming a professional footballer was seen as a quick way of making lots of money. Since Ronaldinho's Brazil debut, the numbers of trialists at Grêmio had greatly increased.

Grêmio also attempted to absolve Ronaldinho from the chore of being the world's hottest property and fielding questions from interested parties left, right and centre. They fixed set hours each day when he would attend to media enquiries. Designed to ensure Ronaldinho wasn't under too much stress, it was presumably also supposed to dampen speculation and put off would-be suitors.

On the football field, Grêmio had been desperately missing their young talisman. Roth attempted to calm some of the hysteria and wild expectations that accompanied Ronaldinho's return by warning there was no guarantee he would walk straight back into the team.

Of course he did, though he couldn't shake the heavy marking employed by Vélez Sársfield in a Mercosul game and was fairly anonymous as Grêmio won 1–0. Soon after, on 26 September 1999, Grêmio lost to Guarani at the Olímpico and the question of how much responsibility it was fair to place on Ronaldinho's young shoulders was suddenly no longer Roth's concern. He was unceremoniously sacked.

Cláudio Duarte had played for Internacional throughout their glorious run in the 1970s and had gone on to coach them too. He had also been in charge at Grêmio before, winning the Copa do Brasil with Assis in 1989 but then overseeing the relegation season of 1991. Known for his defensive tendencies, Grêmio turned to him again to revive the club's fortunes.

The Duarte era got off to a bad start: Grêmio were thrashed 4–0 by Palmeiras and the coach controversially substituted Ronaldinho. The scoreline was harsh with three late goals exaggerating the difference between the two sides. Unfortunately for Duarte, it had been just 1–0 when Ronaldinho left the pitch, so all the ire of supporters and press focused on the curious decision to replace him, given that he had hit the post and come close to scoring on several occasions. Duarte claimed Ronaldinho was injured; Ronaldinho replied that he was not. The manager then attempted a show of strength and declared that no player was untouchable under his stewardship but, for many observers, he had lost the confidence of the *gremistas* before he had even got started.

The situation went from bad to worse as Grêmio lost 1–0 to Independiente of Argentina to exit the Mercosul, with Ronaldinho absent on international duty, and then went down 6–0 to Palmeiras. Ronaldinho did play in that one and, exasperated with his hapless team-mates, was seen haranguing them during the match for all the world to see. Any chances of making the play-offs were gone.

The season drifted along with Grêmio in inconsistent form. They finished fourth from bottom and, with four teams being relegated, should have been headed for the second division, Série B. However, in one of Brazil's many experiments with differing league formats, it had been decided that relegation that season would be based on the average number of points accumulated over the last two seasons. Grêmio had enjoyed a much better campaign the previous year (reaching the play-offs) and so were saved. State rivals Juventude, who had finished level on points with

Grêmio but had a better goal difference, were sent down instead. The two teams that had been promoted the previous year could only take that season's points tally into account and both headed back down again. Gama, a team from Brazil's Federal District, were relegated in this manner, despite finishing a respectable 15th out of 22 in real terms.

In another quirk of the rules, the eight best-placed teams outside the play-off places (also numbering eight) entered a knockout tournament called the *Séletiva* (the Selective). Those successful here would meet the losing teams from the play-offs to dispute a place in the next season's Libertadores Cup. Relegated teams were excluded as were Palmeiras who had already secured a berth by virtue of winning the competition that year.

So Grêmio, who had actually finished in the relegation zone, now found themselves playing for a place in the continent's premier club cup. They promptly beat Santos home and away in the first round (though without Ronaldinho, who was away on international duty in Australia with the Under-23s) to earn a tie with Inter in the second.

With Ronaldinho arriving back in time, *gremistas* were confident of success: in the previous three *Gre-Nals*, Grêmio had come out on top, with Ronaldinho tipping the balance each time.

However, both games were drawn 1–1. Rather than play a third match, extra-time or even penalties, Inter went through by virtue of the fact that they had finished higher in the league table in the first place, which did make one wonder what the point of the play-offs really was. Ronaldinho was unable to make much impact and looked tired and jet-lagged, though he did manage a penalty in the first leg.

Unsurprisingly, 1999 ended with coach Duarte given the boot. His replacement was Émerson Leão, a former Grêmio goalkeeper and then a recent coach of Inter. He was known for his sizeable ego and had clashed with several star players in the past, Dunga being the most recent, and *gremistas* worried how he might handle Ronaldinho.

Leão did his best to dismiss such concerns when he was unveiled to the press and declared that Ronaldinho would be a key man in his scheme. Nevertheless, many commentators recognised that stormy times lay ahead.

In fact, Leão's time at the helm was short: he lasted just 82 days, leaving a record of nine games in charge and just one victory. Ronaldinho played in only two of those nine due to his various Brazil commitments.

By now in partnership with ISL (International Sports Investment), a Swiss investment fund, Grêmio were able to attract players of a higher calibre. World Cup winner Zinho and former *tricolor* favourite Paulo Nunes were drafted in. This raised the bar of expectations and, even with Ronaldinho away, Grêmio were supposed to perform much better than they did in the Copa Sul-Minas (a cup that evolved from the Copa Sul of the previous year by incorporating the teams from Minas Gerais state, which lies just above São Paulo and Rio states, who already had a combined tournament of their own).

Grêmio travelled to Europe to play a money-spinning friendly in Catalonia against Lleida (some agents did use the trip to try and get Barcelona interested in signing Ronaldinho but their efforts came to nothing). Grêmio lost and Leão was sacked. Under pressure from all sides, he lashed out at his players and blamed them for denting his reputation. Ronaldinho in particular was made to carry the can: 'I am just the coach; I can't take the penalties too,' sniped Leão in reference to a penalty missed by Ronaldinho in the Lleida match. In Leão's mind it seemed Ronaldinho's miss had cost him his job.

Free from Leão's somewhat suffocating presence, Grêmio won their next game, a friendly at home to Santa Cruz, 5–0 with Ronaldinho scoring four. As an indication of just how much time Ronaldinho had been dedicating to the *canarinha*, this match, played on 11 March 2000, was his first game of the year at the Estádio Olímpico.

The new manager was Antônio Lopes, a quirky and superstitious coach who had just enjoyed a highly successful few years at Vasco.

Lopes, formerly part of the national team set-up, said that he had no problem with Ronaldinho's *Seleção* commitments, but this was not true of the club generally. Requests were sent to the CBF that he be excused from certain Brazil friendlies.

Under Lopes, Grêmio made a decent start to the *Gauchão* and reached the last eight. The competition then took the format of two rounds of mini-leagues involving all the teams: the winner of each round would meet in the final.

A bad run of form concluded with Grêmio losing 2–1 to Caxias, to give the first-round title and first place in the final to their opponents, and being dumped out of the Copa do Brasil following a 4–1 home defeat to Portuguesa.

In the second-round of the *Gauchão*, Grêmio were dragged along by Ronaldinho, who had by now made the number 10 shirt his sole property (having alternated it with 7, 9 and 11 in previous campaigns). They topped the table and headed for the final decider.

However, Ronaldinho couldn't reproduce the heroics of the previous year: the first leg was lost 3–0, the second finished goalless – Caxias were proclaimed champions for the first time in their history. Although he made little impression in either games of the decision, Ronaldinho still walked away with the player of the championship trophy in recognition of his Herculean efforts in taking his team to the final in the first place.

This didn't go down too well in the *tricolor* camp. Club captain, Zinho, complained of regionalism (he was a *carioca*, as those from Rio are known) and press double standards: 'When we lose, they want me to explain why. When we win, I am ignored and it is all about how wonderful Ronaldinho is.'

Earlier in the campaign, jealousies were roused in the squad when the club's president declared that the only non-negotiable player on the roster was Ronaldinho. Cleison took offence and announced that if that was the case and the club didn't value him then he wanted out.

Again, Ronaldinho missed Grêmio's preparations ahead of the Brazilian league due to national duty but on his return he asked new signing Adão, who had been signed from Caxias, how he liked to receive the ball. Adão was said to be dumbstruck: nobody, certainly not someone of Ronaldinho's standing, had ever before sought to adapt to his game.

That year the Brazilian league took a format unconventional even by its own standards. The aforementioned Gama, who had been relegated despite finishing eight places off the bottom, refused to go down. They had a fair point.

In 1997, Fluminense and Bahia, two important and popular teams and members of the *Clube dos 13*, a group of the thirteen most powerful clubs in Brazil, had been relegated. The *Clube dos 13* wished to avoid this happening again and brought in the complicated relegation system based on average point tallies over two seasons (the idea was that a big club may have a one-season blip but not a two-season slump).

Unfortunately, in 1999, the new system wasn't enough to prevent Botafogo qualifying for the drop. But Botafogo had played (and lost) to a São Paulo side fielding Sandro Hiroshi, a Japanese player who had not been registered properly. Botafogo (and Inter) successfully appealed that they should be awarded the three points lost in their matches with São Paulo and the league backed them, thus salvaging Botafogo from relegation and dragging down Gama in their place.

Gama were outraged and took their case to the courts. A long and drawn out legal process at first threw Gama's appeal out, then found in their favour. Fifa became involved and forbade any team in Brazil from playing against Gama.

Amidst the chaos and lack of league format, the *Clube dos 13* drew up an alternative competition. Called the João Havelange Cup, named after the Brazilian former Fifa president, it featured all 116 teams in Brazil who had been waiting to start the league campaign in one of the top four divisions. The teams were split into three groups: the groups were basically divisions one, two and three, but in order to avoid further protest and to get around recent promotion and relegation problems, the criteria for the three groups were kept classified. The first group, the Blue Group, featured 25 teams and included all those who should have been in the top flight, plus Gama, Fluminense and Bahia for good measure. The second was the Yellow Group, which was split into two sections of 18 and featured the teams who had been expecting to play Brazil's Série B (minus Gama, Fluminense and Bahia). The third was split regionally into the Green Group of the north and the White Group of the south and comprised the remaining 55 teams in 8 mini-groups.

After a regular 'league' season, the twelve best teams from the Blue Group would be joined by the three best from the Yellow Group and the winners of a play-off between the champions of the White Group and Green Group. This would make a last-sixteen knockout tournament.

The criteria was not only secret but also highly suspect, yet nobody put up much of a complaint as it seemed the only chance of actually having a league that year. Just as importantly, it meant that every team, no matter how big or small, had a theoretical chance of becoming national champions.

After a poor start, Grêmio were propping up the Blue Group table after four games and Antônio Lopes was shown the door. The club's directors turned to a trusted hand in Celso Roth to come and sort out the mess. He had to make do without Ronaldinho for his first month, who was away playing for Brazil at the Olympics.

Ronaldinho returned in October 2000 with Grêmio's position improved, although they remained outside the top twelve qualification places. After the disappointment of Sydney, there were fears that Ronaldinho would return subdued, his confidence shattered.

They needn't have worried: he played like a man possessed and the fans favourite chant, '*Ah, é, Ronaldinhôôô!*' – nothing more complicated than 'Oh, it's Ronaldinhooo!' – was once again ringing round the Estádio Olímpico. He was clearly desperate to wipe the Olympic fiasco from his memory and prove his worth anew.

There had been talk of giving him a rest, but Roth was keen to get him playing again. The manager eased Ronaldinho back into the training routine with a session among the reserves, but selected him to face Coritiba and was rewarded with a stellar display and goal in a 2–1 win. When he scored, Ronaldinho ran over to the dugout to celebrate in Roth's arms.

'In 2000, Grêmio came to get me again but this time they had a technically stronger team already,' says Roth. 'There was Zinho, Paulo Nunes, the Argentines Leonardo Astrada and Gabriel Amato and Warley, along with Gavião and Polga whom I promoted as first-teamers. So a better team but one once again bottom of the league,' he recalls.

'Ronaldinho was very impressive in that championship. He was now a world star and his manner of doing certain things had obviously changed;

it was such a quick rise. But we didn't have any problems in terms of ego because I had known him at the start, before his stardom. He knew what I was like, how I worked, what I expected and he was just great.'

But it wasn't all smooth running. After a disappointing defeat to Guarani, Roth claimed that some of the supposed best players didn't always perform and that Ronaldinho was sometimes an 'exceptional player' in inverted commas only. There was also a feeling that some players, Warley in particular, played much better without Ronaldinho, that they felt somehow inhibited or even intimidated alongside him and froze.

Grêmio's form remained up and down but they did eventually qualify for the play-offs. At the last-sixteen stage, Grêmio faced Ponte Preta. The first leg was at home and a very defensive Ponte Preta were only beaten 1–0 thanks to a free-kick from Ronaldinho. Grêmio then lost the away leg 2–1 but the away goal, scored by Zinho and set up by Ronaldinho, saw them through.

In the next round, Grêmio faced a Sport side managed by Émerson Leão. A few old scores were settled as Grêmio won 2–1 with two goals from Ronaldinho, including another free-kick. The Porto Alegre newspapers talked of Ronaldinho-dependence; that without their main man, Grêmio were nothing. Ronaldinho dismissed this as nonsense and said he only scored two because his colleagues won him the ball.

The return leg was drawn 1–1 via a Ronaldinho penalty and suddenly Grêmio, having proved their prowess in cup football once again, were in the semifinals. They would face São Caetano, a team that had emerged from the Yellow Group and surprised everybody.

At São Caetano, the home side's pressing game was too much for Grêmio and they were soon 2–0 down. Ronaldinho then picked up the ball, skinned the centre-half and slid it past the advancing goalkeeper. São Caetano restored their two-goal advantage but Ronaldinho rose to the occasion again and drilled home a second.

The post-match talk turned once more to the team's reliance on Ronaldinho. He had scored six of Grêmio's last seven goals and all but single-handedly rescued them from disaster against São Caetano. His strike partner Warley hadn't found the net in seven games, but again Ronaldinho chose to highlight the team ethic. 'Warley plays a fundamental role in opening spaces up for me,' he insisted.

The return leg didn't go to plan, however, and Grêmio were beaten 3–1. Ronaldinho had teed Zinho up to take the lead and, 1–0 up at half-time, Grêmio had the advantage. At that stage in proceedings, Ronaldinho created a great chance to put the game out of reach but elected to take the shot himself instead of pass (for which Roth would chastise him afterwards). Then came the São Caetano response. Grêmio were out of the

João Havelange Cup final and had missed out on a Libertadores berth in the process.

Ronaldinho had enjoyed a fine season, though, and was named by *Placar* in its prestigious team of the season. The influential football magazine awards marks out of ten for every player in every match throughout the championship. An average match rating is then calculated (for those players who have played enough games to qualify) and the highest ranked player in each position is named in the team of the season and awarded the Silver Ball. The player with the best average overall wins the Golden Ball. Ronaldinho was named as one of the two strikers next to Romário, that season's Golden Ball winner. The Juninhos Paulista and Pernambucano occupied the *meia* positions.

Roth decided to call it a day at Grêmio and, though it was not known then, the Copa Havelange would also prove to be Ronaldinho's last tournament in a *tricolor* shirt.

Ronaldinho and Roth's relationship had, at times, been tempestuous but it had also proved rewarding: Ronaldinho had helped Roth's teams overachieve, while Roth had undoubtedly installed certain disciplines into Ronaldinho's game that would benefit him for the rest of his playing days.

'Ronaldinho never needed any pampering; he always had very high self-confidence,' explains Roth. 'He was always, as a player and person, level-headed and confident in himself. Even when he is serious, before a key match or a penalty, he is not tense: he has an inner belief.

'In the dressing room he was always calm, singing, acting the joker, keeping a sense of fun just as he does playing football. This was because he came from a strong family. He was always an extrovert, always happy, content with life and this shone through in the dressing room,' says Roth.

'He knew of his own potential, his own rising importance, but he still acted the same way he always did, treated people no differently; there was no big-headedness, which is something you always have to watch out for.

'I've worked with some great players in my time and all at a very interesting period in their careers, nineteen to twenty years old. But, with due respect to the others (principally Christian and Lúcio at Inter, Robinho and Diego at Santos), Ronaldinho was a cut above the rest. He was always capable, even when playing badly, of getting the ball, dribbling past two or three and scoring a goal.'

And yet, the legacy of Roth's time with Ronaldinho is scarred slightly; most people remember Roth, probably unfairly, as the coach who tried to make Ronaldinho defend. Roth takes up the story. 'He basically missed out the junior level at Grêmio, going straight from the *Juveniles* to the professionals on merit. This creates certain problems for a young player, problems which, if not dealt with early, would result in serious deficiencies for the rest of their careers.

'I was criticised because I said that Ronaldinho had problems with his participation in marking, his tactical participation. Sometimes I left him on the bench, sometimes dropped him altogether. People didn't understand why I did it then and they still don't. How can a coach leave a player like Ronaldinho out?

'But I had a methodology which I used, not just on Ronaldinho but on all the young players I worked with who shone early. In the *Juveniles* you work on your technique and on the basics of tactics, positioning etc. But Ronaldinho had been promoted so fast he hadn't even really done this work. So he needed to be educated tactically. So when he was with us at Grêmio, and not travelling with the *Seleção*, we did a lot of tactical work with him.'

Roth is keen to justify his thinking. 'People confuse *marcação* (pressing) with marking; you can't make a player like Ronaldinho – or Maradona, Messi, Schevchenko, Kaká – mark. But what you can get them to do is participate in the tactics of marking when the team doesn't have the ball. They cover space, close down players who have the ball and force them into making a bad pass. That is *marcação*. Pressuring the opponent into making a pass which your colleague might then be able to steal.

'But fans don't understand this, nor does it seem do journalists.

'Anyway, Ronaldinho began to participate and, let's not forget, he was top scorer playing as a *meia*, a position that requires much more participation than does striker. He covered ground, got on top of players and benefited from us stealing the ball and breaking.'

This didn't come naturally to Ronaldinho, as Roth recognises. 'It was hard for Ronaldinho. Obviously, it was easy for him to get the ball at his feet and play. Running back and covering didn't come so naturally.

'He was always receptive and wanted to learn but at the same time you live and work in a collective environment and read and hear so many things about what is supposed to be good, what he need and need not do: "Ronaldinho should just be left alone to play." It creates a barrier to his learning,' Roth says, disapprovingly.

'He had to overcome these things and in order to get the message through, the coach has to be very firm and have the courage of his convictions. And I did.

'In Europe, you have to participate in collective pressing when you don't have the ball and he does that. But I was heavily criticised for insisting on it at the time,' concludes Roth.

While covering Grêmio for various news agencies, Pelotinha saw most coaches come and go at Grêmio. 'Roth helped Ronaldinho a lot but he used to claim that Grêmio were as effective without Ronaldinho as they were with him because what they lost in his ability they gained in collective efficiency,' he comments. Pelotinha feels this was possibly pushing it.

'I remember Luiz Felipe Scolari knew Ronaldinho was very good but when we used to try to persuade him to throw Ronaldinho into the first team he would say to us, "Why? So that some big centre-half can kick him into the stands?"'

'Leão didn't like anyone being a bigger star than him so that didn't work. Perhaps the best coach for Ronaldinho,' concludes Pelotinha, 'was Antônio Lopes: he treated him like a grandson. Lopes was the coach who focused most on Ronaldinho, who gave him total freedom and actually organised his teams to suit Ronaldinho's game.'

The worst might have been Edinho. Ronaldinho has spoken to the local press about the one and only time he truly lost his cheerful disposition. Early in his professional career, during Edinho's time as coach, Ronaldinho drew heavy criticism in one particular game and was compared in the papers to Pedro Verdum, a player who had been a star in the Inter youth system but who never fulfilled his potential.

Ronaldinho became depressed, imagining himself going the same way as Verdum and ending up playing in the minor leagues of the state interior. For the first time in his life, he began to head straight home once training sessions had finished, instead of hanging around, practising and messing about with his mates.

Then one day, he put on an old shirt and headed for the Periquito and played in a kickabout. He scored a few goals, rediscovered both his passion for the game and his confidence, and was back in business.

PLAYING THE KILLER PASS

One could argue that Brazil's two most successful export goods are male footballers and female prostitutes. In these two spheres, Brazil's image as a tropical, fun-loving, samba-dancing carnival-land perfectly captures the world market's imagination.

Between 1994 and 2006, the transfer of players overseas brought Brazilian clubs in excess of US$1 billion (£530 million). In 2005 alone, 804 Brazilian players moved abroad, spread over the five continents. As well as the very top stars found in each of Europe's giant clubs, the level below them are employed in leagues in the likes of Russia or Japan. There is then a lower tier where average players earn a living in countries such as Moldova and India.

By buying Brazilian, you are buying into the glamour and romance of the beautiful game. As an agent told Alex Bellos in his book about soccer in Brazil, *Futebol – The Brazilian Way of Life*, it is much easier to sell a bad Brazilian player than it is a brilliant Mexican.

All this leaves the Brazilian domestic league in a fairly sorry state. The best players are veterans (Romário was top scorer in the league in 2005 aged 39), raw youngsters yet to be tempted abroad or middle-rank players in limbo: having failed at their first attempt abroad they have been loaned back to Brazil to regain form and confidence before giving the promised land another try. The remainder are merely mediocre by anyone's standards.

Despite all this, the supply line shows no sign of slowing in Brazil. Comparison with the success of poor black athletes in US professional sports is valid: in both instances one could argue that the opportunity to escape poverty through a sporting career gives such players the edge in terms of competitiveness and determination.

In Brazil, being a professional footballer means you are no longer a nobody, but playing abroad means you have really made it. '*Jogou fora*' (he played abroad) is a phrase used to distinguish between someone who was a good player and someone who really was exceptional. The implication is that almost anybody worth his salt could play for a professional team in Brazil if he really wanted to.

The Brazilian footballer will typically hope to play a couple of seasons in the domestic league and then catch the eye of a scout who will take him abroad, allowing him to tap into unheard-of riches and, in this way, help his family towards a better life.

Carlos Gavião, who eventually left Grêmio to play for Júbilo Iwata in Japan, explains how a young player thinks, showing that, even in this regard, Ronaldinho seemed to stand out. 'We were all thinking of developing as best we could in our own ways and then heading abroad, for sure. We spoke a lot about playing overseas. But Ronaldinho always had the competitive edge, an ambition that he would play in one of the big clubs in Europe.

'When we were starting out, Romário was at Barcelona, then Ronaldo after him and Ronaldinho used to say that he was going to do the same and become the best in the world. Which is what he did.

'He was certain that he would be a great player. I remember him saying that he looked at all the best players in the world and he wasn't scared of confronting them or their situations. He believed in himself a lot.'

So, there was an early suggestion that Ronaldinho's destiny would lie with Barcelona, but the first foreign team to really show an interest in him was Sion of Switzerland. In his teens, Ronaldinho would spend several months at a time visiting his brother who had signed for Sion in 1992. He used to accompany Assis to the ground for training sessions and joined in with Sion Juniors. Around 1994, Sion evidently enquired about signing him up for real.

Assis had toyed with the idea of taking the family over to live with him in Switzerland in any case, but Dona Miguelina insisted they would stay in Porto Alegre. She similarly gave little serious consideration to Ronaldinho upping sticks to the other side of the world at such a young age.

It was no doubt for the best. In choosing to go to Sion, Assis had jumped at the first good-money offer abroad that came along, and as a result disappeared off the football radar. He should perhaps have been more patient; Ronaldinho would benefit from the lessons learned by his brother. When Ronaldinho was being inundated with invitations to join the pick of Europe's top clubs, the family were careful in considering all their options and picking the right move at the right time for Ronaldinho.

Assis' switch to Switzerland wasn't without its benefits: there he became interested and learned about finance and economics, for which Ronaldinho would one day be grateful. He also met Eric Lovey, a Swiss who became his friend and helped broker Ronaldinho's eventual transfer to Paris Saint-Germain.

The first time Ronaldinho's ultimate departure from Grêmio was discussed came not long after he had signed his first contract in February 1998. The following month, local press reports claimed that Grêmio had sold 30 per cent of the rights to any transfer fee received for Ronaldinho to various business interests: 10 per cent was used as a guarantee on a loan the club would pay off by the end of the following year but the other 20 per cent remained in the hands of investors for a longer period. Assis tried, unsuccesfully, to buy the share off them a few years later.

Ronaldinho began to attract overseas scouts from almost as soon as he turned professional. Early European suitors were mainly Italian, with Milan sending an observer during the *Gauchão* of 1999 and Fiorentina said to be keeping tabs on him even before then.

But it was after his debut for Brazil in the 1999 Copa América that transfer speculation really took off. Some commentators were calling his goal against Venezuela the most valuable goal ever scored: Grêmio had been made a £10 million offer for Ronaldinho before that game and were then offered £14 million afterwards.

Spanish papers suggested diverging scenarios, both plausible: Barcelona, acting on a recommendation by former player Ronaldo, were preparing an offer; Real Madrid had already negotiated first refusal with Assis the year before.

In Italy, the head of the pack appeared to be Inter Milan, where President Massimo Moratti was desperate to unite Ronaldinho with Ronaldo, then at the Italian giants. Inter's proposed package, it was believed, included Rafael Scheidt heading out to Milan with Ronaldinho.

Ronaldo's agent, Reinaldo Pitta, had also been heard wheeling and dealing, trying to put an early package together to send Ronaldinho to PSV Eindhoven, just like Ronaldo had done before him.

Grêmio had announced a rise in Ronaldinho's salary from BR$19,000 to BR$90,000 (£4.7,000 to £21,000) following the *Gauchão* triumph and it was said that his new contract featured a bonus payable if he stayed at the club to the end of his contract. This ran to February 2001 and the club repeatedly stated that their man was going nowhere before then.

Amidst all the speculation, Ronaldinho claimed that he was happy at Grêmio and didn't want to move, although reports from foreign climes suggested otherwise. It appeared that Ronaldinho was telling local pressmen one thing, European reporters quite another.

Ronaldinho's spectacular displays in the Confederations Cup had brought with them a whole new wave of interest and rumour. Spanish broker José Minguella made a £15 million offer and Maurício Pinheiros, supposedly representing an English club, arrived in Porto Alegre and bandied around the same sum. The club refused to speak with him. Although £15 million was an extraordinary amount of money for a transfer at the time, it was felt that, with Brazilian league games then set to be transmitted to Europe the following season, his stock could only rise.

Grêmio president, José Alberto Guerreiro, was adamant he would not sell Ronaldinho. He was anxious to avoid the fate of José Asmuz, the president of Internacional in the early 1980s: although Inter came second in the Libertadores of 1980 and won the *Gauchão* in 1981 under his jurisdiction, he will be forever remembered in Porto Alegre as the man who sold Falcão.

Eventually, Guerreiro lost his patience with all the transfer rumours and took the bizarre measure of erecting a giant banner across the gates at the main entrance to the ground, which warned away anyone come courting. Written first in Portuguese, the words were then translated into English underneath, lest anyone should be in any doubt: '*Não vendemos Craques. Favor não insistir* – We don't sell our best soccer players. Don't you dare insist.'

All these deterrents seemed to work and the rumour-mill more or less ground down for the rest of the year.

But the New Year brought new ideas. Clubs in Europe were resolute, determined to mark 2000 as the start of a new era. Juventus were the first to make overtures about Ronaldinho with Barcelona not far behind. According to Spanish sports daily *As*, Barça were ready to pay up to £37 million. The Catalan giants were about to sanction a big-money move to Lazio for Ronaldinho's national team colleague Rivaldo and were looking for a replacement on whom to splash the cash. Ex-Barcelona star José Maria Bakero led a scouting mission to the Olympic qualifiers and had reported back favourably on Ronaldinho.

The figure was huge and, although Grêmio directors said the question of Ronaldinho's transfer was not about money but principle, the offer did bring with it the first murmurs of acquiescence among groups of fans.

For a sum such as this, the argument went, Grêmio could buy at least three great players. Besides, £37 million might represent the top of the market; his price could easily fall given an injury or poor run of form. Then there was his contract: it had another year to run but Ronaldinho would likely be with the *Seleção* as much as with his club during that time, leaving Grêmio constantly unsettled.

Muddying the water yet further was the *Lei Pelé*: this was a new law proposed in Pelé's name that was to come into effect at the start of the following year and strengthen a player's rights at the end of his contract. The exact details were still uncertain and, although Grêmio felt confident it wouldn't have any impact on their relationship with Ronaldinho, some observers suggested that the law's unknown quality was yet another argument in favour of cashing in on their star asset early.

However, *Rádio Guaíba* ran a poll and over 70 per cent of respondents voted in favour of turning the Barcelona offer down. In the event, all such debate proved hypothetical as no official offer was made, but such was the climate when a serious approach did come in from an English club.

Sheffield United fans will constantly wonder what might have happened, both to the club and to the player, had they actually decided to sign Diego Maradona when they set up a deal to buy him as a seventeen-year-old. The name of Ronaldinho can be added to the list of nearly-Yorkshiremen. How would Ronaldinho's and Leeds' fortunes have differed had the nineteen-year-old Brazilian come to live the dream after a big-money offer was made in the Elland Road club's name? Leeds back then were on their way to finishing third in the Premier League and qualifying for the Champions League.

In February 2000, a fax arrived at the Grêmio offices proposing a then world-record transfer of £42 million. It was signed on behalf of a Fifa-approved agent and the Leeds vice-president of finances. Grêmio, as they had done many times before, stated that they wished to keep Ronaldinho for another three years but, given the extraordinary size of the fee, asked for more details. Ronaldinho's value had almost tripled in six months (it was eventually revealed that Real Madrid had made a firm £14 million offer back in August 1999) and Grêmio's directors agreed that they would be doing the club a disservice if they didn't at least study what was being proposed.

The plot thickened when Leeds denied making any such offer. Leeds claimed that Grêmio were using them to try to increase Ronaldinho's market value. Grêmio questioned why on earth they would seek to do that when they were actually trying to extend his contract and any rise in value would result in them having to offer him better terms. But Grêmio then announced that the scheduled meeting, supposedly with representatives from Leeds who had flown into the city, was cancelled. So had Grêmio been making it up all along?

Grêmio denied such slander and said they had the fax to prove it. Curiously, they then refused to show the fax to the media. Grêmio claimed it was an internal finance affair and that the fax, or in fact faxes – there were suddenly said to be three – had been shown to those at the club who needed to see them.

Meanwhile, *Época*, one of Brazil's several weekly news magazines, published details of the supposed contract: Leeds would pay Grêmio £42 million with Ronaldinho entitled to pocket 15 per cent (£6.3 million) and an annual wage of £2 million.

Who to believe? Had Leeds, as many in Porto Alegre suspected, arrogantly gone over thinking they could take their pick from whichever players they wanted in that remote corner of Brazil, then, on discovering they couldn't, denied the whole affair in an attempt to save face? Or had Grêmio, as Leeds were claiming, been victim to a game of bluff on the part of a group of agents?

In the meantime, *gremistas* set up a website petition begging Ronaldinho to stay: it soon had some 20,000 names to it.

Eventually, Grêmio showed the faxes to the press and it appeared that Leeds had been half-right. The first fax was stamped 'Global Transfer' and had been signed by agent Gerd Butzeck, offering £27 million plus Mário Jardel (former Grêmio hero, then of Porto in Portugal) in exchange for Ronaldinho. The fax asked Grêmio to acknowledge receipt of the offer by sending a signed copy back.

After asking for more details, a new offer with the same request followed, this time for a straight £42 million. Again, Grêmio asked for more information. A third fax followed and said the deal was off due to Grêmio's lack of discretion.

As it turned out, Butzeck, along with colleague Christian Flick, had been attempting to manipulate Grêmio into sending them a signed document that would effectively give them permission to broker a transfer of Ronaldinho to England. They then intended to approach Leeds, along with several other teams they thought might be interested. It seemed that somebody at Leeds had agreed to consider such an offer and, in this way, Leeds had been used as a smokescreen.

Grêmio had acted correctly and with caution; if they had been taken in by the proposal and permitted the agents to put together a possible package, agreeing so in writing, the agents would then have been entitled to a share in the proceeds of any transfer Ronaldinho might have made to England at any date in the future, be it arranged through them or not.

In late May, new gossip had Ronaldinho on his way to Real Madrid once more, then in September it was Barcelona's turn again. The fact that rumours were constantly cropping up involving these two clubs seemed to have as much to do with the fact that both Madrid and Barcelona were cities that supported two daily sports newspapers – with a lot of column inches to fill – as any genuine interest from the clubs.

In the meantime, the new *Lei Pelé* finally entered Congress: it was approved in principle in May 2000, voted upon in June and became law in July. Grêmio were happy with its contents, which seemingly laid their concerns to rest. For one thing, it stated that any contracts signed before the new law was enacted retained their original terms and conditions; some observers had suggested that the new law would make all old contracts null and void.

Grêmio's other cause for celebration was the confirmation that the *Lei Pelé* would not come into full force until 26 March 2001, 37 days after Ronaldinho's contract had expired. Grêmio were satisfied that during those 37 days the old law would still apply, meaning that the club was entitled to set a transfer fee and any club hoping to sign Ronaldinho would be obliged to pay it.

Doubts remained with regard to what might happen should the club and Ronaldinho not agree on a new contract, but it was believed that a transfer fee would then be calculated as a multiple of the salary being offered to him.

Club lawyer Vincente Martins was convinced Grêmio would not lose out. 'Let's wait until his contract ends and then we can come to an agreement which suits all concerned,' he said ominously.

Assis, representing his brother, always repeated the same mantra: Ronaldinho was going nowhere until his contract ended. Deise agreed and told reporters, 'There is no need to discuss a new contract until the old one expires.' They claimed they preferred to wait (at first until after the Olympics, then after the World Cup qualifiers) to see if Ronaldinho's market value would rise, allowing them to demand better terms. However, it seemed that Ronaldinho's party were extremely confident he would become a free agent.

Representing Assis and Ronaldinho, lawyer Sérgio Neves warned that the player could still transfer to Europe if he signed a pre-contract with a club at any time within the last six months of his contract. This, he argued, was because Brazilian legislation was not protected from Fifa regulations; if a contractual agreement is good by international law then Fifa would overrule any objections the CBF might make.

Rumours immediately emerged that this had already happened and that a European club had a pre-contract with Ronaldinho's signature on it. Ronaldinho was quick to deny the legitimacy of any such deal if not, bizarrely, his own name being on it: 'My signature means nothing unless it is complemented with my mother's and she has signed nothing, I can assure you.'

Assis also swept aside such suggestions. He claimed that such a move would provoke and alienate the fans and they had no intention of doing that. (This was in reference to the case of Athirson, who had played for Brazil at the Olympics with Ronaldinho: a Flamengo player, he had announced a pre-contract with Juventus and the fans turned upon him, hounding him for the rest of his time in Rio, before a legal dispute erupted between the two clubs.)

Around this time, the latest speculation involving Barcelona hit the headlines. Assis had been heard to say that his brother's future ultimately lay in Spain where the offensive and spectacular style of play would best suit him. Barcelona were reported to have paid £15 million to acquire 50 per cent ownership of Ronaldinho and Assis was forced to explain that he had been speaking in general terms of Spain, and besides, 'Barça have an office in Brazil. Why would they pay all that money knowing full well that he could soon become a free agent?'

Assis and his entourage were evidently increasingly convinced that the new law would free Ronaldinho. Grêmio seemed equally content that it wouldn't. Clearly, somebody had miscalculated.

Grêmio initiated attempts to persuade Ronaldinho to renew his contract early. The benefit to the player would be an insurance against injury; a serious injury would make his working liberty meaningless while any new deal signed beforehand would be valid even if he could never play again. Ronaldinho and his camp refused such approaches. A compromise was then sought with a new contract featuring a clause that allowed Ronaldinho to leave should an offer come in at a predetermined value. Again, Ronaldinho's representatives weren't interested: aside from a sudden dramatic injury, viewed as too remote a risk, there was no incentive to sign as they had very little to lose by waiting to see what happened with the new law; either Ronaldinho would be free to move wherever he wanted or he could negotiate a paid transfer.

As December began, Jaime Eduardo Machado, Grêmio's vice-president who had been in Brasília carefully following every development of the *Lei Pelé* through Congress, launched a new book on the subject. Called *O novo contrato desportivo profissional – Manual da Lei do Passe*, 'The new professional sports contract – Manual for the law of the transfer', it claimed to be an analysis of the new law with clear explanations of what it meant for football clubs and what they would have to do to adapt and comply. Grêmio would soon be needing it.

On 13 December 2000, French newspaper *Le Parisien* broke the story that Paris Saint-Germain (PSG) were negotiating a deal to sign Ronaldinho. Initial reports suggested that Ronaldinho had signed a pre-contract and would leave Grêmio in June. Grêmio, it was said, were to receive £33 million.

Ronaldinho and Grêmio denied the story and the club was furious that such speculation should surface when it did (the eve of Grêmio's cup semifinal with São Caetano) and distract from their match preparation.

Grêmio then presented their own definitive renewal package: a three-year contract worth £80,000 monthly as well as a percentage of any future transfer fee. This last part was Grêmio's trump card: under the existing law, players were entitled to 15 per cent of any transfer fee, but the new *Lei Pelé* did away with such a practice. Grêmio proposed to increase Ronaldinho's percentage each year, offering him an incentive to stay longer.

But those PSG rumours wouldn't go away. Confusion reigned but it was widely felt that if Ronaldinho had already signed a pre-contract then there was nothing Grêmio could do to keep him. They simply had to seek compensation from PSG.

The New Year came and went amidst rumour and counter-rumour: as extra motivation for Ronaldinho to stay, Grêmio had offered to sign his brother Assis too, for £20,000 per month; meanwhile it would appear that PSG had been hyping up what was a far-from-done deal in order to appease their fans, who had been protesting about PSG's disastrous league form.

What was known was that in Grêmio's presidential elections José Alberto Guerreiro was returned and started 2001 with one top priority: keeping Ronaldinho.

The *Lei Pelé* was really an extension of measures ushered in via the *Lei Zico* in 1991. Zico had been elected Secretary for Sport under the doomed government of Fernando Collor in March 1990. In an attempt to drag Brazilian football into the modern era, he had drawn up a motion that would alter the state of the game in several fundamental ways: force clubs to be run like businesses; break the links between club and state; formulate a more transparent electoral process within the CBF; and end the *Lei do Passe*.

The *Lei do Passe* ('the law of the transfer') had come into being in 1976 and classified a player's *passe* as a sporting link between the player and his club, separate to a working contract. In order to sign a player, you had to acquire his *passe* (perhaps best understood as his right to move to – or pass on – another club) and this was sold to the highest bidder.

Zico wanted to give players greater contractual freedom and, aware of the Bosman case unravelling in Europe, prepare Brazil for what was likely to be a new environment in which laws such as the *Lei do Passe* would become obsolete.

The Bosman law is something so sensible that it seems absurd it hasn't always existed, yet it only became applicable in 1996. Jean-Marc Bosman was a Belgian player at RFC Lège who wished to transfer to US Dunkerque in France in 1990. Dunkerque wanted to sign him but the two clubs could not agree a transfer fee. Bosman's contract at Liège had ended, so he took his case to the European Parliament and demanded he be granted the freedom of movement and worker's rights of any European citizen. He argued that if he was out of contract then he was free to sign a new one with whomever he pleased.

After several years at court, the judiciary agreed and the transfer system was turned upside down. In January 1996, the European Commission informed Uefa and Fifa that a transfer fee was no longer applicable for a player out of contract and wishing to move within the EU. From then on, players ceased to be viewed as the property of a club but as employees. Any footballer who chooses not to renew a contract but move elsewhere for free once it has expired is still said, in football parlance, to move on a Bosman.

Ronaldinho would, in his way, become the Bosman of Brazil.

The Zico law didn't quite have its desired effect. Amendments weakened it and strong resistance from the clubs meant they were only obliged to study and prepare an end to the *Lei do Passe* but not actually implement one. But another famous football figure soon adopted the cause.

Pelé had been elected the Extraordinary Minister for Sports in January 1995 by Fernando Henrique Cardoso. Wishing to leave a lasting impression, he decided that the end of the *Lei do Passe* would be his legacy. The *Lei do Passe* was clearly archaic and unjustifiable in the modern world: players argued that in effect they were treated like slaves. Why should they belong to anyone if their contract was up?

However, clubs were fiercely resistant and claimed that its removal would prejudice against those who invested in a youth academy. It was impossible to compare Brazil with Europe, ran the argument, because the market was so unbalanced. Laws such as the *Lei do Passe* were vital to thwart greedy, rich European clubs from stealing all Brazil's best young talent.

Nevertheless, Pelé sent his motion straight to Congress in 1998 and lobbied for it himself. Clubs and coaches criticised the lack of consultation and called Pelé an authoritarian.

The matter was a delicate one and a new proposal was drawn up in 2000 seeking to protect the rights of a club that had nurtured a player. If a player had been on a club's books as a non-professional for at least two years, the club would have the right to offer the player his first professional contract. If the player refused this contract or signed but failed to fulfil it, his new club would be forced to pay a compensation package to his original club for the money and time invested in him.

The first contract could be as long as five years and signed by a player as young as sixteen. If broken, compensation could theoretically be as much as two hundred times the player's annual salary.

Claudinho of Ponte Preta was the first player to really exercise his worker's rights and follow Bosman's example to earn his freedom, but Ronaldinho's case gained the greater notoriety.

It would emerge that Ronaldinho had signed a pre-contract agreement with PSG on 22 December 2000, a deal that would begin on 1 July 2001. Assis and Sérgio Neves claimed they had informed Grêmio directly.

In Ronaldinho's case, he had decided not to renew his contract with Grêmio, which terminated mid-February 2001. He then opted to wait until 26 March and the implementation of the new legislation, when any link, sporting or otherwise, would evaporate. Grêmio were outraged: given that they had drawn up his first contract years before the new law had even been mooted, how could they have possibly made allowances for future unknown legislation? It was outrageous that they could invest so much money and energy into a player only for him to be stolen from them just as they were ready to reap their rewards from him. They demanded compensation for the investment made in training the athlete.

But, although Grêmio acted the aggrieved party well, everybody knew that it was more than mere compensation the club was protesting about. Grêmio had fixed Ronaldinho's *passe* at £44 million, a figure way above anything Grêmio could possibly have spent in training him. The *passe* was seen by clubs as a right of ownership and sold not for compensation but to make as much money as possible in the transfer market.

Perhaps a better argument from Grêmio would have centred around the implications for Brazilian football: without the possible reward of a fat transfer fee at the end, there was a lack of incentive to train and reveal new players. Nevertheless, although the new law was certainly more justifiable, its timing was awful for Grêmio, who were basically being stripped of their prize assets. Their whole financial future had been planned with proceeds from a Ronaldinho transfer in mind.

As compensation, Grêmio at first demanded around BR$40 million (some £9 million); PSG felt they should pay nothing. Some people agreed with PSG: as far as compensation was concerned, weren't the trophies in the cabinet that Ronaldinho had helped win or, perhaps more accurately, won single-handedly reward enough?

Another element of the new legislation was that a player was entitled to renegotiate and ultimately terminate a contract if his club failed to meet its wage obligations. Grêmio had apparently already had difficulties in paying players' wages on time and Ronaldinho wanted to know how, therefore, they could possibly claim to be able to afford to compete with what PSG were offering him.

In September 2000, Grêmio and ISL had signed a new extended partnership, set to last fifteen years. This meant, they claimed then, that the club would be able to hang on to Ronaldinho until the 2002 World Cup at least. But it would emerge that the new deal being offered to Ronaldinho was nowhere near as good as the contracts players who had signed via ISL were on. It was thought that Zinho and Paulo Nunes enjoyed particularly lucrative salaries and that Ronaldinho's package would not match their terms.

Grêmio were playing the role of the righteous and casting Ronaldinho and Assis as villains, and the fans were lapping it up. They knew supporters were always likely to side with the club in such circumstances and by turning *gremistas* against Ronaldinho, observers suspected, they hoped to disguise some of their own short comings and less-than-noble dealings. Besides Paulo Nunes and Zinho, some said Ronaldinho wasn't even being offered as much as the Argentines Astrada and Amato.

It also remained unclear how much of Ronaldinho's *passe* Grêmio even owned with those percentages of transfer-rights negotiated back at the beginning of his career coming back to haunt them. Agent Eltamar Salvadori claimed he was still entitled to 10 per cent of Ronaldinho's *passe* left over as a deposit from a loan made in October 1997. It was also speculated that an extra 20 per cent had been sold in similar fashion to an investor linked to metal concern Grupo Gerdau. If nothing else, such sideshows smacked of incompetence on Grêmio's part and offered further evidence that the club had not properly prepared for events now unfolding.

Given Ronaldinho's popularity, fans were reluctant to blame him and sought scapegoats elsewhere. Assis had been using his old friend from Switzerland, Eric Lovey, as an advisor. Lovey at the time lived up the coast from Porto Alegre in Florianópolis, Santa Catarina, and Grêmio discovered that he was in Brazil only on a tourist visa. They attempted to get him thrown out of the country for working and breaching the terms of his stay in Brazil, but Lovey claimed to be acting only as an observer on the case.

Others saw Assis as the villain of the piece and a petition was set up to declare him *persona non grata* in Porto Alegre.

The whole drama dragged on and on. In January 2001, Ronaldinho completed the formalities of signing for PSG but Grêmio took their case to the courts to try and prevent him from being allowed to move to France. So long as there was a legal process against him in motion, Ronaldinho was forbidden from playing. He was forced to leave the city and began to train on his own in Rio.

Fifa finally took over adjudication of the affair in July 2001 and organised a series of meetings between the two clubs at Fifa headquarters in Zurich. Grêmio presented a report compiled by the now defunct ISL in which they concluded that the Brazilian club was owed US$27.5 million (£14.5 million) in damages. Grêmio suggested the sum as a fair compensation figure, though it is thought that by then they had resigned themselves to no more than half that sum.

In August, Ronaldinho was finally cleared to start playing in France and then, in November, Fifa came to the conclusion that PSG should pay Grêmio £3 million in compensation. The clubs disagreed.

Finally, in February 2002, a full year after Ronaldinho had left Grêmio, it was resolved that PSG would pay Grêmio £2.2 million, roughly BR$10 million, as well as 5 per cent of any future transfer fee PSG might receive. The agreement appeared to reach a conclusion partly because Grêmio had fallen behind in paying their players' wages and were in desperate need of cash flow, forcing them into an imperfect compromise.

Even then, the matter wasn't completely closed. Several years later, with Ronaldinho having long since moved to Barcelona, an investigation into accounting irregularities at PSG uncovered a secret bank account in Switzerland said to have been opened in 2001 by the Parisian club in the Brazilian player's name and into which, it was claimed, had been deposited some US$11 million (£5.8 million). The implication seemed to be that Assis might have agreed to fix it so that his brother left Grêmio for free provided that a share of the transfer money that PSG would save went to the player.

Such accusations remain unproven but, if nothing else, they do serve as a reminder that the saga of what has to be one of the most troubled transfers of all time is still able to stir bad blood and ill feeling.

BETTER TO HAVE LOVED
AND LOST

In January 2001, amidst all the confusion of Ronaldinho's transfer, Grêmio had to play a home match against Figueirense. The atmosphere at the Olímpico was very tense with fans divided on the Ronaldinho issue.

The *sociós* booed Ronaldinho as soon as he set foot on the pitch. The *sociós* are club members who pay a monthly subscription fee and therefore consider themselves part-owners of Grêmio; if Ronaldinho was doing the club out of what it had rightfully earned, then Ronaldinho was swindling the *sociós* as much as anyone. Someone threw a suitcase full of supposed banknotes on to the pitch and coins rained down from the stand all afternoon. A banner accusing Ronaldinho of being a mercenary was later unveiled.

Meanwhile, the *organizadas*, the organised fan groups who co-ordinate support in certain sections of any Brazilian crowd, tried to protect Ronaldinho. For example, *Super Raça* (Super Tribe – though *raça* in a more general football sense suggests playing with passion and spunk), Grêmio's biggest *organizada*, unfurled a giant flag painted with a caricature of Ronaldinho.

The president of *Super Raça* is Giovanni Martins Dos Santos, though at the time of the Ronaldinho saga he was simply another member of the troupe. He explains the group's stance thus: 'When Ronaldinho played his last match at the Olímpico he was still a Grêmio player. There were rumours but we didn't know if he would stay and we supported him because he was wearing the Grêmio shirt. As a supporters group, our objective is to support the team, do what's necessary to get the best out of them. That is why the *organizadas* tried to protect Ronaldinho. What happened afterwards? Well, that is a different matter.'

Ronaldinho began the game very nervously indeed, miscuing passes and earning himself a pointless booking. But opportunity knocked in the form of a free-kick and Ronaldinho arrowed it into the corner. Kissing the badge on his shirt, he then ran up to a microphone at the side of the pitch and screamed into it: '*Esse gol é pra gente como nós de Vila*' – 'this goal is for people like us from Vila Nova.' Given that even his goal had been booed by the members area but cheered by the cheap seats, he was acknowledging the support of those he could depend upon now the going was getting tough.

The game ended and it turned out that Ronaldinho's booking was not so pointless after all: it meant he would be suspended for the next home game and, with his contract due to expire before another one was scheduled, he would not have to endure the miserable experience of his own fans turning on him at the Olímpico again. His last match for Gemio would be away versus América of Minas Gerais in the Copa Brasil on 31 January 2001.

That didn't, though, spell the end of his troubles: on his last day at the club, security had to intervene to prevent two fans coming to blows while watching his final training session; one was insulting Ronaldinho, the other defending him.

Antônio Carlos Verardi's title at Grêmio is Superintendent of Football but in truth he is more a general manager. He first joined the club in August 1965 as part of the overall administration team but has specialised in running the club's football affairs for most of his time. Grêmio, as with most Brazilian clubs, is a general sports society that includes, among others, volleyball and rowing divisions; football is obviously the most popular and important element but it is dealt with, at least in theory, as one other department within the club structure.

Immensely respected, especially among the players, Verardi is also known as a sort of 'Mr Grêmio' and it is said that the gates at the Estádio Olímpico couldn't open without him.

He remembers Ronaldinho when the boy was just seven years old because of his brother. 'Assis was an incredible player; a left-footer, very talented. Ronaldinho used to accompany his brother and his father, who was a worker here at the club too – we often do this, bring someone from the family to work at the club alongside the player – so there was always a very big link between Grêmio and the family of Assis. I remember his dad telling us that Ronaldinho would become the better player,' recounts Verardi.

'His exit was traumatic. The fans were livid, and completely under-standably so. The point of view of the club was one of much frustration. He was well represented and his transfer was a great piece of business for his family but not for Grêmio. So, from Grêmio's side, there was a sense of resentment. But I couldn't say – I'm not an expert in law – if a fraud took place. We have to assume not, as Fifa approved the transfer.' Grêmio certainly felt cheated.

Verardi is quick to recognise that an atmosphere of uncertainty regarding the new law contributed to Ronaldinho's departure. 'His exit came at a moment of transition in Brazilian football and drew everyone's attention to the *Lei Pelé*. It was designed to give freedom to the athlete but wasn't absolutely clear. Brazil had very precise laws in place designed to protect a player's connection to a club but I was never completely convinced by them either. Unforeseen circumstances could always end up with the club having to let the player go and many clubs lost players in this way, though never Grêmio. So when the process began, I had a feeling Ronaldinho would probably end up free, even under the previous legislation. But then came the *Lei Pelé* and we had no chance.'

Clearly appreciative of the financial implications Ronaldinho's non-transfer had on the club, Verardi more readily looks at the affair from the perspective of the Grêmio fan he is. 'A multimillion-pound deal that could have benefited the club would have been another achievement of Ronaldinho's and, therefore, another source of pride among us *gremistas*.

'He was forged here. He learned his trade here, received his physical preparation, medical help, health care, all that he needed to transform him into what he is today. If you look at photos and videos of him playing *futebol salão* (the five-a-side of his formative years) he was fragile and now he is a fine, strapping, perfectly formed athlete. There is a lot of Grêmio in him and I know that his family know this.'

Celso Roth shares the view that others are now benefiting from the groundwork laid by Grêmio. 'Nowadays, playing for Barcelona, he is strong and can hold off players and that comes from where? From his training at Grêmio. When he arrived at Barcelona and PSG before that, he was already tall, already strong, already able to participate tactically in the collective work of the team, which you have to do in Europe, all of which he got from Grêmio.'

Speak to many Grêmio fans and they will agree. Some even suggest that Ronaldinho would likely be stacking shelves in a supermarket or attending cars if it had not been for Grêmio's careful nurturing. The fans still feel Ronaldinho betrayed their club.

At this time football in Brazil vitally needed restructuring to meet the requirements of the modern world, but most people – fans and media – were not ready to view themselves as clients or consumers, the players as simple employees, the club as a business. In football, uniquely, there are other factors at play; most important of all, there is an emotional link between fan, club and player and, although this may be impossible to define in law, it is the very foundation of the game itself. Fans do feel, rightly or wrongly, that the backing they give to a player should be repaid in kind; that the player has a moral obligation to respect the fans who have given him support.

Giovanni of *Super Raça* takes up the theme: 'For us fans, Ronaldinho will always be seen as a traitor. He was loved by us and we identified with him. He used to swear affinity for the club and the shirt. But a good deal is one that helps the club and the player. His deal helped him but left Grêmio with nothing.

'He claimed to love Grêmio so much that he wanted to stay, that he would even play for nothing. But he left Grêmio with nothing and they are still suffering for it. For us, he is a liar and a traitor.

'Ronaldinho may be the best in the world for Barcelona now but he started here, he was formed here. And Grêmio got nothing to show for it. He showed no gratitude, just treachery, and that is why he is still not welcome here.' Giovanni doesn't mince his words.

'When Grêmio were relegated to the second division a few years ago Ronaldinho said in an interview that it was a very sad day for him, a *gremista*. Yet it was thanks to him that we did go down. If he truly was a fan then he would have allowed the club to maximise his worth and benefit from the transfer. With the money being talked about, Grêmio could have created a great team to see them right for years to come. But no, he walks away for free.'

Fans do invest a great deal of emotion in supporting their team and it is always difficult to discover that a player, especially an idol, doesn't share the same sense of duty to the cause. It is even harder when the player in question is a local boy and one whose popularity has always been founded on empathy, the presumption that here, representing us, is a player who loves the club as much as we do.

The main beef *gremistas* have with Ronaldinho is not that he left Grêmio but that, if he truly did love the club, he would have arranged things differently; he could have made it so that his departure benefited the club financially but he didn't.

Says Giovanni, 'Not so long ago, he was presented with a shirt with his name on by Internacional. They asked him to put it on but he refused and said he couldn't as he was *gremista*. But he accepted the shirt. He only didn't wear it because he knew that that would have been the final straw; then he really wouldn't have been able to set foot in Porto Alegre again.'

If Ronaldinho is still hated in some quarters, Assis is positively abhorred. 'One of the main reasons Ronaldinho left was because Assis wanted to sign for Grêmio again but Grêmio didn't want him. He was past it by then, it would have just brought trouble, having to play his brother just so we could play Ronaldinho. So Assis made Ronaldinho leave for nothing in spite,' suggests Giovanni. 'There are many issues with Assis and the club, a club which took both him and Ronaldinho in at very young ages and gave them an opportunity. He certainly isn't welcome around here.'

Verardi likes to reflect on matters slightly differently. 'I am lucky enough to consider myself a friend of the family, of Dona Miguelina, of Roberto (Assis), of Ronaldinho himself. So for me, personally, my first reaction was one of sadness to see them, as people, leave.'

With Ronaldinho being a hugely popular figure with everyone involved in the day-to-day running of the club, Verardi wasn't the only one for whom his departure was a personal loss as much as a footballing one. There were security guards Pedrão and Leandro, Bete in the bar at the ground where Ronaldinho had always stopped for refreshment since he was a junior; all would miss the cheerful young man they had known since boyhood, who always had time to speak to them, always remembered them with a gift at Christmas.

'Despite the circumstances of his exit, there is no way of ever taking away the link between him and Grêmio,' continues Verardi. 'As a *gremista*, you want your best players to stay forever and if they can't then to be sold for millions. This wasn't the case and Grêmio suffered. But who can blame Ronaldinho for looking after his family? They are a family of humble origin and everyone has to look after their future.'

With regard to opinion some five years later, Verardi believes the resentment largely to have passed. 'These days, speaking as a fan myself, I think if you did a big survey among *gremistas* and said, "Do you like or dislike Ronaldinho?" then the vast majority would say they liked him.

'I saw an interview with him recently in which he said that after leaving Grêmio he couldn't be seen out in public places in Porto Alegre because he would always be challenged by outraged *gremistas*. I think that has probably changed by now. Time heals everything. The sorrow passes.'

Throughout the whole sorry episode of his transfer, Ronaldinho did indeed have to keep a very low profile within the city. There were rumours that he was booed on entering nightclubs and ended up fearing for his safety if he wandered the streets.

After Brazil won the World Cup in 2002, those members of the *Seleção* delegation who were from Rio Grande do Sul were rewarded with a parade through the Porto Alegre streets. Coach Luiz Felipe Scolari was there, as well as several members of the backroom staff and Anderson Polga, a squad member who played in the group games and was then still a player at Grêmio. But Ronaldinho was conspicuous by his absence. He headed straight for Rio and didn't show up in Porto Alegre until a week later, and clearly wasn't comfortable about how he would be received.

In an interview with *Playboy* magazine a few years later, Ronaldinho justified his actions thus: 'The transfer was complicated. With all the lies, everybody started giving me a hard time and I had to leave Porto Alegre. I went to Rio alone to train and I made friends there. After the World Cup, I went first to see those who had stood with me when times were tough.'

As regards the transfer itself, he concluded: 'I have never regretted my choice of going to Paris. For one thing, it helped me win back my place in the *Seleção*.

Grêmio never really valued me. I was distinguishing myself with the *Seleção* but they never came to talk to me, see if I needed anything.' He also accused Grêmio of lying to the fans: 'They claimed I was on BR$100,000 a month (£23,000) but it was a lot less than that and I never asked them for a cent more. I was on BR$20,000 (£4,750), one of the lowest in all the squad. The others deserved to earn what they did but Grêmio didn't value me and then the *Lei Pelé* presented an opportunity and I took it. I have never regretted anything. I'm happy.'

In June 2005, Brazil played Paraguay at Inter's Beira-Rio stadium in a World Cup qualifier. It was Ronaldinho's first appearance in his home city since being crowned World Footballer of the Year in December 2004. Brazil won 4–1 to all but guarantee their participation in Germany and Ronaldinho scored twice (both penalties). He was cheered enthusiastically, even rewarded with a special ovation, and the occasion evoked memories of the Argentina game there several years ago, with the blue and red halves of the city united in acclaiming the *canarinha* and its Gaúchos.

The match seemed like his first step on the road to redemption in the city. Inter fans were free to admire the skills of the best player in the world, formed in their home town and no longer tainted by playing for the enemy. Of course, he still evoked too many painful memories for them to truly worship him, but the very fact that he had caused their rivals so much suffering elevated his status in their eyes.

Gremistas had begun to come to terms with their loss and also better appreciated how much the club was also to blame in the whole debacle. Other players came and went: Ronaldinho's successor, Anderson, slipped through Grêmio's hands and left for Porto in Portugal in 2006 aged just seventeen. Fans bemoaned another loss and pointed accusing fingers at the board.

As Giovanni would have it, 'For the *Seleção* it is a different matter. We support Brazil and hope they win and therefore hope that he does well. That is a very separate issue.'

But Pelotinha believes people better understand the circumstances now. 'Ronaldinho left Grêmio just at the right time; the club was getting itself into a mess and people realise that. They see that by leaving he was able to develop into what he has now become.'

As for Verardi, he says, 'Fans will always want their best players to stay for ever and get angry when they leave. In the last *Gre-Nal*, Tinga, a former idol of Grêmio now playing for Inter, was booed every time he touched the ball. That's just the way it is. When you lose a lover to another you are not going to cheer them on. You are going to boo them always.'

Continuing the jilted lover theme, perhaps one philosophical *gremista* put it best when he said, 'Better to have loved and been betrayed by a rare beauty than to have the eternal faithfulness of an ugly one.' Ronaldinho may not be the prettiest but we all know what he means.

PARIS SAINT-GERMAIN

Ronaldinho arrived in the French capital for the first time in early April 2001 and was received at the airport by a sizeable throng of pressmen and supporters. As his court case rumbled on, PSG had given up any hope of his appearing for them competitively until the following season, which would begin in August. In the meantime, PSG drew up a special training programme for their new star to follow.

Once his contract at Grêmio had run out, Ronaldinho had tried to keep in shape by training with Esporte Club São José, Porto Alegre's third club. It soon became obvious that the spat between Grêmio and PSG would not be reaching a swift conclusion and so Ronaldinho tactfully chose to leave Porto Alegre. His future still in the balance, uprooting to Paris seemed premature and instead he set up residence on the outskirts of Rio in Barra da Tijuca. Zico had a training centre in the area and Ronaldinho had been told he was welcome to use the facilities whenever he wished. Meanwhile, Antônio Lopes, the former Grêmio coach who was then working as a co-ordinator for the *Seleção*, arranged for him to join in training sessions with Bangu, a second division team in the Rio state championship where Lopes' son was the assistant coach.

Throughout this period, Ronaldinho was accompanied by his cousin Joaquim Valdimar Gonçalves Garcia. A qualified physical instructor, Valdimar co-ordinated Ronaldinho's exercise routine and, when the player finally relocated to Paris, Valdimar went with him.

Luis Fernandez was PSG's coach and he was looking forward to incorporating the Brazilian into his plans. 'We hope to be able to have him as soon as possible,' he said. 'To help his adaptation, the sooner he arrives in Paris the better. As far as the player is concerned, I have only seen him play on TV but it seems like PSG has got itself a very talented young boy, full of potential.'

The coach also sounded a note of caution. 'Now, it will all depend upon his adaptation to the European game, which is quicker but, if he is in the line of the great Brazilians who have come here in the past, everything will be fine for him.'

Fernandez was referring to the club's rich recent history with regard to Brazilian players: Ricardo Gomes, Valdo, Rái and Leonardo had all distinguished themselves at the club during the 1990s.

These days, almost every major team in Europe builds their team around a Brazilian star but it wasn't always thus. In the early 80s, Brazilians in Europe were few and far between in the leagues of England, Germany and Spain and this despite the *Seleção* possessing an incredibly talented generation of players. Italy was home to Brazil's dream midfield of the decade but even there the situation wasn't as it is today: although Falcão and Toninho Cerezo played at Roma, Zico and Sócrates, two of Brazil's all-time greats, found homes at Udinese and Fiorentina respectively – both teams of stature, certainly, but hardly the European top tier.

In France, Brazilians were even more scarce. In 1974, Olympique Marseille signed Jairzinho and Paulo César, two stars of Brazil's magical 1970 World Cup winning team, amidst much fanfare. The experiment proved a costly failure, with both players heading back to Brazil after just one year, and French clubs would take a long time to shake the memory. There were a few exceptions – centre-half Mozer became a legend at Marseille after signing in 1989 – but French clubs tended to look elsewhere for their talent, to Africa in particular.

It was PSG and their owners, Canal Plus, who would lead the rehabilitation of the Brazilian reputation in France. When Canal Plus took over the club in 1991 they installed the Portuguese Artur Jorge as coach. He came to PSG following a successful spell at Porto and persuaded the Parisians to sign the Brazilians Ricardo Gomes and Valdo, who had impressed him for rivals Benfica. Their success at PSG led to the incorporation of two more Brazilian internationals, Rái signing in 1993, Leonardo in 1996. All would play a role in the club's golden era: PSG won the league in 1994, the cup in '93, '95 and '98, and reached the semifinals of European competitions three seasons in a row between 1993 and 1995 before lifting the Cup Winners Cup in 1996. Lyon soon took PSG's lead and built teams based on Brazucas (as Brazilians abroad are often called). To a lesser degree, Ajaccio, Rennes and Bordeaux all followed suit.

As examples of successful travellers, both Leonardo and Rái offered advice to the Brazilian footballer moving abroad: the player who tries to embrace the whole experience will always fare better than the one who treats the exercise as a means to make money before returning home as quickly as possible. Any foreign player will encounter difficulties, typically climatic (in France the winter can be very cold indeed) and performance-related (criticism of the French kind can be cruel and blunt in the extreme). For the player looking to make a quick buck, such problems rapidly lead to homesickness. By treating the adventure more as a whole package – learning the language, appreciating the culture – then such setbacks carry less weight and are more easily overcome. PSG had chosen well: in Rái et al. they uncovered a group of players with character enough to surmount all obstacles. They were celebrated as much for their brilliance on the pitch as for their supreme dignity off it.

By the time Ronaldinho packed his bags for Europe, playing abroad was less of a leap into the unknown. Brazilian footballers were employed all over the place and their experiences had filtered back home. Ronaldinho was also lucky enough to have a brother who had done it all before and could prepare him for what lay in store.

Nevertheless, the legacy of Rái's generation was priceless. 'The Brazilians before me did a fantastic job. They were great on the pitch and an example off it. They left the door open for others and now I just have to follow their footsteps,' Ronaldinho would later acknowledge. 'People warned me that the French were cold. It's quite the opposite. From the moment I arrived at the airport, there were people waiting for me, treating me with kindness,' he added.

As his transfer – if not yet his freedom to play – eventually got the green light, Ronaldinho began to settle into his new life in France. He started French classes, went house-hunting in Paris and, once a property took his fancy, turned his hand to a bit of painting and decorating. Ronaldinho chose a house located in Bougival, a small town on the Parisian outskirts towards Versaille. It was close to PSG's training centre at Saint-Germain-en-Laye and most of the other players lived in the area too.

Situated at the top of a hill, the house had five bedrooms over two storeys, a veranda, garden with tennis court and a ping pong table in the garage. The place was designed very much to Ronaldinho's tastes with a minimalist approach, meaning no pictures on the walls but a giant TV equipped with Playstation and karaoke machine.

His sister Deise moved in with him and, although retaining residency in Porto Alegre, Dona Miguelina never let too much time elapse without an extended visit. His cousin Bárbara and her baby Nátalia were also semi-permanent boarders throughout his time in Paris, not to mention Assis, then also playing in France at Montpellier. Valdimar, his cousin and personal trainer, added to the full house, as eventually did Tiago, his boyhood friend. Ronaldinho and Tiago had become buddies as juniors at Grêmio but Tiago's career had stalled on his suffering an injury: Ronaldinho invited him over to see if PSG's doctors could help. The idea was that Tiago might find a French team to play for once he recovered. He never did, but has remained Ronaldinho's right-hand man in Europe ever since.

As Ronaldinho would tell *Playboy* magazine when they visited him in the European autumn of 2002, there were usually no fewer than ten people at his home at any one time. As always with Ronaldinho, a four-legged friend (this one called Tiger) completed the posse.

In that *Playboy* interview, by which time he had been in France for over a year, Ronaldinho described how well he had adapted to life in the City of Light. He loved to venture to the Champs-Élysées or visit the Eiffel Tower (though he had never been able to go up it due to the crowds).

All was going well at PSG too. 'The organisation here is great. Even before the start of the championship, you know when and where you are going to play, not like in Brazil where it is always changing,' he enthused. 'In Europe, you also know that come pay-day you will get paid. That's the sort of benefit of being here. Things are more structured. You can plan your life. It is one of the things I like most about France. In fact I like everything,' he concluded.

Ronaldinho was enjoying a few of the cultural differences too. 'Fans are more restrained here in the streets,' he told the men's magazine. 'They'll say hello, ask for an autograph, then be on their way. In Brazil a fan always wants to chat.'

He enjoyed French food, though he tended to eat this at the club and preferred the city's Brazilian restaurants if he ate out; O Brasil Tropical, O Terra Samba and Pau-Brasil were all favourites. Yet whenever he might get homesick, he didn't necessarily have to venture out to kill the *saudades* (a very Portuguese word meaning 'longings'). He had Brazilian television transmitted via satellite direct to his house and would regularly invite his Brazilian friends over to watch the soap operas or football. Most Sundays, if PSG had played on the Saturday, he would throw a huge barbecue and samba party for the Brazilian fraternity. They would usually attract up to thirty people.

There were four other Brazilian players at the club during Ronaldinho's spell in Paris. Vampeta and Christian departed as he arrived but Alex Dias and Aloísio were signed in the summer of 2001 and André Luiz and Paulo César the following year (though Alex Dias moved on at that same time).

Aloísio, now back in Brazil playing for São Paulo, looks back on the period fondly. 'Sundays were *churrasco* and *pagode*,' he reminisces, *churrasco* being the barbecue, *pagode* a modern and popular version of samba. 'All of us there together, with our families, enjoying a great friendship, it was very important, something to remember forever and look back upon.'

Having already been playing in France for two years, Aloísio was able to aid Ronaldinho somewhat in assimilating to life in the country, though the younger player was already more familiar with the city. 'Really, we helped each other. I was more adapted to France having played for Saint-Etienne but I arrived in Paris when he had already signed his contract with PSG,' explains Aloísio. 'We joined our families together and created a bond which was very important in his adaptation, which was very quick,' he says.

'All his family were there with him and this is very important for a player who arrives abroad straight from Brazil,' Aloísio continues. 'You don't really know anything about where you are yet, nor speak the language and it is important to make sure you are not stuck at home alone, feeling sad, on the phone to Brazil all the time saying: "Mum, it's cold here".'

In terms of picking up the local lingo, Ronaldinho was evidently quite adept. 'He spoke very good French,' according to Aloísio. 'I played in France for four years, Ronaldinho just two, but he spoke much better French than me. Perfect, it was as if he had already been there for ages.'

Learning the language was evidently a top priority for Ronaldinho. He told *Playboy*: 'I had French classes in Brazil then (in Paris) for three months with a private tutor. It is good in every sense, to integrate, to develop as a person. To live in someone else's country, you have to learn their language.' PSG seemed to have found themselves a worthy successor to Rái and the gang.

Ronaldinho's best friend while in Paris was probably Talal El-Karkouri, a Moroccan and native French speaker. 'It is amazing because Ronaldinho really did speak very, very good French. After two months he started to communicate, which is amazing for a Brazilian player; it is not easy for them to come to France for their first time abroad and learn the language straight away,' confirms El-Karkouri who, after PSG, transferred to Charlton in 2004 and speaks good English himself.

El-Karkouri would certainly agree that Ronaldinho spoke better French than Aloísio. 'Yes,' he laughs, 'Aloísio did have a few problems, as did Alex. But Ronaldinho and Paulo César really learned quickly and spoke very well.

'Sometimes I used to go to the barbecues on a Sunday too,' continues El-Karkouri. 'Brazilian players have the same mentality as Africans, as Moroccan players, so it was easy for us to become close, to go out for dinner, enjoy spending our free time together. Not just me and Ronaldinho but others too.' As well as El-Karkouri, Ronaldinho's other main man in France was Selim Benachour, a Tunisian who ended up at Vitória Guimarães in Portugal. The three of them, along with the rest of the Brazilian contingent, would frequently socialise together.

El-Karkouri again: 'Sometimes we went out for meals and we enjoyed ourselves. The Brazilian players love meat (beef) – too much meat – and their second choice is chicken. I don't understand why they don't eat fish. But anyway, I went with them for nice Brazilian food and Brazilian music.'

The Brazilian reputation at PSG had been slightly tarnished by Ronaldinho's two immediate predecessors: Vampeta and Christian had earned notoriety for flamboyance off the pitch if not necessarily on it. Ronaldinho would also eventually be criticised for going out on the town a little too often, but El-Karkouri is quick to dismiss such suggestions. 'People say that he went out too much but he went out just like the other players. When we are free we might go out, especially after the game. It's normal.'

Ronaldinho certainly gave the impression of being a dedicated footballer when *Placar* magazine called upon him in September 2001. A van used to pick the players up from their houses and take them to the training pitch (a strange echo of a pub-team structure). Ronaldinho would then be the last to leave, practising shots and free-kicks long after the session had finished. When *Placar* was there, he arrived at training for 4 p.m. and left sometime after 9 p.m.

French football fans had read a lot about Ronaldinho during his enforced rest from competition. They had been led to expect a Youri Djorkaeff type, the French World Cup winner of 1998 who had enjoyed a successful spell with PSG before winding up at Bolton. There was also much excitement about Ronaldinho's potential partnership with Nicolas Anelka. The ex-Arsenal man was back at PSG – where he had initially started his career before heading for London – after a recent passage through Real Madrid. Tellingly though, a few observers did wonder how a Brazilian superstar would fit in at a club that had just completed such a dreadfully unsuccessful season.

At the time news of Ronaldinho's capture first broke, December 2000, PSG were in the middle of a dreadful slump that ended with manager Philippe Bergeroo being sacked and Luis Fernandez taking over. Fernandez was a legend in Paris: as a player he had formed part of France's magical midfield of the 1980s along with Michel Platini, Alain Giresse and Jean Tigana. Together they had lifted the European Championship in 1984. For PSG, Fernandez had won the league as a player in 1986, their first league title, and then guided them to Cup Winners Cup glory as manager ten years later. With such a figure back in charge (he had stepped down after that European triumph), decent players already on the roster (such as Jay-Jay Okocha and Gabriele Heinze) and the latest thing out of Brazil to add to the mix (Ronaldinho himself), there were plenty of grounds for optimism among the PSG fans.

Form had been patchy throughout the 2000 season but PSG did clinch the consolation prize of Intertoto Cup qualification. Over the summer, PSG thrived in the Intertoto and ended up as one of the three annual winners of the tournament (there is no outright winner – the prize is qualification for the Uefa Cup). Importantly, this meant Ronaldinho would have an international competition in which to cut his not-insignificant teeth.

Ronaldinho didn't take part in the Intertoto triumph as his clearance to play for PSG had come too late for him to be registered: although PSG and Grêmio continued their dispute, Fifa gave Ronaldinho permission to start playing competitively again on 2 August 2001. Two days later, he made his official PSG league debut. In the second match of the French championship – *Ligue 1* – away at Auxerre, Ronaldinho entered the fray in place of Aloísio with half an hour to go. He made a solid impression and PSG held out for a 1–1 draw.

In fact, draws would very much mark the beginning of Ronaldinho's career in France: PSG tied six of their first eight matches, culminating with a 0–0 at home to Montpellier. Assis didn't line up against his brother that day; indeed he only played for Montpellier five times before hanging up his boots for good. Commentators weren't impressed: how could a team that possessed the attacking flair of Anelka, Okocha, Ronaldinho, Alex Dias and Aloísio be struggling to kill teams off? PSG's front line, whatever the combination, was said to be too slow, too careless, too lightweight and too noncommittal.

Ronaldinho had appeared in all but the first league match and had started three times. He was yet to score but had been involved in all the goals of a 3–0 home win over Rennes. However, after spending six months on the sidelines, the player clearly wasn't match-fit: Ronaldinho showed no sign of being able to accelerate away from a defender, lacked all-round sharpness and was far too easily pushed off the ball. He also regularly chose the wrong option, too prone to overelaborate when a more clinical contribution was required. *L'Équipe* warned that PSG couldn't afford to indulge him for too much longer.

He soon learned to get more involved and improvement followed. With PSG losing 2–1 at home to Lyon, Ronaldinho came off the bench in the seventieth minute and his dribbling and overall movement changed the game. He put Bartholomew Ogbeche clear to win a contentious penalty and then took on the responsibility of equalising from the spot himself. In his ninth appearance, Ronaldinho had finally scored his first goal for PSG.

A further notable performance came a few weeks later. PSG were losing 1–0 at half-time away at champions Nantes and were down to ten men; Ronaldinho and El-Karkouri were brought on at the break and prompted a battling performance and turnaround which culminated in Ronaldinho drilling home the winner.

The Uefa Cup also inspired the more steely side to the PSG character. After defeating Rapid Vienna to reach the last sixteen, PSG were pitted against Rangers. The first leg in Glasgow brought one of the season's most spirited displays to earn a goalless draw. The return tie was just as hotly contested but remained deadlocked too and, after extra-time, went to penalties: Ronaldinho tucked his away but PSG's captain Mauricio Pochettino was less ruthless and the Glaswegians went through.

Although epic in their way, those European performances had ultimately yielded nothing and were being overshadowed by more tepid displays in the league. By the time they had drawn 0–0 at home to Auxerre, in what was their last game in Paris before the winter break (*Ligue 1*, as with most championships in Europe, pauses for a fortnight over New Year) seven of PSG's ten league games at the Parc des Princes had finished all square, three of them goalless.

Fans and reporters were not impressed and PSG's forwards copped most of the blame. Anelka had fallen out with Fernandez and been loaned to Liverpool at the start of December, but the other forwards had been equally insipid. For all his flashes of genius, Ronaldinho was proving far too inconsistent and had notched up just two league goals by Christmas.

Ronaldinho resolved to turn over a New Year leaf: determined to put a problematic twelve months behind him, 2002 would prove to be much more rewarding. A match versus Guingamp in the last sixteen of the League Cup began inconspicuously enough with Ronaldinho on the bench but, when he came on as a substitute, the time had evidently come for him to kick-start PSG's season along with his first in Europe. In what would be remembered as one of his finest performances in the PSG red and blue, he set up Edouard Cissé for PSG's first goal, scored from a free-kick for their second and then embarked upon a dribble that would become his trademark in Paris, beginning in the centre-circle and finishing with him one-on-one with the keeper and putting the game safe at 3–1.

Ronaldinho got on the score-sheet in the next game too, an away win at Rennes, then notched up PSG's goal in a 1–1 draw away at league leaders Lens. Having found his stride, there was suddenly no stopping Ronaldinho. PSG swatted Lorient aside 5–0 at the Parc des Princes with Ronaldinho scoring from a free-kick and setting up two of the other goals. Ronaldinho's form boded well as Marseille came to town.

The biggest games of the season for PSG fans are their fixtures against Olympique Marseille. The rivalry between the two is intense, although this is something of a relatively new phenomenon. Matches between the two sides passed with little fuss throughout the 70s and 80s, with the intensity seen today only emerging in the 1990s. Bernard Tapie was the Marseille president when Canal Plus took over Paris Saint-Germain in 1991. Both camps concluded that what they needed as clubs was a serious rival against whom to focus the energies of their own fans and stir new passions: an enemy against whom to rally the troops. For Canal Plus, which transmitted *Ligue 1* games on its pay-per-view service, upping the ante between the two biggest teams from the two biggest cities in France could only increase interest and viewing figures.

Marseille were the established power and PSG suddenly had the spending power to compete with them. There was also plenty of potential for rivalry given the traditional non-football antagonism factors: north versus south; province versus capital; down-at-heel Marseille versus haughty Paris. Such feelings were easily manipulated by the clubs' respective owners and the games between PSG and L'OM soon developed an extra intensity. The rivalry may have been artificially engineered but its instigators had soon created a monster.

L'OM's visit to Paris in November 2001 had produced the habitual animosity in Ronaldinho's first taste of hostilities – and he had been subjected to some fairly rough tackling – but all the huff and puff ultimately led to nothing and the match finished goalless. Fate then conspired to give Ronaldinho and the rest of the players another go in the last sixteen of the French Cup. Ronaldinho was a lively presence throughout the tie in what was the most emotionally charged atmosphere of the season. Losing by a solitary goal, PSG equalised with five minutes remaining, forcing extra-time and then penalties. Ronaldinho tucked his spot-kick away confidently but the contest dragged on until El-Karkouri fired home to give the Parisians a 7–6 victory.

PSG were enjoying themselves in the knockout tournaments and a League Cup semifinal versus Bordeaux followed. Despite being presented before the match with the *Ligue 1* player-of-the-month trophy for January, Ronaldinho started among the substitutes (it was still felt that his contribution was greater in short, sharp bursts). He entered the contest with half an hour to go and, surrounded by three defenders, somehow still managed to tee Didier Domi up for a great chance. The defender failed to finish off Ronaldinho's good work and the miss proved costly: Bordeaux held on to win 1–0 and head for the final.

PSG would soon be crashing out of the French Cup too: although they had beaten Lorient 5–0 at home in the league just a month previously, the same fixture in the cup ended with a 1–0 win for the visitors, despite Ronaldinho starting the game.

There was now just *Ligue 1* to focus on and Champions League qualification via a top-three finish was the target. Ronaldinho scored twice in a 3–1 home win over Troyes and again in a 2–0 victory over Metz. PSG played away at Lille in the last game of the season knowing that a win could bag them the coveted third spot. There was so much travelling support for the team from the capital that it almost seemed like a home match, but such backing was all in vain: Lille's goalkeeper had an inspired evening and PSG conceded a late goal.

So Champions League qualification proved elusive, but fourth place in the league, with its ticket to the Uefa Cup, was no mean achievement for Ronaldinho in his first season in Europe. He had even managed to play his way into the *Ligue 1* team of the year at the end-of-season awards ceremony, known as the *Oscars du Foot*. Ronaldinho also finished as PSG's top scorer, hitting the net thirteen times. This tally was all the more impressive considering his slow, transitional start to the season and the fact that he had generally occupied a midfield position and begun many games on the bench. The prospect of a fully acclimatised Ronaldinho going full steam ahead the following season filled the PSG faithful with glee.

WORLD CUP WINNER – *O PENTA*

Brazilians like to consider theirs to be *the* football country. The huge inequality between rich and poor in Brazil – plus all the accompanying problems this situation brings – means that its citizens have little to be genuinely proud of on the world stage. Football is different. Brazil are the best in the world at football and everyone likes to emphasise and be defined by what they do best, particularly a people with little to cheer in other spheres.

Perhaps as a legacy of their love of sport, Brazil is also a country obsessed with measuring achievements and, in this way, uncovering a winner. This is perhaps most obvious in the complicated and competitive scoring systems used to judge samba schools at carnival parades, in which points are awarded in ten different categories, ranging from costume design to flag bearing. Non-sporting events that receive similar treatment include the various firework displays marking New Year. They are not so much analysed for aesthetics as for how long they last and how many tonnes of explosives are used. It is thus possible to compare displays in different cities and find some sort of winner: the longest this, the biggest that.

When the *Seleção* heads to a World Cup, they don't go simply to win the cup but rather in search of *o penta*, Brazil's fifth, and then, once that had been achieved, *a hexa*, the sixth. The tally is important, paramount even. No other country has won five World Cups and so it provides Brazilians with categorical proof that they are the best, that they are *the* football country. Only with this in mind is it possible to understand why, for example, finishing as runners-up to France in 1998 was considered disastrous. Adding another star above the Brazilian badge was all that mattered.

There are those who believe that how Brazil play is as important as what they achieve. Brazilians like to try to make virtues out of what might otherwise be considered shameful problems: corruption dressed up as a cheeky creative streak; immaturity as being fun-loving; passivity as a laid-back approach. Linking Brazil's exciting style of play to the country's supposed character is convenient in providing an excuse for a lack of social improvement, for not trying harder. Yet such a façade only works if the *Seleção* keeps winning.

Football is the most popular game in the world and Brazilians – possibly due to some of the characteristics cited above – are the best at playing it. This is, quite rightly, a source of national pride and it is said that only when getting behind the *canarinha* during a World Cup does the Brazilian population, diverse and vastly dispersed, feel any sense of common brotherhood. The World Cup unites the country in a way nothing else can.

Brazil's 1994 triumph (*a tetra* – their fourth) was pivotal to Ronaldinho's life in this respect. As he told the *Independent*: 'I watched every second of that tournament. Finally we were world champions again. Then came the party – a massive national party. That victory made me understand that I was going to dedicate my life to playing football and trying to become a world champion with Brazil. From that precise moment I was crystal clear about my objectives for the first time in my life.'

Following the fiasco of Brazil's 2000 Olympic campaign, Vanderlei Luxemburgo was sacked as manager of the *Seleção*. His former assistant, Candinho, took over for the next game, a World Cup qualifier against Venezuela. Ronaldinho, evidently being punished for his role in the demise of Candinho's former master, was not called up.

In late October, Émerson Leão was named as the new national coach. Having had his differences with Leão back in the manager's Grêmio days, it came as no surprise when Ronaldinho was omitted from the first squad of the new regime. Leão did call him up for a couple of friendlies and a World Cup qualifier with Ecuador at the end of March 2001, but Ronaldinho then entered his state of limbo between Grêmio and PSG and was no longer considered a realistic option for selection.

Leão's term proved short-lived. Performances were poor and a hopeless showing in the Confederations Cup (Brazil drew 0–0 with Canada and Japan and lost to both Australia and France) brought his reign to an end. He was sacked at the airport before even boarding the plane home.

Brazil's football federation, the CBF, approached Luiz Felipe Scolari and the former Grêmio man agreed to take over.

Although a popular choice with fans, his appointment was not met with widespread approval within the press. Scolari, or Felipão (Big Phil) as he was known, had a reputation based on tactical discipline and teamwork and certainly not the individual flair many Brazilians saw as an almost patriotic duty of the national team. He had been quoted on numerous occasions demanding more fouls from his team. More importantly, despite a brief yet successful spell with Palmeiras, he had largely worked away from the São Paulo/Rio media axis. He was seen as gruff and uncouth by these city slickers. While Ronaldinho could take comfort from the fact that a fellow Gaúcho was at the helm, a familiar face who would undoubtedly be monitoring his progress, the media jury was out and they waited for the new boss to embarrass himself.

They didn't have to wait too long: Brazil were dumped out of the 2001 Copa América by Honduras.

More sympathetic observers recognised that Scolari had taken over at an impossible time, with the Seleção's form patchy and confidence low, but Honduras lacked pedigree and Brazil's exit was, therefore, considered a disgrace. There were now very real fears that Brazil might not qualify for the 2002 World Cup, a catastrophe that had never previously befallen *the* football country.

Amid such hostility, Felipão insisted on the key qualifier against Paraguay being played in Porto Alegre at the Estádio Olímpico where he knew he was guaranteed local support. To make doubly sure, he selected three Grêmio players in Marcelinho Paraíba, Eduardo Costa and Ronaldinho's mate, Tinga. Ronaldinho himself was still recovering his rhythm after his enforced competitive break and, besides, his presence would almost certainly have provoked the opposite of the desired effect.

The tactics paid off and Brazil ran out 2–0 winners in a positive and vocal atmosphere.

The next game was away to Argentina, runaway leaders of the qualifiers, and Brazil were beaten 2–1. Although there was no disgrace in this, losing to Argentina never goes down well in Brazil and their qualifying prospects were delicately poised with just three games to go.

Argentina had been the most formidable international side of the previous two years and were a model of collective brilliance. They were more organised than Brazil, more of a team; in short, more Argentine and this also meant more Gaúcho. Felipão began to think in terms of basing his Brazil side on the Argentine model and drew up a list of like-for-like players: Cafu–Zanetti, Gilberto Silva–Simeone, Rivaldo–Verón, Ronaldinho–Ortega.

With this in mind, Felipão went to Paris in September 2001 to visit Luis Fernandez, where the PSG coach told Scolari that Ronaldinho was progressing well. Ronaldinho was recalled to the squad for the next match, at home to Chile in early October. Brazil won 2–1 and, although Ronaldinho played no part in the match itself, Scolari said later that he sensed a change in the mood of the camp as soon as that squad came together: it seems likely that Ronaldinho's good nature would have contributed to the positive vibe.

With two games to go, Brazil faced a tricky test in the altitude of La Paz and were defeated by Bolivia 3–1 in the thin air. Ronaldinho was again in the squad but never stirred from the bench.

All this meant that the final match at home to Venezuela was a must-win game. Venezuela had won four on the trot and were suddenly no longer the pushovers of old. But the World Cup wouldn't be the same without Brazil and most of the football world were pleased to see them come out on top 3–0. Luizão was the star of the show, scoring twice and setting the tone with his committed display, but Ronaldinho had come on for the last twenty minutes and made a good impression too, in his first appearance in the *canarinha* in seven months.

What's more, the omens were good: every time Brazil had left qualification to the last match (in 1958 and 1994) they had won the resulting tournament.

The *Seleção* now played a series of friendlies with Scolari alternating his squads between Brazilian and European-based players. When Ronaldinho got his chance against Portugal in April 2002, he was the star of the show. For most commentators, he was unrecognisable from the Ronaldinho of old. For one thing, he had let his hair grow long and filled out physically, but he had also matured into a more all-round performer. The feeling was that, having adapted to European football, he had become a more imposing player; the tricks and trademark smile were still there but were now married to a more consistent and participatory approach.

People liked what they saw, especially Felipão. Whenever he made comments in the press, and particularly if he singled out a player for praise, he did so for a reason: to reward a player he felt had worked hard or to nurture their confidence. For Ronaldinho it seemed to be a bit of both when Felipão declared, 'The way he is playing – the tactical conscience he is demonstrating – means he is ready to become one of the main figures of the World Cup. He has an amazing physical presence which, when coupled with his talent, means he is a candidate to be one of the real stars.'

In some eyes, Ronaldinho's image was still tainted by his poor Olympic tournament in 2000. If Ronaldinho was hoping to leave such a sorry episode behind, he wasn't helped by the similarities being drawn between the announcement of the World Cup squad and the naming of the Olympic party two years previously. Once again, Brazilians were clamouring for Romario's inclusion and, once again, the coach of the *Seleção* refused to bow to fan pressure.

Romario had been in Scolari's first squad for a World Cup qualifier in Uruguay but had upset the coach by sneaking out of the team camp to hook up with an air hostess he had met on the flight down there. He then declared himself unavailable for the Copa América tournament of 2001, claiming he was due to have an eye operation. He was soon seen turning out for his club side Vasco in a series of friendlies in Mexico before he left for his holidays in the Caribbean. Felipão was appalled by this betrayal of the cause and refused to pick him ever again. He cited tactical reasons but it was clear that he was sending out a message to all players: if they wished to be involved in his World Cup project, then he expected full commitment.

Brazil's World Cup warm-up began in mid-May in Catalonia. The squad assembled for a series of fitness tests and to play a friendly against the autonomous region's representative side. It also allowed them a gradual adaptation to the new time zones: Barcelona was five hours ahead of Brazil – Korea and Japan, where the 2002 World Cup would be held, was twelve.

The friendly itself finished 3–1 to the South Americans and Brazil looked impressive. Ronaldo, the former Barcelona man, had been struggling with injuries for so long that his form was the great unknown but his mobility, alongside the directness of Ronaldinho, boded well. Ronaldinho scored twice, Edmílson bagged the other; unknown signs of things to come for the Nou Camp faithful. For the opposition, Luis García, who scored, and Víctor Valdés would both be future Barcelona colleagues of Ronaldinho's and they contributed to a solid display by the Catalans, who were never embarrassed. Rivaldo, then of Barcelona, missed the game through injury.

Next stop for the Brazilian delegation was Malaysia for more of the same: Felipão planned to build up fitness levels gradually and time adjustment came in the same manner. A friendly against Malaysia resulted in a comfortable 4–0 triumph.

While in Malaysia, a minor controversy broke in the Brazilian press. It was alleged that the CBF had distributed masturbation kits, containing pornographic magazines and other items, to the players to help them cope with chastity during the tournament. (Scolari had recommended, though not insisted, that players travelled alone.) The story proved to be something of a tall tale and Felipão lost his temper before calling a meeting with the press to establish some ground rules and appeal for co-operation. The result was that everybody knew where they stood: pressmen could talk to the players whenever they liked, although no recording equipment was permitted; the players were not to be given access to news reports from back home unless Felipão said so.

This meeting led to much better relations – in fact the whole travelling troop became known as the *Família Scolari* – and the players enjoyed the extra company of the journalists, though they used to coo like a pigeon whenever near the reporter who had written the porn story, suggesting he fed on rubbish.

The *Seleção* were drawn in Group C and would play all their opening-round matches in Korea. The Brazilian delegation had chosen the city of Ulsan as its base. Ulsan was known as Hyundai City as it was home to the car manufacturers and Brazil were holed up at the Hyundai Hotel. Some four hundred well-wishers were waiting at the hotel to meet the team coach as they arrived on what was a cold and rainy day. The chaotic reception, from a mixture of exiled Brazilians and local followers, lifted the players' spirits. Ronaldo and Ronaldinho were clearly the most celebrated of the group, with fans eager to touch the former's bald head or get a photo of the latter's ear-to-ear grin.

The *Seleção* took up two floors of the hotel and all players had their own room. However, the footballers were certainly not sealed off: there were other guests in the hotel, including the Brazilian press corps, and all mixed together freely. The main entrance was open to the public and visitors were entitled to come and go as they pleased. Felipão didn't want the players to feel they were incarcerated and indeed it was the most relaxed World Cup atmosphere anyone could remember.

The Mayor of Ulsan, Hwan Ku Shim, went to meet the Brazil players and declared his support for the team. Ronaldinho was chosen for ambassador duty and the mayor was thrilled when presented with a number 11 Brazil shirt (Ronaldinho's squad number) but such distractions were rare and the players soon grew restless and desperate to get the competition under way.

Felipão had contracted someone (a Spaniard whose name, curiously, was never revealed) to gather footage and assemble videos of all Brazil's opponents. It is also interesting to note that this editor, as well as the team psychologist, was paid for by Felipão himself in order not to draw unwanted attention to their influence and usefulness and allow them to simply get on with their jobs. The first montage lasted forty minutes but this proved to be longer than the players' attention spans, so future videos were a tighter twenty minutes.

Ronaldinho was interviewed before the opening match with Turkey and talked of what the tapes had revealed. 'Turkey's centre-halves are strong and play hard: we will have to use our speed to beat them. It will not be an easy match.'

The squad's training had focused a great deal on team shape and collective pressurising. In terms of tactics, Ronaldinho and Rivaldo practised interchanging positions. Everything seemed set until, on the eve of the first game, the team captain, Émerson, injured himself while playing in goal. As part of a meticulous attention to detail, Émerson had been practising with the gloves in case at any stage the regular goalkeeper had to leave the field when all three substitutions had already been used: as captain and midfield linchpin, it was felt that Émerson would always be on the pitch and hence was the most sensible contender to be emergency keeper.

The injury was serious and Émerson was forced to withdraw from the tournament. Cafu was hastily promoted as captain, Gilberto Silva given Émerson's role in the starting eleven and Ricardinho, then of Corinthians and latterly of Middlesbrough fame (if only for the club not registering him properly), called up as a late replacement to the squad. The whole squad felt sad for Émerson but Ricardinho raised morale on his arrival with tales of the excitement building back home.

Brazil struggled greatly against Turkey. Having missed several first-half chances, they conceded just before half-time before rallying in the second half. Ronaldo equalised from a Rivaldo cross and then substitute Luizão was pulled back by Özalan Alpay, who was dismissed, and a spot-kick was awarded (though the incident was clearly outside the box). Rivaldo duly slotted home the winner for Brazil. The game ended in further injustice for the Turks when Rivaldo's theatricals (having had the ball kicked at his knee, he fell to the floor clutching his face) got Hakan Ünsal sent off.

Ronaldinho had started the game as the left-sided *meia* (Juninho Paulista was on the right) behind Ronaldo and Rivaldo leading the line. As had been rehearsed, he and Rivaldo switched position regularly to disrupt the Turkish man-to-man marking. Besides flunking a chance from close range, scuffing his shot straight at Turkish goalkeeper (and future Barcelona colleague) Rüstü Reçber, Ronaldinho had been anonymous. He made way for Denílson midway through the second half.

The Brazilian media were heavily critical of his performance. In a post-match press conference, Ronaldinho was asked bluntly if he had bottled it on the big stage again. Ronaldinho looked taken aback but kept his cool and reminded everyone that he had been a successful tournament player for the *Seleção* at several junior levels. He nevertheless admitted that he had played badly and regretted his missed chance: 'If I'd have scored, the game would have been much easier for us and I'm sure I would have gone on to play well.' He put it down to an off day. As regards his detractors he had this to say: 'There is constructive criticism, which I welcome and pay attention to. Then there is the more passionate criticism, which comes from those who only think they understand football.'

Turkey had proved themselves very able opponents – in fact they would go on to reach the semifinals – but their lack of football pedigree on the world stage meant that Brazilians saw them as an easy touch. Felipão was eager for such thinking not to permeate his players ahead of the next match, versus China. He printed off a short story called 'The Lion Hunter and the Magic Flute' and slipped a copy under each of the players' hotel doors. They then discussed the morals of the fable the next day, ahead of the game.

A 7-year-old Ronaldinho practices his ball skills.

Left to Right: Ronaldinho's father João, his mother Dona Miguelina, his sister Deise and
Ronaldinho himself.

Before and after: Above is 73, Rua Jerólomo Minuzzo, Vila Nova, Porto Alegre, Brazil, the wooden bungalow Ronaldinho called home as a young boy; below is the imposing entrance to the private road in Porto Alegre where Ronaldinho, his mother, brother and sister have recently had luxury homes constructed.

Roberto lifts up a young Ronaldinho at a Grêmio training session. Roberto became the father figure in Ronaldinho's life following João's death.

Ronaldinho and his brother, Roberto, kick a ball around the garden of 215 Rua Murá, Guarujá, Porto Alegre: the new house was bought for the family by Grêmio when Roberto signed for them as a professional. Behind them, the swimming pool which would prove to play should a tragic role in the family history can be seen.

Sérvia is a team comprised exclusively of Ronaldinho's family members. Here 'The veterans' line-up for a match at the Perequito in Vila Nova, the same pitch where Ronaldinho first learnt to kick a ball.

The Sérvia name honours Ervino Assis, Ronaldinho's grandfather, and the club badge is a tree to symbolise the club's family roots.

Ronaldinho quickly established himself as the Grêmio fans' favourite.

Ronaldinho wriggles clear of Dunga in the final of the Gaúcho state championship in 1999. The match was defined by the young pretender, Ronaldinho, outsmarting the veteran, former Brazil captain. Dunga is these days Brazil's national coach.

Ronaldinho celebrates scoring what would prove to be the winning goal in the final of the Gaúcho state championship in 1999.

A 19-year-old Ronaldinho kisses the Gaúcho trophy after the match above, a victory which marked the player's coming of age.

Ronaldinho celebrates his first call-up to the Brazil senior squad by trying the famous shirt for size.

Ronaldinho's departure from Grêmio was traumatic in the extreme. Some of the club's fans have still not forgiven him for the manner in which he departed the club. Here, supporters hold up a banner accusing him of being a mercenary.

After a 6-month legal dispute between Grêmio and Paris SG, Ronaldinho was finally cleared to play for his new club in August 2001.

While Ronaldinho became a hero to the Paris SG fans, his talent didn't bring success to the club and his time in Paris was marred by accusations of a lack of professionalism.

Ronaldinho celebrates scoring a penalty in Brazil's 4-0 win over China at the 2002 World Cup.

The 22-year-old was a key performer as Brazil went on to win the tournament. Here he celebrates after Brazil had beaten Germany 2-0 in the final.

Ronaldinho lifts the World Cup trophy aloft. He was voted fifth best player of the 2002 tournament.

If Ronaldinho's true passion is football, music comes a close second. Here he plays the drum with his band Samba Tri.

The role of Ronaldinho's mother, Dona Miguelina, cannot be underestimated in his success story. Here she revels at a carnival parade organised in Ronaldinho's honour. The player himself was not permitted to attend by his then team, Paris Saint-Germain, in whose section of the parade Dona Miguelina can be seen.

A global megastar, Ronaldinho has even been transformed into a cartoon character in Brazil.

Ronaldinho advertises dozens of products and has his own ice lolly.

Ronaldinho salutes the heavens after scoring the second of his two goals in a 3-0 victory over Real Madrid at the Bernabéu. So impressive was his performance that the Madrid fans rose to their feet and began to applaud.

The Barcelona team line-up ahead of the Champions League Final against Arsenal in Paris in May 2006. Back row (from left to right): Txema Corbella (kit-man), Ronaldinho, Edmílson, Rafael Márquez, Marc van Bommel, Oleguer Presas, Víctor Valdés, Samuel Eto'o; Front Row: Giovanni Van Bronckhorst, Ludovic Giuly, Deco, Carles Puyol, Àngel Mur (masseur).

Ronaldinho tries to find a way through the defensive attention of Ashley Cole and Sol Campbell in the pouring rain during the Champions League Final in Paris. Barcelona ran out 2-1 winners to lift the trophy for just the second time in the club's history.

The Barcelona team parade through the city atop a Trio Elétrico truck following the Champions League triumph in 2006.

Ronaldinho playing for Brazil in their opening match against Croatia in the 2006 World Cup. The tournament proved to be a major disappointment for both player and country.

The story told of a lion hunter who invited two friends to go hunting with him. Before they set off, he visited a witch who presented him with a magic flute: when played, a lion would start to dance and then freeze still; the hunters could walk up and kill it with ease.

The first lion they encountered was slain in this way, as a monkey observed from a tree. The second lion suffered a similar fate, again under the monkey's gaze. The third lion ignored the flute and devoured the hunter and his two friends. The monkey exclaimed, 'I was waiting for them to come across a deaf lion.'

The message was clear: Brazil must be on their guard; China could be a deaf lion. Whether such caution was required seemed academic as Brazil raced to a 3–0 lead by half-time. The Chinese threat tamed, Ronaldinho was withdrawn at the interval (Denílson again his replacement) and Brazil went on to register a further strike and run out comfortable 4–0 winners.

Ronaldinho had begun the game on the left again but this time as part of an attacking trident involving Ronaldo and Rivaldo, with Juninho dropping deeper. Ronaldinho's performance was greatly improved and he was involved in all three first-half goals: he was brought down for the free-kick which brought Roberto Carlos' opener; he crossed for Rivaldo to tap home the second; and he scored the third himself from the penalty spot.

Two wins meant that qualification for the second round was secured and so Scolari elected to rest those players already on a booking for the next game against Costa Rica – another yellow card would rule them out of the second round tie. Ronaldinho had picked up a yellow card versus China and so watched from the bench as the *Seleção* brushed Costa Rica aside to win 5–2.

For the second round, Brazil would play Belgium in Kobe, Japan. To stress the importance of teamwork for this game, Felipão handed round a printout that detailed how and why geese fly in a V formation while, to get the players in the right mood, he urged them to play their samba instruments on the bus on the way to the game. Ronaldinho led the musical proceedings.

Once the match began, however, Brazil lacked both rhythm and direction. The *Seleção* created and spurned a few chances in the first half but it was Belgium who actually put the ball in the net, only for the header from Marc Wilmots to be inexplicably ruled out by the referee.

Belgium began the second half much the brighter and Brazil's goalkeeper, Marcos, was forced into making a series of key saves. Then Ronaldinho got hold of the ball on the edge of the box and laid it off to Rivaldo, whose strike flew in via a slight deflection. Brazil had to absorb strong Belgium pressure until a counterattack was finished off by Ronaldo with three minutes to go and the game was made safe: 2–0 it finished. Ronaldinho played most of the game, making way for Klebérson with ten minutes to go.

Ronaldinho had plenty to cheer: as well as being in the quarterfinals of the World Cup, his family had come to visit. Assis, familiar with the country having played in Japan during his own career, had established the clan in Tokyo and they travelled to matches from the capital via train. When Ronaldinho got back to the hotel after the match, his brother, Dona Miguelina, Deise, Carla and Diego were all there to greet him.

Brazil may have reached the last eight but they had been far from convincing and the Brazilian media were harshly critical, feeling the midfield was failing to ably link defence and attack. Many Brazilians also recognised that they had only got as far as they had thanks to two favourable and dubious refereeing decisions: the penalty award against Turkey and Belgium's disallowed 'goal'.

England were to be Brazil's opponents in Shizuoka. The winner would go on to play either Turkey or Senegal in the semifinals and, especially when considering that the likes of France, Argentina and Italy were already out, would be in a great position to win the whole thing.

As past winners and inventors of the game, England were considered by the Brazilians as worthy challengers. Much time was spent in training preparing to defend David Beckham's crosses, and dead-ball situations were generally viewed as the main danger. As they watched the video montage of England's earlier games, Ashley Cole was signalled out for special attention and Klebérson was brought into the right side of midfield to combat his raids down the left. Felipão also noted that Rio Ferdinand and Sol Campbell defended much higher up the pitch than the Brazilians were used to and Ronaldinho and Rivaldo were again instructed to switch positions regularly, the idea being for one of them to suck the English centre-backs out too far so the other might sneak in behind (this is more or less what happened for Brazil's first goal).

To motivate his players, Felipão had no need to resort to fairy tales this time: he simply made use of the fantastical English press. The *Daily Star*'s headline of 'We'll Thrash 'Em' was reproduced alongside the *Daily Mirror*'s 'Is That All You've Got?' and passages from a preview in *The Times* that argued that if the Brazil defence played as poorly against England as they had against Belgium, then England wouldn't just win but might even do so comfortably were taken out of context. These were all pasted on a sheet entitled: 'British press bank on a massacre'.

In what was a cagey opening period, Brazil began with a 3–4–3 formation, Ronaldinho playing up front on the right. Before long, however, they were chasing the game: Lúcio's slip let in Michael Owen and England were 1–0 up. For Ronaldinho, there were echoes of that Under-15 game at Wembley back in 1995.

Felipão then switched the team's shape, with Ronaldinho moving into the middle and playing in the hole. Improvement was almost immediate. As half-time approached, a less-than-fit Beckham shirked a challenge and the ball ended up at Ronaldinho's feet. He began to run at the heart of the England defence and, via a swift change of feet, danced past Ashley Cole. Ronaldinho's pass to Rivaldo, who had slipped in behind England's back line, was perfectly weighted and the finish was clinical.

The second half began in much the same vein and Ronaldinho was soon lining up a free-kick some forty yards out. He consulted with his captain, Cafu, and then lofted a high ball above and beyond England's goalkeeper David Seaman and into the back of the net. Brazil were winning and playing their best football of the tournament, with Ronaldinho the mastermind.

But not for much longer. Ronaldinho went into a tackle high on Danny Mills and England's right-back collapsed in a heap; the referee took out his red card and Ronaldinho was heading for an early bath.

With over half an hour to play and against just ten men, England were now in a great position to get back into the match. Yet Sven-Göran Eriksson's cautious approach, a solid defensive base with sporadic attacks, was little use now that England were chasing the game. In the not entirely misguided belief that Brazil's centre-backs weren't up to much, England launched a succession of long balls down the middle but, on a windy afternoon, these punts proved useless. England failed to conjure a shot at goal against the ten men and Brazil held on to win 2–1.

While it had certainly been a victory of the collective hard work of those ten men and Ronaldinho's status as the match's central figure came not all for the right reasons, the Brazilian press rejoiced in Ronaldinho's performance. Finally, an individual had been able to shine and display the flamboyant characteristics that make Brazilians proud. He had been the one who had opened up the spaces, found room to dribble, brought a little of the magic and art which the *canarinha* required to keep its legacy alive. Brazilians say that tight games are won by details and the detail had been in Ronaldinho's skill. His step-over on the way to setting up the first goal and his spectacular second had been the defining moments.

Much debate, in England at least, centred on whether or not Ronaldinho's goal had been a fluke. Ronaldinho claimed that it was definitely a shot, that Cafu had told him in training the week before the game to keep an eye on England's goalkeeper because he often strayed from his line. Some commentators backed up this argument by noting that Cafu had been a member of the Real Zaragoza team that had beaten Arsenal in the Cup Winners Cup final when Nayim had lobbed Seaman in similar fashion. Others pointed out that Ronaldinho certainly had the skill and audacity to have tried to score direct. He dedicates a great deal of time to practising free-kicks and furthermore, if it had been intended as a cross, it is unlikely he would have got it so badly 'wrong'.

The mystery rumbled on until three years later, in an interview with the *Guardian*, Ronaldinho tried to put the matter straight. 'I wanted to shoot in the left-hand side of the goal. Maybe I hit it harder than I thought and as the goalkeeper was standing out in front of his line, it ended up going in behind him. It was better than I thought! I'd practised it at training but always aiming for the other side of the goal. When it went in, well, I felt something completely out of the normal.'

So he had taken a shot but not aimed exactly where the ball ended up: half deliberate, half fluke.

Ultimately, whether or not he had intended to put the ball precisely where he did was beside the point: taking a shot was so ambitious an option that Seaman hadn't even considered it; the game turned out to be a victory of Ronaldinho's optimism over England's lack of imagination.

His sending off had, of course, marred his performance. The referee's decision had been harsh but justifiable. In a delicious piece of engineering on Fifa's part, Ronaldinho and Mills were chosen (along with Cafu and Ferdinand) to give the post-match doping tests, a process that took them three hours, finishing long after the rest of the players had returned to their hotels. Ronaldinho questioned Mills about the incident and the England defender said he couldn't understand the red card. Ronaldinho was full of lament but denied any ill intent. 'I regret it but I don't think it was a sending off. I have seen it on TV and I think it should have been a yellow. I didn't mean to hurt him, just protect myself because I thought he was coming in stronger than he did do. But I won't go in like that again with my studs showing.'

All there was left to do was await his punishment: if his misdemeanour was deemed serious it would warrant a two-match suspension and his World Cup would be over. In the end, Fifa's disciplinary committee were lenient and he was banned for just the one game, the semifinal.

In the semifinal Brazil faced a rematch with Turkey, who were having a remarkable tournament. Brazil ran out 1–0 winners in what was a very tight game thanks to a lone goal from Ronaldo at the start of the second half. Ronaldinho watched from the sidelines but in Felipão's teams those on the bench still had a duty: they were expected to make plenty of noise in shouting encouragement.

The *Seleção* were in the World Cup final and the players in celebratory mood. Scolari, however, insisted that they establish themselves in

Yokohoma, where the final would take place a week later, as soon as possible. The whole entourage flew to their new base that very night, not arriving at their hotel until 3.30 a.m. The squad drank beers and played music on the plane but in such a controlled environment that the party was a low-key affair. Felipão had successfully managed to ensure that nobody was celebrating too much too soon. They had won nothing yet.

The players' partners and families joined the squad for the final, all bringing news from home. Felipão also arranged for a news feature from Brazil's TV Globo to be shown to the players: it showed a nation united in their support for the *verde-amarelo* and stimulated the players with a sense of responsibility and pride. Felipão also got his editor to splice together a mix of Brazil's goals in the tournament so far with the celebrations in the streets back home, all to a samba soundtrack.

For the more high-brow members of the squad, Scolari selected a quote from German poet Christian Morgenstern: 'If you don't have the will to re-conquer the world every day then on most days you will lose it.'

Scolari asked the players to get an early night on the eve of the final and for them to go to sleep fantasising about the final, visualising the game and lifting the cup.

On the morning of the match, fresh from their World Cup-winning dreams, the players set off to the ground after a special ceremony orchestrated by the hotel staff. '*Aquarela do Brasil*', a Brazilian song performed by Gal Costa, was pumped from speakers and the hotel workers clapped the players all the way from their rooms on to the coach.

Driving to the ground, the roadside was full of Japanese waving. At first it was assumed they had come out to salute Emperor Akihito, who would be travelling through the city to attend the final, but then someone realised this wasn't part of his route and that they were actually all there to salute the *Seleção*.

As the bus approached the stadium, a quirk of fate saw the Brazil and Germany team coaches meet and the contrast between the two could not have been more striking: the German players looked deadly serious with manager Rudi Völler one of few to even muster a smile; the Brazilians were in party mode, singing along to the samba as Ronaldinho, Edílson and Denílson led the drumming. The match, curiously the first between the two countries in any World Cup, was being billed predictably as a contrast between efficiency and flair: the scenes on the two buses captured this notion perfectly.

In fact, neither side was viewed as a vintage one when compared with these nations' illustrious footballing pasts, but both countries were playing their seventh final and so it was certainly a clash of World Cup titans. Brazil were bidding to win their fifth cup (*a penta*), Germany to match the

Seleção's current tally of four. Brazil, *the* footballing country, were desperate to avoid anyone matching their *tetra*.

The Brazil of 2002 had yet to produce the beautiful game synonymous with previous sides, particularly the 1970 or 1982 versions, but they had shown more imagination than the 1994 side that lifted the trophy. They had also demonstrated the importance of the collective with few people remembering a *Seleção* and all its delegation – the Scolari Family – quite so united.

A demonstration of this spirit arrived just before kickoff. As the two sides lined up for their team photos, all those Brazilian players not in the starting eleven suddenly ran on to the pitch to join in the picture; instead of a team photo, as Fifa stipulates, for the final Brazil's was a squad shot.

Ronaldinho was in that starting eleven. Some observers had suggested that Brazil had looked slightly more solid without him against Turkey but the World Cup final was likely to be a tight encounter and Scolari banked on Ronaldinho's creativity as a potential deciding factor. Indeed, caution ruled in the opening exchanges and, although Brazil did show extra adventure, it was a more even game than had perhaps been expected. Brazil began with a 3–4–1–2 line-up with Ronaldinho playing on the left of the two. He managed to put Ronaldo in on goal with a one-touch pass on two occasions in the first twenty minutes, but openings generally proved rare. Felipão then tinkered with his formation and switched to a 3–4–2–1 with Ronaldinho on the right of the two. Brazil's play improved, and Klebérson hit the bar after being fed by Ronaldinho, but it was all square at the interval.

Germany were the first to threaten in the second half as Oliver Neuville had a free-kick tipped onto the post by Marcos. Then, on 67 minutes, Ronaldo dispossessed Dietmar Hamann in the midfield and Rivaldo was able to fire off a shot. Ronaldo followed up and, as Oliver Kahn parried, tucked home the rebound. He was obviously not put off by his new bizarre half-moon haircut, on which Ronaldinho would comment, 'Ronaldo is my mate so when he asked me what I thought I said, "Yeah, it looks great." But I think deep down even he knew it didn't.'

The goal relaxed everyone – a mistake would no longer be crucial – and Brazil were able to open up more. After 79 minutes, Klebérson broke free on the right wing and put in a cross that Rivaldo dummied before Ronaldo scored his second of the match and eighth of the tournament (enough for him to top the scoring charts). With five minutes to go, Ronaldinho made way for Juninho but the job was by then done: Brazil had won the World Cup.

There were emotional scenes of celebration on the pitch and tears of joy. Ronaldinho was at the heart of things, draped in a Brazilian flag. At one point all the Brazilian delegation, at the prompting of Marcos (the most vocal Evangelist in a very religious squad), formed a giant circle and knelt in prayer on the pitch.

Back in the dressing room, Ronaldinho and Roque Júnior led the percussion celebrations. Vampeta, who was performing a sort of *capoeira* dance with Juliano Belletti, demanded beer and two crates soon arrived. French football legend Michel Platini came to offer his congratulations and Brazil's president, Fernando Henrique Cardoso, did likewise via the telephone. Scolari and the players took turns to attend to the media, then gradually began to shower and get changed. Ronaldinho just sat there playing music.

Ronaldinho is never in a rush to leave the dressing room, be it after training or a match, and is usually among the last to depart. After the final, he was even less inclined to budge. TV cameras captured him saying, 'I'm not leaving here. I'm not showering or getting dressed or anything. I'm staying right here forever.' His words, though simple, seemed to sum up the euphoric state of bliss he had entered.

Yet he did finally leave and, once returned to the hotel, everyone was completely free to do whatever they pleased. A celebration was organised in one of the hotel reception rooms. Ronaldinho was the life and soul of the party, which lasted well into the early hours, keeping the samba beat going with Denílson and Dida.

The magnitude of their achievement didn't sink in straight away. 'It was the next day, when I woke up and went down for breakfast, when it hit me,' Ronaldinho would later admit. 'It is hard to explain. I was another person, I felt somehow different.'

That day, the party continued on the flight back to America: the trophy itself was passed around everyone – players, coaches, journalists – as drum beats echoed throughout the plane, but Ronaldinho, somehow, managed to sleep through the chaos. Once back in Brazilian air space, the *Seleção's* plane was met by five military fighter jets and other aircraft, which flew in circles and wrote *penta* (fifth) in smoke in the sky. The air-force commander's voice then came through the Tannoy addressing the players: he called them warriors who had brought honour and pride to their country. Ronaldinho was reduced to tears.

A military troop and orchestra welcomed the players off the plane and they were ferried to an audience with the president on a *Trio Elétrico* – a truck-come-float used by bands as a moveable stage as they parade through the streets at carnival. The 15km from the air base to the Planalto presidential palace took three and a half hours to navigate, with some two million fans lining the streets. Ronaldinho spent the entire time at the front of the *Trio Elétrico* playing drums.

In order to present the right image to the millions more watching at home on television (not to mention promoting their sponsors), the players had to drink *guaraná*, a popular Brazilian pop made from Amazonian red berries. However, *guaraná* appears golden when in a glass, so the players struck upon the cunning ruse of swapping the pop for beer when out of sight. This meant that one or two of the players were pretty merry by the time they met the president (Vampeta performed a forward roll on the palace steps).

From Brasília they flew straight to Rio for another parade there. They were welcomed by state governor Benedita de Silva (the first black woman to reach the Brazilian senate) who presented them all with medals. Ronaldinho was evidently her favourite player – he was lavished with attention and told that she had dedicated many prayers to him.

Ronaldinho remained in Rio for several days (he missed the parade in Porto Alegre arranged to honour the conquering Gaúchos) but when he did finally return to his home city he was met by three hundred people at the airport, over a hundred being direct family who had hired coaches to head straight for yet another party.

Brazil had won *a penta*, their fifth World Cup, and Ronaldinho had been a key component, even being named Fifa's fifth best player overall (Ronaldo was first) and top midfielder in the team of the tournament. He hadn't quite set the world on fire but his contribution, above all versus England, had been vital.

Before the tournament, with Ronaldo and Rivaldo both coming back from injuries and Ronaldinho having played so well in the warm-ups, people began to talk of him as the team's main man, a possible star of the tournament. Ronaldinho himself tried to play down such expectations. 'I'm not thinking or worrying about this. I don't want to be the best player or the top scorer or anything. I just want to be a World Cup winner, help the team achieve its objective.'

Yet the pressure and responsibility did weigh and he wasn't at his best for the group games. Felipão persevered with him and then, as the other two Rs found their stride and took the lead, Ronaldinho warmed to his supporting role. He was absolutely fundamental against England and throughout the competition his positional interchange with Rivaldo offered the constant element of surprise vital to Brazil's attacking scheme.

As Ronaldinho himself would eventually summarise: 'I did well for it being my first World Cup – I participated in the victory – but I can do a lot better.'

That remained to be seen.

SOUTH AMERICAN IN PARIS

The PSG pre-season training camp had begun while Ronaldinho was still on World Cup duty, so he was afforded special dispensation to enjoy an extended holiday, or at least one that started and finished after everyone else's. Some observers suspected the World Cup winner may be tempted away from France, with Inter Milan, Barcelona and Manchester United said to be interested, but Ronaldinho returned to Paris on 21 July 2002.

The mayor of Paris, Bertrand Delanoë, invited him to the City Hall for a civic reception. Ronaldinho had hobnobbed with the hierarchy in Paris before, having been invited to a reception for Fernando Henrique Cardoso when the Brazilian president had visited the previous year, but this time Ronaldinho was the one being honoured: he received the Grande Médaille Vermeil de la Ville de Paris, the city's highest accolade. Thinking it only appropriate to involve a Brazilian, the mayor also invited him to take part in the inauguration of *Paris Plage*, a summer initiative to create an artificial beach on the banks of the River Seine.

Everyone had high hopes for PSG in the 2002–03 season: the defence had proved to be the meanest in *Ligue 1* the previous year and was a solid foundation on which to build, while Ronaldinho was now an established world beater and fully adapted to the French league. The PSG fans dared to dream of a first league title win since 1994.

But PSG's first game of the season came and went without Ronaldinho's involvement and, although it resulted in a 1–0 home win for the Parisians over Auxerre, the abject attacking display only served to show how much they would once again be relying upon Ronaldinho. Yet he was behind on his fitness schedule, complaining of aches and pains and fatigue after the World Cup tournament.

A goalless draw at Bordeaux followed and then PSG threw away a two-goal lead at home to Ajaccio, overshadowing Ronaldinho's return (he came on with 25 minutes to go). His next performances were also of the cameo kind: when asked if he was not tempted to rush Ronaldinho back into the team, coach Fernandez replied that it was unnecessary as the Brazilian had enough quality to change a game in a matter of minutes.

Performances and results steadily improved, even if PSG were again drawing more often than they should (five from the first nine games). By the time of the visit of Olympique Marseille to the Parc des Princes, PSG had nudged up to third place in the table and Ronaldinho was back in the team. He rose to the occasion and was the driving force behind a convincing 3–0 win, scoring from a free-kick after a quarter of an hour, then again from the spot before half-time. More than that, he was a constant menace, quick, powerful and, most important of all, decisive. The PSG faithful could pay him no greater compliment than to leave the Parc that night saying that Ronaldinho had reminded them of Rái. He had also provoked a response from the L'OM fans, who pelted him with several missiles, including a firecracker that appeared to strike him.

A very contented Ronaldinho gave the post-match press conference. 'It was one of my best matches in the red and blue,' he beamed. 'I knew about the rivalry between the two teams and that winning against L'OM is like entering the history books of PSG. That is what motivates me, and bringing pleasure to the supporters.'

The win moved the Parisians up to second in the table and the future looked bright: PSG's fans could never have imagined that it would be downhill all the way from there. In both of the next two matches PSG would have gone top of the table had they won, but each opportunity was squandered: they had entered their annual autumnal slump.

Ronaldinho had been in and out of the team all season, sometimes starting on the bench, often ending up there, and his understanding with Fernandez was becoming increasingly strained. As the *Ligue 1* campaign began, Ronaldinho had insisted on travelling back to Brazil to play a friendly match for the *Seleção* against Paraguay, a sort of homecoming homage to the World Cup winners. Fernandez thought the player should get his priorities right and stay in Paris to work on getting fit. This disagreement set the tone for the whole season.

Fernandez claimed that Ronaldinho had returned from the World Cup too big for his boots and said he no longer merited an automatic place in the team. Ronaldinho, meanwhile, questioned Fernandez's tactics: the

Brazilian was not being played in his preferred free-floating role but having to lead the line.

One of Fernandez's main sore points was that Ronaldinho dedicated too much energy to chasing women and not enough to football. With this in mind, the timing was poor when the coach discovered, on the eve of a match away at Lens, 17 November 2002, that Ronaldinho had smuggled a girl into his room at the team hotel. The coach blew his top and told Ronaldinho he could forget about playing, but the decision was overruled from above: the club president, Laurent Perpère, acting on behalf of the Canal Plus directors who owned the club, instructed Fernandez to play Ronaldinho or else. As well as this being a vote of confidence in their Brazilian star, the game was also to be transmitted live on Canal Plus and the audience would be tuning in to see Ronaldinho in PSG's line-up. Ronaldinho duly started, PSG lost 3–2 and, to add insult to injury for the coach, Perpère came into the dressing room after the game to congratulate Ronaldinho on his performance.

A feeling of mutual animosity between player and coach now reigned supreme and something was bound to give. Ronaldinho began the next game on the bench, a 1–0 home defeat to Nantes. After the match, Fernandez and Ronaldinho were said to have got into a massive row and the relationship between the two would never recover. More generally, PSG had picked up just one point in four games and an air of crisis descended upon the club.

Respite came in the form of a Uefa Cup tie with Boavista. PSG had been making efficient progress through the tournament: back in September, Ronaldinho had scored the first goal of the campaign with a header in a 3–0 win over Újpest of Hungary and since then a two-leg victory versus National Bucharest had followed. This time, PSG again showed good European form in sending Boavista back to Portugal with a 2–1 defeat.

However, such was the climate of introspection at the Parisian club that many commentators managed to find the negative in victory. PSG had been on top and wasted chances to put the tie beyond doubt before a defensive lapse gave Boavista a consolation goal. The pessimists predicted that PSG would live to regret the goal they conceded.

The convincing win over Olympique Marseille, achieved only a few weeks earlier, that had PSG looking like title contenders was now long forgotten. Performances were in decline and one of the main problems was Ronaldinho. He had started just eight games all season and looked tired or, worse, disinterested. Were PSG's ambitions too modest for him, asked some observers? Speculation linked him with a winter move to Italy and there were those who thought this might be for the best.

PSG lost their next game on 30 November 2002, away at Monaco:

Ronaldinho opened the scoring, ghosting into the area and firing home a deft cross-shot, but *les Monégasques* fought back to win 3–1, including a goal from Mexican defender Rafael Márquez, a future colleague of Ronaldinho's at Barcelona. This meant that PSG had earned just a single point from their last five games and there were suggestions that Fernandez's days were numbered.

The directors of Canal Plus and PSG president Perpère seemed to agree. Perpère was quoted as saying, 'For now, Luis Fernandez is the PSG coach and he will not be replaced providing he fulfils certain criteria, these being results and maintaining the image of the club.'

His choice of words was telling: 'maintaining the image of the club' related to his spat with Ronaldinho. The club and its board considered Ronaldinho as integral to their project and indispensable: if they had to chose between Ronaldinho and Fernandez, their commitment was to the Brazilian. Everyone expected Fernandez to be sacked if PSG failed to beat Lyon, the league leaders.

Club captain Pochettino had missed the Monaco game through injury and Fernandez had surprised many with a bold gesture: he gave Ronaldinho the armband. Ronaldinho had relished the responsibility and done enough to earn a second chance as captain against Lyon.

The gamble paid off and Ronaldinho was in inspired form as PSG put in their finest display in months. They harried and chased and generally played as if keeping Fernandez as coach was vital to all of them. The 2–0 victory came courtesy of two Ronaldinho free-kicks: the first was whipped in from the right to Heinze who scored from near the penalty spot; the second was a shot from the left that the goalkeeper pushed straight to El-Karkouri to return with interest.

El-Karkouri remembers that evening very well. 'Playing against Lyon was a very important game, especially for the manager because, if we lost, he was going to get sacked, but we won 2–0 and I remember I scored. It was me and Heinze, so two defenders scored. Obviously, the manager was delighted.'

In his role as captain, Ronaldinho addressed the press afterwards. 'This evening, we thought only of victory and that is why we are all so happy.' As to his relationship with Fernandez, Ronaldinho refused to be drawn. 'He is a good coach, one I respect. Personally, I have no problem with him and it doesn't seem to me that any player at the club does. I hope we can continue to win together.'

Ronaldinho was also keen to suggest that the victory hadn't been a matter of a different mental approach. 'Sometimes everything comes off whereas sometimes nothing goes right. For example, we had success from free-kicks today, something which has deserted us recently,' he explained.

The Brazilian was famed for his dedication to free-kick taking, practising them over and over again on the training pitch, but before the Lyon game he prepared himself in a different manner. Benachour told *So Foot* magazine that he, Ronaldinho and El-Karkouri had rehearsed free-kicks on the Playstation until two in the morning the night before the game. El-Karkouri concurs: 'I don't really like the Playstation but Ronaldinho really plays very well and before that very important game at home to Lyon we played for, like, five hours – but not the game, just the free-kicks.'

Victory over Lyon may have saved Fernandez's skin but it proved something of a false dawn: PSG crashed out of the League Cup 3–2 to Nantes (a game in which Ronaldinho missed a penalty) and lost 1–0 away to Boavista to exit the Uefa Cup on away goals. PSG ended 2002 on a low.

Ronaldinho was given permission to spend the winter break back home in Brazil, with training due to restart on 28 December. However, the date came and went with no sign of the Brazilian. He contacted the club and informed them that he had remained in Brazil as he needed to have some work done on his teeth. While nobody could deny this to be the case, the whole episode undermined his commitment to the French club.

Ronaldinho eventually showed up on 2 January, five days late. Fernandez was furious and announced that the Brazilian would sit out the first few games of the New Year, but Xavier Couture, owner of Canal Plus, was much more understanding. 'It is all a storm in a teacup. Besides, the weather is good in Brazil right now. It's summer. I can understand Ronaldinho wanting to spend a few more days there.' The player was fined a measly €2,000 (£1,350) for his tardiness.

With comments and disciplinary measures like these, many observers thought PSG's owners were giving Ronaldinho licence to behave just as he pleased. Inter Milan were believed to be ready with a bid and some fans hoped the Italians would take Ronaldinho off PSG's hands. It was also said that some of the players had tired of his antics too, as they had before with Anelka. When Ronaldinho breezed into training almost a week after his colleagues, wished them a 'Happy New Year' and then sauntered off to make a phone call, goalkeeper Lionel Letizi had seen enough – he collared Ronaldinho and demanded that the Brazilian explain himself to his team-mates. Ronaldinho stuck to the teeth excuse, even though PSG had already issued a statement saying that all players have their teeth examined once a fortnight and, while Ronaldinho did have dental problems, this had always been the case and treatment was not urgent.

Ronaldinho played no part in PSG's first four games of 2003, but the French Cup tie versus Olympique Marseille at the Parc des Princes was too big a game for Fernandez to continue to prove his point: the Brazilian was named among the substitutes and, with the game hanging in the balance, was introduced midway through the second half. Although his performance was sluggish and he was clearly not fit, Ronaldinho was still able to make the difference: his perfect pass put Fabrice Fiorèse through to score the winner in extra-time.

Ronaldinho remained a fringe player for the next few league games as PSG stumbled along – his main contribution was to get sent off for violent conduct towards the end of a home loss to Bastia. However, the French Cup was bringing the best out of him and he made a decisive contribution away at Laval in the quarterfinals. Playing in black tights and gloves, despite the spring sunshine, Ronaldinho combined once again with Fiorèse to give PSG a 1–0 win against the run of play.

Back in favour for an away fixture at Guingamp, Ronaldinho opened the scoring with a marvellous individual goal following a mazy dribble. However, he was eclipsed that day by Didier Drogba, who scored twice, including Guingamp's last-gasp winner.

This latest loss saw PSG slump to eleventh place in the table. There was trouble in the camp and the supporters were rebelling. Certain fan groups were boycotting matches at the Parc des Princes in protest, others from the Auteuil area of the ground were on a singing strike. Some in the Boulogne segment had even turned hostile towards Ronaldinho. The inability of coach and star player to get along was seen as the root of all the team's problems and the issue had divided the PSG support: some favoured Fernandez, others backed Ronaldinho.

They were tricky times, as Aloísio testifies. 'Fernandez said Ronaldinho came back with a big ego but I think it was just part of the problem between the two of them,' he says. 'Fernandez was a star in France, one considered an idol by many still to this day. But Ronaldinho won over the fans too and they took him as their new idol. So, you had a situation with half the fans ending on Fernadez's side, half on Ronaldinho's.' It affected the players in the end, as Aloísio appreciates: 'I had no problem with Fernandez, he was great. But it was difficult for us because in the group we could see this problem between them and it made us sad.'

At the home game versus Troyes, all such issues would come to a head. Aloísio remembers it well. 'We had lost four or five on the trot. The fans were getting on our backs and were angry, particularly concerning the problems between Ronaldinho and Fernandez. At the start of that game, we went two down and the fans went berserk. Then I scored and we managed to turn it round.'

PSG won 4–2 in the end but the problems weren't over. After the match, Ronaldinho was getting into his car when some fans asked him for an autograph: ever obliging, he got out to attend to them but was suddenly surrounded by a mob of disgruntled supporters and insults began to fly. Paulo César and Aloísio arrived on the scene to back up their friend and the argument escalated: Aloísio had his phone stolen in the confusion and there were even reports that Ronaldinho was punched. The incident only cooled when Heinze and Éric Blondel, the assistant coach, emerged to mediate.

Aloísio recollects the fracas thus: 'On leaving the stadium there was an incident in the car park between the fans who had been waiting for us there. They attacked us Brazilians as we got in our cars but they were angry with the whole team. We appealed for calm, admitted we had been out of form, on a bad run, and in the end nothing really happened.'

The next match was away at Marseille. PSG had not won at the Vélodrome for fifteen years and victory for L'OM would take the southerners three points clear at the top of the table, and exact sweet revenge for losing twice already that season to their rivals from the capital.

But they came up against a Ronaldinho in magisterial form: he scored one and set up another as PSG ran out 3–0 winners. He had been on fire all evening with an explosive display of skill, speed and power and after the game told reporters, 'Ever since I started playing football, people have always said that I thrive on the big occasions. This evening, the whole team played well too and if we carry on like this we can still think of winning the league.'

In fact, his performance had been so good that it only served to remind everyone of what they had been missing. Commentators pointed out that Ronaldinho did indeed rise to the big occasion, but that this was perhaps as much to do with a dismissive attitude as his mental fortitude: if he didn't think the game was big enough for him, he simply didn't bother. In lesser games, he seemed content so long as he pulled a few crowd-pleasing party tricks out of the hat.

A French Cup semifinal versus Bordeaux at the Parc des Princes awaited, a fixture certainly prestigious enough for Ronaldinho to wish to impress. And impress he certainly did. In perhaps his finest display in front of the PSG faithful, he scored both goals in a 2–0 win and, many would say, single-handedly dragged the Parisians into the final. His first goal was a wonder strike: he knocked the ball through one defender's legs then performed a step-over and feinted to pass before beating the keeper with a shot to his right. The second was no less flamboyant: having been put clear by Fiorense, he perceived the keeper advancing off his line and lobbed the ball over him, seemingly without looking. The supporters bowed to his genius and the stadium rocked to chants of his name.

Afterwards, Ronaldinho had this to say: 'I feel on top of the world. In that atmosphere, I can try almost anything and know it will come off. I feel like the happiest boy in the world. I have many good memories in France but that there was a bit special. We reached the final, I helped my team-mates and brought pleasure to the fans and therefore leave satisfied.'

PSG carried on their good form against the top teams with a 2–1 win at home to Monaco, via a penalty from Ronaldinho. Monaco, led by their captain Ludovic Giuly (Ronaldinho's future colleague at Barcelona), had been aiming for the title but this defeat effectively ended their chances. It also meant that PSG had beaten the top three placed teams (Lyon, L'OM and Monaco) at home. Fernandez summed up the feeling of many Parisians when he said: 'I am very happy with our performance but the win also brings regrets. It shows that we have the means to be competing for the title.' All these wins against the top teams certainly added weight to the theory that the real Ronaldinho only showed up for the big games.

The league season petered out and with the French Cup final versus Auxerre on everyone's mind, an away *Ligue 1* match at Auxerre to finish the campaign was of little interest to anybody. A second-string PSG went down 2–0 and this meant that PSG finished eleventh, their worst position in fifteen years and the first time they had been placed outside the top half during the Canal Plus era. They had finished fourteen points short of league winners Lyon, ten outside the Uefa places and even three shy of Intertoto qualification. They had to win the French Cup to rescue their season.

PSG took the lead when a Ronaldinho cross aimed at Fiorèse ended up instead at the right boot of Hugo Leal, but Auxerre equalised in the last quarter of an hour making for a grand finale. A Ronaldinho back-heel resulted in a last-gasp chance for Francis Llacer but his shot was weak. Then, in the very last minute, Jean-Alain Boumsong got on the end of a free-kick for Auxerre: his first header was saved but the future Newcastle defender scored with the rebound. PSG had lost the French Cup and, though it wasn't immediately known then, Ronaldinho's period in Paris had ended without a trophy – he would leave for Barcelona later that summer.

Making an overall evaluation of Ronaldinho's spell at PSG is no easy task. He finished overall top scorer at the club in his first season with thirteen strikes and joint-top PSG marksman in *Ligue 1* in his second, level with Aloísio on eight. Yet his efforts ultimately yielded nothing.

Most PSG fans would name Ronaldinho as the best player to have ever played for the club, but whether that is a judgement based on his performances for them or what happened afterwards is difficult to tell. In any case, if he can lay claim to such an accolade for PSG then it is as the individual who reached the loftiest heights in isolated moments of the sublime rather than as the most consistent performer who made sure his performances contributed to the team actually winning things.

Ronaldinho's time in Paris will perhaps best be remembered for his tempestuous relationship with Fernandez. The coach himself, not someone afraid to mince his words, has been asked to address the subject on several occasions. In an interview with the *Guardian* in May 2006, he summed things up thus: 'He was very young when he came to Paris. He wanted to learn, he wanted to work, he wanted to make progress. He came with his family, with his brother and his mother, and the first year went very well because he accepted that he had to work if he was going to develop.' However, circumstances soon changed, according to Fernandez. 'The second year was different because in the meantime he'd become champion of the world. That can make a difference to the head of a player. You understand? He was still young but now he thought he knew everything.'

Talking to *So Foot*, Fernandez explained how the success of his own coaching methods may have contributed to Ronaldinho's downfall. 'I used to make him train in fractions, that's to say short sharp bursts. He will never be a marathon runner, a Valdo, so there is no point in making him train like one. But he also had to learn European football. He was lacking in terms of tactical positioning.' The Brazil national team would reap the rewards: Scolari said to me: 'You've changed him for me.' But then he became world champion and he knew he was the only star of the team, it was a difficult situation to manage,' concludes Fernandez.

Fernandez to the *Guardian* again: 'I coached Rái, I coached Ginola, I coached many other internationals. And it's not hard to integrate a young player when you have the experience. Ronaldinho has the talent. It's easy for him. At Barcelona, where he is surrounded by great players, he seems to be working hard again.'

That after the World Cup Ronaldinho only managed to motivate himself for the big games does seem a fair charge. How else can one explain that PSG, suffering their worst league season in fifteen years, could win four of their six games against the top three placed sides? The problem was that the French League didn't throw up enough big games.

After beating Lyon, Ronaldinho suggested to *L'Équipe* that it was because PSG coped with pressure better than other teams. 'Truly, the motivation is independent of the opposition. For sure, I like to play against the best players in packed stadiums. OK, we have better results against the big teams. The figures prove it. But the reasoning stops there. I love pressure, it doesn't scare me. The group neither. The team knows how to use pressure as a means of motivation and we thrive.'

Following his inspired performance against Bordeaux in the French Cup semifinal, he was accused of picking and choosing in which games to perform. 'It is impossible to choose your matches. The big games are more difficult to play but in such games things go well for me because there is more space, less individual marking. That perhaps explains my success.'

The other main criticism stemmed from his supposed lack of professionalism. In his second season in Paris, there were suggestions, not least from the coach, that Ronaldinho dedicated too much time to exploring the City of Light's nightlife. Ronaldinho's PSG team-mate and buddy Benachour told *So Foot*, 'It's clear that in Paris he went out a lot and that created problems with Luis. But Ronaldinho is one of those players who needs to go to a nightclub, to have a drink, in order to be right in his head. If it doesn't affect his performances then what's the problem?'

Meanwhile, Deise backed up her brother, saying, 'I lived with him in Paris and he went out just like anyone his age, no more, no less. Mostly, he just organised Playstation competitions.' Both Benachour and El-Karkouri can testify to that.

'He was not going out all the time because he respected his job and he knew that he had a big responsibility,' says Talal El-Karkouri, defending his friend from such accusations again. 'He is Ronaldinho and he needs to score, to run with the ball, to pass (to) players, to show his skills and enjoy himself on the pitch because that's what the fans expect of him. He knew he had to be prepared for all that.'

El-Karkouri has a different theory as to why Ronaldinho's passage through Paris wasn't one long success story. 'PSG is a special club. I can't recall a single star player who has gone to PSG and had a fantastic time. The problem with PSG is the fans, because some of them don't really know what football means,' he accuses.

'When they go to a game, they think they are going to a nightclub or something, just passing the time. Some people come with a packed lunch and start eating. They don't talk about the game, they are often drunk and talk about something else and sometimes I would be sitting close to them and I could hear them ask each other, "Who is the number ten?"'

'They didn't even know Ronaldinho; I mean come on, this is crazy. Then, if someone lost the ball, they started booing him, insulting him. That is really the problem.'

The Moroccan feels Ronaldinho's unproductive second year in Paris will prove to be a one-off. 'That is why that "bad" season of his is going to be the worst in his career, because look what he is doing now: a really good job for Barcelona,' he declares. PSG may not have been the perfect first team for Ronaldinho to join in Europe after all. El-Karkouri even suggests he might have been better off signing for their rivals. 'The PSG fans are totally different. If he had, instead of PSG, gone to Marseille, it might have been different, he could have had a big season there, but he started at PSG and it is really difficult there.'

Difficult perhaps, but the Brazilian Aloísio for one looks back fondly on that time in Paris. 'They are great memories. For me, it was very good to have played next to Ronaldinho. When he went to Barcelona, I went to Russia, and that was when he became the best in the world and nowadays I am very happy to say that I played with the best in the world.' But he has regrets too. 'It was just very sad that we didn't win something for PSG, for the great fans, for the directors and the great respect we were treated with by everyone at the club. Especially Ronaldinho, who was taken by the people into their arms. That Cup (the French Cup of 2003) would have been a very important conquest for us Brazilians. We did win the Intertoto Cup in Brescia, so we did at least add to the honours list there.'

Whatever the reasons, and probably everyone – coach, club, fans and player – are equally to blame, Ronaldinho's time in France was not as successful as it might have been. While he did capture their hearts, PSG fans are entitled to feel that a solitary Intertoto Cup win – in which Ronaldinho wasn't even involved – perhaps represents something of an under-achievement from a period with the world's best player in their midst.

MUSIC AND PASSION

If football has always been Ronaldinho's first love, music has come a close second. In these two main interests he is typically Brazilian: football and music are defining national passions. Nor are they entirely unrelated. Both celebrate freedom of expression and reward improvisation, and there are those who can see links between the fancy footwork of a samba dancer and the dribbling style of a player such as Ronaldinho.

He grew up surrounded by football and music; no post-match gathering of the family football team or indeed gathering of any sort was complete without several relatives picking up their instruments for a samba session.

For an example of how important music is to Ronaldinho's family one need look no further than the surprise present the footballer bought for his mother's fiftieth birthday. The doorbell rang at nine in the morning and Dona Miguelina couldn't believe her eyes when she opened the door to find Alcione, the famous samba singer – her favourite, she had all her CDs – waiting on the step. The singer grabbed a tambourine and gave a mini-concert of some of her hits in the lounge.

For Dona Miguelina, the surprises kept coming. That evening, Ronaldinho, Assis and Deise took her to a *churrasco* restaurant for what she thought was to be an intimate birthday celebration. When she got there, four hundred family and friends were waiting. Bebeto, a samba singer from Rio, had been hired to provide the music along with two *pagode* bands but, when the band had finished, Ronaldinho and his mates took to the stage and played until 5 a.m.

Over the years, Alcione has retained her popularity in the Ronaldinho household. As a promotion for the 2006 World Cup, he launched a CD of his favourite tunes called *Samba Gol*, and Alcione was there at track thirteen with a song called '*Um ser de luz*' ('A being of light'). Number four on the album was 'Deixa a vida me levar' ('Let life take me') by Zeca Pagodinho, Ronaldinho's absolute desert island disc.

Ronaldinho also sings on the album himself. Samba Tri is a band that began in the late 90s in Rio Grande do Sul, playing samba but incorporating musical influences and instruments from the Gaúcho state too. Ronaldinho met one of the band members, Paulista, at a party at Tinga's house and they have been friends ever since. Ronaldinho is the group's patron and sings on 'Goleador', the opening track on *Samba Gol*. Samba Tri are usually present if Ronaldinho throws a party, flying over to Europe especially to perform at birthdays and other special occasions. After helping to knock Chelsea out of the Champions League in March 2006, Ronaldinho performed on stage with Samba Tri at Barcelona nightclub Bikini as part of its carnival celebration. In order not to attract too much attention or take the limelight away from the musicians, Ronaldinho played the bongos wearing a big mask.

Ronaldinho used to have all the *pagode* instruments himself back in Porto Alegre and used to throw parties at his home in Guarujá, often in the garage, complete with barbecue and even beers if Dona Miguelina was in a tolerant mood. Valdimar Garcia, cousin and these days Ronaldinho's personal fitness coach, was a little older but still one of the gang: Dona Miguelina used to rely on him as a go-between to make sure nothing got out of hand. Valdimar obviously wasn't too strict: as neighbours might testify, those boys, even once they'd become professional footballers, knew how to party long and late.

Sometimes they would go to *pagode* nights at the Restinga samba school headquarters near Tinga's home. In fact, the gang became such regular faces on the Restinga *pagode* circuit that in Carnival 2000 they represented the district's samba school.

Carnival in Brazil takes many shapes and forms. While it does mean general revelry in bars, homes and on the streets, the official parades are another thing entirely. They are highly organised events in which samba schools (more strictly speaking, clubs) compete against each other, parading down the *sambódromo* (a purpose-built carnival avenue lined with stands for spectators on either side). Each school chooses a theme for its parade and then writes a song and designs floats and costumes accordingly. When they parade, a panel of judges rates each school in a variety of categories including costumes and flag-bearing (as mentioned previously), the quality of the song, the rhythm-making of the drummers and the co-ordination of the various dance wings (a school may be composed of literally thousands of performers). The contest is fun but also taken extremely seriously.

Rio hosts the country's biggest and most traditional parade but every major city has its own competition. Porto Alegre's *sambódromo* was only opened in 2004: past parades took place on Avenida Augusto de Carvalho, a wide thoroughfare in the downtown district.

In 2000, Ronaldinho, Tinga and Claiton led a fifteen-strong group of footballers from Grêmio and Internacional who paraded for the Estado Maior da Restinga samba school. Their presence helped propel the school to the runners-up spot.

A few years later, the Escola Estado Maior da Restinga chose to honour their most famous reveller and named Ronaldinho as their carnival theme for 2003. The idea was to celebrate Ronaldinho as the humble local boy who had gone on to conquer the world but it was a controversial subject: despite him being a World Cup winner, wounds were still raw following his troubled departure from Grêmio. Adding to the tension, 2003 was Grêmio's centenary year and the Bambas da Orgia school chose to honour the football club by making it their carnival theme. Grêmio donated funds to the Bambas da Orgia to help with the cost of costume and float-making, but it was money given on the understanding that there would be no mention of Ronaldinho in any part of the production. Meanwhile Ronaldinho, who was proud to have been chosen by Restinga, similarly stumped up BR$200,000 (£48,000) but on condition that they make minimal reference to his Grêmio days. This was a truly Brazilian spat.

Composer Adairton Guedes, otherwise known as Dadá, was charged with writing the Ronaldinho carnival ditty for Restinga and gave it the somewhat lengthly title, '*Vida e arte de um pequeno ser que cresceu nas glórias de um gramado para o mundo: Ronaldinho Gaúcho*' or 'The life and art of a small being who grew through the glories on the pitch to embrace the world: Ronaldinho Gaúcho'.

Ronaldinho vem aí . . . (Ronaldinho come here . . .)
Prá sacudir toda cidade (bis) (To rock the whole city (repeat))
E a Restinga dá um show (And Restinga gives a spectacle)
Com sua luminosidade (With its luminosity)
Hoje a Tinga vem amor . . . homenagear (homenagear) (Today Tinga
comes with love . . . to pay homage (pay homage))
Ronaldinho Gaúcho (Ronaldinho Gaúcho)
Que com raro talento (With his rare talent)
Contagia corações (He won our hearts)
Em Porto Alegre . . . nasceu (In Porto Alegre . . . he was born)
Na Vila Nova cresceu (In Vila Nova he grew up)
Exibindo nos gramados (Showing on the pitch)
À habilidade que Deus lhe deu (The ability God gave him)

O coração tricolor . . . vai explodir (The *tricolor* heart . . . would
   explode)
De emoção (With emotion)
Tem Ronaldinho na minha convocação (I have Ronaldinho in my
   team)
Moleque danado é bom de bola . . . (The smart kid is great on the
   ball)
Que na Seleção . . . deita e rola . . . (And in the *Seleção* . . . he goes
   forth and lets it roll)
E no Paris Saint Germain (bis) (And in Paris Saint Germain (repeat))
A rede vai balançar (The net is going to bulge)
E gol de placa . . . (And goals be scored . . .)
Alegria está no ar . . . (Happiness is in the air)
Com seu pandeiro agita o pagode (With his tambourine he gets the
   pagode moving)
Ho . . . ho . . . ho . . . (Ho . . . ho . . . ho . . .)
O bom churrasco não pode faltar (Good barbecue is there of course)
Tira o dedo do pudim (Get your finger out of the pudding)
O vídeo game é a sua distração (Videogames are his pastime)
É gol . . . é gol . . . é gol . . . (It's a goal . . . it's a goal . . . it's a goal . . .)
Ele é multi campeão . . . (bis) (He is a multi-champion . . . (repeat))
Com a medalha do penta na copa do mundo a consagração . . . (With
   the World Cup medal his ultimate prize)

However, when the big day finally came, it would prove disastrous for the
Estado Maior da Restinga. Although Dona Miguelina and Assis did parade,
Ronaldinho was unable to participate, having failed to get permission from
PSG to fly home. In his absence, Marcelo, a former *Big Brother* Brazil star,
led the Restinga school. Despite his best efforts, everything went wrong: two
of their floats broke down and blocked the route for two others. This meant
that only three of seven floats completed the circuit and even they were
thirty minutes behind schedule (there are strict time penalties at carnival).
Restinga's fans wept in the stands: they knew the fiasco could mean
disqualification, maybe even relegation (in most of the big carnival parades
there are different divisions).

The three floats that had made it through had been the ones
celebrating Ronaldinho's childhood, his time at PSG and his World Cup
win. The first included a football pitch with lots of children running
around in Grêmio and Internacional kits while the others featured giant
papier-mâché models of Ronaldinho's head. Dona Miguelina took part in
the PSG section of the parade.

Carnival voting takes several days to gather and decipher but, when the results were announced, Restinga's worst fears were realised: they had finished rock bottom and were dumped out of the top flight. To make matters worse for Ronaldinho, the Bambas da Orgia with their Grêmio theme were voted champions.

Restinga had been severely hampered by Ronaldinho's no-show. When he was first considered as a theme, it was taken as given that he would parade. In this way, Restinga were banking on the presence of the city's most famous son. However, carnival fell just a few days before PSG's league game with Marseille and there was no way the Parisians would excuse the player from that particular engagement. Ronaldinho pleaded and pleaded and there were hopes of him escaping right up to the day of the parade, even rumours of a last-minute surprise appearance. Yet it wasn't to be and the anticlimax cost Restinga dear, even if the technical faults would ultimately prove more damaging.

The timing of carnival (early March 2003) wasn't great for Ronaldinho. Revelations in the French press at the time claimed that he spent more time in strip-clubs than at the training pitch and his commitment to PSG was called into question. The climate certainly wasn't right for the club to give him permission to go carnivalling in Brazil.

Ronaldinho's penchant for gentlemen's clubs had first surfaced the previous summer. In a story published to coincide with England's World Cup quarterfinal match with Brazil in 2002, supposedly in an attempt to put Ronaldinho off his game – a fat lot of good it did – the *Sun* ran with a front-page splash detailing Ronaldinho's sex romps with an English stripper. Lisa Collins, a 23-year-old former shop-worker from Altrincham, had danced for Ronaldinho at Stringfellow's in Paris. According to the British red-top, Ronaldinho asked Miss Collins (or Ash, as was her stage name) out for dinner and several dates followed. They had remained in contact while he was at the World Cup and, she reported, had spoken after Brazil's win versus Costa Rica.

Apparently, he had claimed to be Ronaldo when they first got talking but the busty blonde soon 'got to know' the real Ronaldinho. They even did it eight times in one night. 'By the eighth time I was exhausted. He had worn me out. He is a brilliant performer in the penalty box, like a pneumatic drill.'

Ronaldinho would later deny the story and, in an interview with *Playboy* magazine in November that same year, he revealed that the tabloid gossip was proving difficult to live up to. 'After that it has been very hard for me. Every woman I'm ever with now expects eight in a row. It's not possible. It has created unfair expectations.'

In the *Playboy* interview, Ronaldinho also revealed a few of Dona Miguelina's ground rules. 'My mum always wants to know what I'm up to –

she doesn't sleep until I get home.' Be that as it may, the Dona wasn't always around and observers suggested that Ronaldinho's night-time antics grew wilder when she was back in Brazil. The fact that he met Miss Collins at Stringfellow's certainly came as no surprise to the French press: they claimed he spent a good deal of his time there, sometimes just hours before a match.

When at Grêmio, aside from his *pagode* parties, he was spotted in the Chalet Bar enough times for locals to speculate that he had bought the place, but generally he tended to conduct his private life away from the media glare. Pelotinha recalls his time as a journalist covering Grêmio in Ronaldinho's era. 'He always was a clean guy. He didn't go in for orgies or anything like that, just the odd girlfriend like any adolescent. There were no scandals.'

However, his personality also helped him avoid press intrusion. 'Ronaldinho was never a man of many words,' continues Pelotinha. 'He always gave simple answers but he always answered, always made himself available. He could be getting into his car and see a journalist asking for a quote and he would get out and be friendly – "Hi, how you doing?" – and comply. He helped and respected us and so we respected his privacy off the pitch.

'But also he was always very reserved,' adds Pelotinha. 'I know that even now he still has a place – though I've never been there – outside Porto Alegre, where he takes girls, his friends, out of sight. He is not one of those who likes to be seen.'

In an interview for the Uefa website, Ronaldinho himself claims that his life 'is so simple it doesn't sell newspapers. It is very similar to everyone else's. When I get up, I see a normal person in the mirror.'

The face staring back at him is not blessed with dashing good looks but, as Ronaldinho himself calls it, '*Sou um feio simpático que acaba bonitinho*' – 'I'm an ugly one who is happy and so ends up looking handsome'.

His teeth have always been his most striking feature and he was teased about them at school but some observers believe them to be a part of his football success: they say he runs the way he does – head held high – because of his teeth; they prevent him from closing his jaws properly and so he always breathes through his mouth, which naturally makes him keep his chin up. In this manner, his sense of awareness and vision on the pitch is better than most.

His haircut is the other trademark of his appearance. As a Grêmio player his locks were always tightly cropped, but he let them grow once he moved to France. 'When I arrived it was starting to get cold and me with my short hair,' he told *Playboy*. 'So I started to let it grow and I'm liking the new style.'

His dress sense cannot so much be described as sports casual as simply sports. Michael Jordan basketball garb is his favourite fashion when not in his football training kit. He is not the sort of footballer who likes to be tailored by the latest designers and only ever wears a suit if attending an awards ceremony. Perhaps his only concession to the flash footballer image is a rather bling-bling taste in jewellery. His neck is adorned with a heavy silver chain with a giant 'R' medallion, and he sports an 'R' stud in his left ear to match.

Whether or not he goes out less in Catalonia than he used to in France is debatable: it seems more a question of excursions being paid less press attention. The Catalan media traditionally stays out of their athletes' private lives, but when newspapers captured Ronaldinho playing with his Samba Tri buddies, some troublemakers did try to make an issue of it. Rijkaard instantly diffused the situation saying, 'I hope he enjoyed the concert because he made a big effort to get there. It wasn't any old party. The players are humans and sometimes they need a bit of music. He works hard in training and enjoys himself outside the game in the correct manner.'

Of course, if neither he nor the team were delivering on the pitch, such incidents might be made more of. Stories of Ronaldinho painting the town red at PSG tended to appear in his second year at the club. The theory was that he had returned to Paris a World Cup winner, no longer committed to the cause, and the night-time escapades were compromising his form on the pitch. Yet it could equally be argued that tales of his socialising appeared only because the team was in poor form and the press went looking for scandal and a scapegoat.

A case in point occurred before, during and after the 2006 World Cup in Germany. The Brazilian pre-tournament training camp was something of a circus in Switzerland, but there was no major complaint back home with regard to how the players were spending their spare time, despite reports of nightclub visits. However, after the *Seleção* had been knocked out, Brazilians were outraged to learn that Ronaldinho and Adriano had been seen partying the day after defeat. An in-depth report detailed where they had been and what they had been up to (in and around Ronaldinho's home in Castelldefels and not much more than enjoying a few drinks and a bit of dancing as it turned out) while the fans back home scorned his lack of mourning.

It was also during the World Cup in Germany that several European press agencies first picked up Ronaldinho's romance with Alexandra Parresant and started to promote them as a new glamour couple. '*L'amour foot*' as some French reports would label them.

Ronaldinho first got together with Alexandra – French catwalk model, L'Oréal Cosmic Hair girl and bit-part actress (a small role in *Asterix 3*) – in February 2006. 'We were both staying in the same hotel in Barcelona,'

Alexandra would reveal in German tabloid *Bild*. 'I saw him sitting down and I handed him a piece of paper with my name and room number on and went upstairs to wait. He called soon after and said he would like to get to know me. We have been an item ever since.'

A significant liaison between the two then came in Paris after the 2006 Champions League final. After the Barcelona official meal and party, Ronaldinho headed for a club to meet up with her. They retired to the team hotel in Versaille in the early hours and made no attempt to hide from the scrum of pressmen and fans camped at the entrance. Alexandra evidently spent the next few days there and was even introduced to Dona Miguelina.

She then joined him in Switzerland and followed him to Germany where the couple were captured on camera dancing in a nightclub. After Brazil's World Cup match with Australia, the players were afforded a rest day to spend however they pleased. It pleased Ronaldinho to check into a luxury suite in Cologne with Alexandra where, rumours had it, their love-making could be heard through the open windows. Indeed, Alexandra declared to the *Sun* that Ronaldinho had sneaked out of the team hotel for a bit of hanky-panky most nights, an allegation the player was keen to deny.

Other newspapers pointed out that Ronaldinho's new squeeze was something of a *Maria Chuteira* (Maria Boots, as football groupies are known in Brazil) who had already had several flings with footballers in France. Indeed, as stories emerged of Ronaldinho admitting to being besotted like never before, of the player considering a move to AC Milan as the city would better suit her fashion career, even of the couple adopting a child in Guatemala, so too did suggestions that the relationship was being promoted more by the model's agency, keen to boost her profile, than the couple itself.

Unlike compatriot Ronaldo, whose love life is played out as a national soap opera in Brazil, Ronaldinho had always kept a low profile where womanising was concerned. Protective of his private life, if asked when he was younger whether he had a girlfriend he would habitually say, 'Yes, the ball.'

With Dona Miguelina putting his career before serious relationships and keeping a check on his liaisons, most girlfriends didn't have much of a chance. By the time the PSG official website interviewed their star player, Ronaldinho would not admit to having ever been in love or at least 'not to the point of suffering'.

The website also asked him about the type of girl he went for. 'As I'm not very cunning, she has to be the clever one,' he told them. 'Joking aside, I don't like foolish girls or groupies.'

An earlier *Playboy* interview asked a young and fresh-faced Ronaldinho (then only twenty) the same question. 'To win me over they have to be like me. The more easy-going she is the more she will catch my eye. I don't go for forward women, much less famous ones.' As for whether he preferred the natural or silicone-enhanced look: 'If it looks good I'm not going to waste my time finding out if it's real or not. What I most like is the Brazilian standard with a big *bunda*.' *Bunda* means bum, and Brazil is a country where the red-blooded male appreciates a shapely posterior even more than an ample bosom.

Playboy continued to probe and asked Ronaldinho about his first time which had evidently been with an elder woman. 'Oh, it was a while ago but it went fine. My brother was always surrounded by girls and I used to pay close attention when he talked to his friends about such matters so as not to mess it up when the big day came.

As for his favourite place to get it on, 'I don't like it in cars, I know that much. I'm not an acrobat. A mattress on the floor will do me. I'm a simple man. I wouldn't like to do it on the pitch as I'd lose my concentration thinking about it next time I played.' Yet the football field and bedroom did bear some comparison. 'Scoring a goal is an emotion as euphoric as an orgasm. It brings the same pleasure.'

He revealed that only twice had he had a serious girlfriend and that both were dark and voluptuous. 'These days I prefer to get off with girls, not fall in love. I chat, invite them to a *pagode*, a barbecue. Despite being shy, I'm unrestrained when on the pull.

'It's too early to consider now but one day I'd like to marry and have kids, seven of them. I'm working hard so I'll be able to support them all.'

Back in Brazil for the close season in 2004, Ronaldinho enjoyed a brief relationship with showgirl Janaína Nattielle Viana Mendes. Their affair was relatively short-lived but, in August the following year, Janaína revealed that Ronaldinho was the father of her child: in February 2005, she had given birth to a baby boy in the Clínica Perinatal hospital in Rio. When tests confirmed the claim, Ronaldinho recognised the boy as his own and arranged to name him João, in honour of his own father.

The revelation that Ronaldinho had a love child was the first whiff of real controversy in what had been a very clean-cut life. Yet no sooner had the tabloid hacks prepared to feast than Ronaldinho had done the honourable thing, recognised the child and declared himself delighted to have become a father. Any sense of scandal was snuffed out before it had even had a chance to develop, and all because of Ronaldinho's honesty and dignity.

Although Janaína and Ronaldinho are no longer together romantically, the footballer is still very much involved with his son's upbringing. He supports João and his mother financially and sees them as often as he can. However, he also ensures that they lead a normal life away from the prying eyes of the media. Ronaldinho has never been one to parade his girlfriends in front of the press and has always been careful to keep his family life private, but in the case of his son he is particularly careful. Neither João nor his mother are ever seen in the papers (*Quem* magazine did publish some paparazzi shots in May 2006) and very little is known about their lives generally.

Janaína is from Realengo, a small suburban overspill half an hour outside Rio, three years younger than Ronaldinho, light-skinned and dark-haired, and was a dancer on hit Brazilian television series *Domingãao do Faustão*, a Sunday variety show aired on the Globo channel. Ronaldinho himself appeared on the programme after the 2002 World Cup win but the couple didn't meet until a few years later at a *pagode* party in Barra da Tijuca, an area of luxury beach apartments, designer shopping malls and exclusive bars and restaurants on the outskirts of Rio. Ronaldinho has his own holiday apartment in Barra, a penthouse suite overlooking Pepê's beach. Janaína, her mother and João now live in the area too, in a flat bought for them by Ronaldinho.

When Ronaldinho is back in Brazil, he makes sure to visit them in Barra or Janaína and João are invited down to stay in Porto Alegre. Otherwise, they communicate over the Internet, with Ronaldinho said to have been able to witness some of João's first steps via webcam. Apparently, João has also begun to speak and says '*bola*' (ball) when he hears his father's voice.

Ronaldinho is proud of his son and takes his parental responsibility seriously. 'Like all fathers, I want to be the very best role model and example for my son that I can be. I am not with his mother but the boy has a normal life,' he told the *Independent*. Ronaldinho has also revealed that João already has a ball. 'My son likes to play with the ball. He is always messing around with it,' he said, before concluding, 'He is the best thing I have.'

FC BARCELONA

That Ronaldinho ended up at Barcelona was as much down to one man as anyone else: Sandro Rosell. A Catalan, Rosell was appointed Nike's man in Brazil shortly after the 1998 World Cup. He got the gig having proved himself a smooth operator for Nike Iberia, securing a shirt deal with Barcelona among other things.

Rosell enjoyed a successful time in Brazil, even forming part of the *Família Scolari* at the 2002 World Cup triumph. In his four years in South America, he developed a superb network of contacts and became friendly with many players. One of his early responsibilities had been to revamp Ronaldinho's Nike contract once the player's profile had rocketed after the Copa América in 1999, and he had remained well acquainted with him ever since.

After the 2002 World Cup, Rosell elected to return to Catalonia and there became involved with a band of young executives preparing a bid to take over FC Barcelona.

In the European summer of 2002, FC Barcelona, or Barça as they are more popularly known, were a club in crisis both on and off the field. Crippled by debts, the team had failed to lift a trophy in three seasons. Joan Gaspart was the then beleaguered Barça president, having taken over from Josep Lluís Núñez in July 2000. Núñez had presided over a period of unrivalled success at the club: with Johan Cruyff as manager, the so-called Dream Team won the European Cup for the first time in 1992 and reached the final again in 1994 while picking up four league titles in a row along the way. However, by the turn of the millennium, the situation had soured.

Barça's club motto is *Més que un club* – More than just a club. In the stateless nation that is Catalonia, Barça has evolved into a powerful symbol of regional identity. Under the dictatorships of General Primo de Rivera (in the 1920s) and General Franco (for a lengthy part of the twentieth century), the Catalans were severely repressed, even forbidden from speaking their own language. They found in FC Barcelona an environment in which they could express themselves freely, their words protected by the allegorical qualities of supporting a football team and sheer strength in numbers. At the same time, as a vehicle representing the people of Catalonia abroad, beyond the borders of its Spanish rulers, there was nothing so big and important as Barça. In all these ways, Barça came to stand for basic human rights and became a political and cultural phenomenon. It remains a club run as a democracy and its president is chosen by ballot of its more than 100,000 members, the *socis*.

In the mid-90s, many *socis* felt that the club's democratic values were being compromised. Núñez, it was claimed, was running things as a despot. A young lawyer called Jan Laporta was one of a band of rebels who formed an opposition group called Elefant Blau (Blue Elephant, the idea being that Barça is a huge but noble beast), whose self-appointed role was to question everything Núñez and his cronies did. The pressure told and Núñez eventually stepped down, only to be replaced by Gaspart, Núñez's long-serving vice-president.

Gaspart's stint proved disastrous. By early 2003, with Barça twelfth in the league, he was forced out and presidential elections were called for the summer.

Elefant Blau had by then disbanded but its former members, Laporta included, were still active and looking for a candidate to get behind. Rosell was introduced to Laporta through a mutual friend: both shared the belief that some radical new life needed breathing into the club. Barça had stagnated at a time when football was modernising its commercial side, and if they didn't act fast the fear was they might be left behind for good. To make matters worse, deadly rivals Real Madrid were moving on quite the opposite trajectory, busily converting themselves into a winning machine on the pitch and a powerful global brand off it.

Eventually, a consortium of over a dozen executives, with Laporta as their figurehead and Rosell his right-hand man, announced their candidacy. Laporta, Rosell and their cohorts promised a revolution of sorts: they would run the club like a business, bringing a professional approach to every element of its operations. They were young, mostly under forty, and promised to be bold and daring. As directors they would work for the club for free and each would put up a €1.5 million (£1 million) guarantee for a place on the board.

They were the new wave but their revitalisation project needed a symbol. When all was said and done, Barça were a football team, and a footballer to personify what they stood for was required. They sought a talismanic new signing, someone who could capture the imagination of the fans and inspire those players already at the club.

Ronaldinho was Rosell's first choice right from the start. He had known the player for quite some time and was on familiar and friendly terms with both Ronaldinho and his agent, his brother Assis. He also knew the player's abilities and character far better than anyone else involved in the new Barça project.

Making the most of a trip to Mexico for a Brazil match, 30 April 2003 – an engagement left over from his Nike days – Rosell sounded Ronaldinho out about joining Barça. As Rosell recounts in his autobiography, *Benvingut al Món Real* (*Welcome to the Real World*), he explained that he was part of a consortium aiming to take over FC Barcelona, that they were planning to form a great new team and that he wanted Ronaldinho to be the key part of it. Rosell asked Ronaldinho to give the matter some consideration and the player said he approved of the proposal in theory.

Back in Barcelona, to comply with the wishes of his colleagues, Rosell began negotiations to try to sign the then hottest property on the market, David Beckham. Rosell was convinced that Beckham's switch to Real Madrid was already a done deal and had even warned Ronaldinho not to worry if he read in the papers that Barça were trying for Beckham: it was highly unlikely to materialise and Ronaldinho would always be Rosell's priority.

Nevertheless, Rosell, who would be in charge of player recruitment in the new regime as sporting vice-president, went through the motions. Talks with the Manchester United chief executive, Peter Kenyon, appeared to go well. Rosell fixed it so the Red Devils agreed to sell Beckham to Barcelona in principle should the Laporta bid be successful, providing Beckham himself proved well disposed to the move. The Manchester United website promptly broke the news and it gave Rosell, Laporta and the gang a huge credibility boost in the eyes of the voters, so much so they were swept to victory in the elections on 15 June 2003.

However, just two days later, Real Madrid officially announced Beckham's capture. Rosell saw it as a blessing in disguise – Ronaldinho remained his top target – and for some observers the episode seemed too good to be true: Laporta and co had got the publicity boost they craved but without having to sign a player they didn't really want. Rumours began to do the rounds that all was not as it seemed. Some people claimed that Manchester United had been paid to publish the Beckham-to-Barça story on its website even though both parties knew Golden Balls was already effectively a Madrid player. Rumour had it that this arrangement had been organised through football agent Jason Ferguson, son of United manager Sir Alex. Part of the supposed agreement was that Barça would sign Rüstü

Reçber in a deal brokered by Ferguson, and the Turkish goalkeeper did indeed sign the following week.

Whatever the goings-on behind the scenes, and nothing was ever proven, Beckham's non-capture did mean the new club directors were suddenly under huge pressure to deliver the star signing they had promised.

Some of the new board, as well as the manager they had just appointed, Frank Rijkaard, favoured raiding Valencia for the spine of its team (Roberto Ayala, David Albeda and Pablo Aimar) while press gossip cited Roy Makaay and even Harry Kewell as potential captures, but attentions and efforts soon focused on Ronaldinho.

Signing him would not be straightforward: although Rosell knew that Ronaldinho was predisposed to moving to Catalonia, PSG, aware of Barcelona's financial troubles, were understandably more tempted by solid offers from Real Madrid and Manchester United.

Real Madrid proposed buying Ronaldinho but loaning him to PSG for a further year: they had just signed Beckham and claimed their squad was complete for the coming season, but thought Ronaldinho represented an investment opportunity too good to pass up. To PSG, this seemed like the best of both worlds: selling him but keeping him. However, the player wasn't keen as he felt his time was up in Paris. There was also the little matter that PSG still owed Real Madrid cash from the Anelka transfer.

The Old Trafford outfit, meanwhile, wanted Ronaldinho immediately and were cash-rich having just traded in both Beckham and Sebastián Verón. The Argentine had signed for Chelsea, a team suddenly with money to burn following Roman Abramovich's takeover. Chelsea emerged as an outside bet to sign Ronaldinho but ultimately had too many tasks to juggle for them to dedicate the time to a serious bid.

Without the financial clout to win a bidding war, Rosell and his team realised they needed to be more creative in order to get to the front of the queue. At first they tried to incorporate two Barça players, Argentine playmaker Ramón Riquelme and French defender Philippe Christanval, in the deal but PSG were not interested. Another idea mooted was that Barça would sign Ronaldinho but, just like Madrid had proposed, loan him back to PSG for another year. The advantage to Barça would be fulfilling their promise of making a star signing without actually having to pay for anything until they had secured a new bank loan. In the meantime, Barça would take Deco from Porto.

Rosell met up again with Ronaldinho, this time at Charles de Gaulle airport as the Brazilian headed off for a *Seleção* friendly with Nigeria. The deal was no longer the hypothetical one it had been when they had talked in Mexico: Laporta and Rosell were now in power. Ronaldinho repeated that the idea of joining Barça sounded great to him but that it was his brother who was studying the offers.

As luck would have it, Rosell then bumped into Assis in a restaurant in Paris. Assis agreed that his brother did favour Barcelona, and even stated that he himself did too, but that the terms being talked of elsewhere were much better and couldn't be easily ignored. Assis told Rosell he would have to improve his offer. Rosell did so there and then: the two men shook hands and Rosell had a verbal agreement with both player and agent; now to work on PSG.

Barça noted that Canal Plus, PSG's owners, was part of Vivendi, the French communications concern. The president of Vivendi was Jean-René Fourtou and he was also a major shareholder in Fomento de Construcciones y Contratas (FCC), a construction firm based in Barcelona. Some Fomento directors were also Barça *socis* while FCC's main competitor, Actividades de Construcción y Servicios, ACS, was owned by Real Madrid president Florentino Pérez. The top brass at FCC were asked by Rosell to have a word in Fourtou's ear about the merits of PSG favouring a Barça bid.

At this point, as if not under enough pressure already to secure Ronaldinho's signing, Rosell received a phone call from Jordi Pujol, President of the Genaralitat, the Catalan government. He told him, 'Bring Ronaldinho whatever it takes. It is very important for the morale of the Catalans.' Rosell was doing his upmost: he even called Dona Miguelina to try and sell the move to her.

The plot thickened as Ronaldinho was spotted in Madrid, but it turned out that he was only making an advert for Pepsi. In fact, Real Madrid's interest cooled and Ronaldinho's future suddenly boiled down to the choice of two: Barça or Man United.

Negotiations hotted up. PSG's directors lodged Rosell and Kenyon in neighbouring hotels in Lyon and walked back and forth between the two, getting one to outbid the other, each oblivious to what was going on behind the scenes. In this way, Ronaldinho's transfer price was upped to €30 million (£20 million). Rosell had to drop out at €27 million (£18.3 million) but Kenyon met the asking price – plus €3 million (£2 million) in add-ons – and the deal was done. Manchester United would send official confirmation via fax as soon as Kenyon returned to Old Trafford.

However, when the fax arrived a few days later, it was for €28 million (£19 million) rather than the €30 million (£20 million) agreed upon. Kenyon had got wind of the fact that Barça wouldn't go beyond €27 million (£18.3 million). Francis Graille, the PSG president, felt insulted and replied with a fax telling the Manchester club that they had broken their side of the bargain and the deal was off.

Old Trafford replied that €30 million (£20 million) was fine but it was too late: Graille had called Rosell and told him Barça could have Ronaldinho for €27 million (£18.3 million). It had become a matter of principle and, while Rosell had acted honourably throughout, Kenyon, it was felt, had not. It was one more reason for PSG to favour Barça. Besides, the bidding war had done its job: before the whole soap opera began, the first bid from Barça had been for €16 million (£10.8 million). Manchester United had started lower, though this was viewed in Paris as a further example of the condescending attitude emanating from Lancashire: Barça's offers were at least respectable right from the start.

PSG would receive a package ultimately worth around €30 million (£20 million) – an initial €25 million (£17 million) plus add-ons – and were comforted in the knowledge that Nike backed Barça and the player, as well as PSG – should the Catalans fail in their financial obligations, the sports brand would honour them. Rosell had also managed to structure the payment scheme so that Barça didn't have to pay anything for almost a year, by which time a bank loan would be in place.

The deal from Old Trafford had been financially stronger. To this day, some Manchester United fans are convinced that Ronaldinho used the Red Devils: he always intended to go to Barça but encouraged the charade of uncertainty to improve his terms at the Catalan club. As the Man United team and entourage boarded a plane for their pre-season trip to the United States, they believed the deal was in the bag. By the time they landed, Ronaldinho had signed for Barcelona. Alex Ferguson was furious and his relationship with the chief executive would never recover: Kenyon left the club two months later, accepting a lucrative offer from Chelsea.

All Rosell's various angles of attack had paid off but ultimately it seemed the fact that Ronaldinho favoured Barcelona proved decisive. Assis had hunted the best deal but also recognised the non-financial benefits of the Barça package and was even said to have forfeited the bonuses normally awarded to agents to ensure the deal went through. Ronaldinho later revealed that he consulted Assis for some brotherly (as opposed to agent) advice: Assis pointed out that, quite apart from issues of language, culture and climate, joining Barça would give him the advantage of entering the scene at the start of a new project, one involving people they knew and trusted, when expectations would be low; in Manchester, Ronaldinho would be replacing Beckham and would have to compare favourably with him right away, and Beckham had been a popular part of a successful side.

On Friday 19 July 2003, Assis and Eric Lovey, the Swiss who had helped broker Ronaldinho's move from Grêmio to Paris, arrived at the Nou Camp to put the finishing touches to the contract. Ronaldinho flew into the city from Brazil later that afternoon, accompanied by his sister Deise, and was met at the airport by thousands of fans. He headed directly to the Nou Camp. While Ronaldinho and Laporta played head tennis with a football in the offices, the rest of the delegation ironed out the final points of contention – the contract stipulated, for example, that Ronaldinho was not to ride motorbikes or jet-skis or go paragliding or skiing without the club's permission – and ensured the translation to Portuguese proved acceptable. At 10.30 p.m., some five and a half hours after landing in the city, Ronaldinho put pen to paper on a five-year deal.

The fly-on-the-wall documentary, *Barça: Inside Story*, captured the moment: Ronaldinho made Laporta sign first, saying he was the one who would be paying. Laporta signed then passed Ronaldinho his own pen and said he would be honoured if Ronaldinho used it, which he did, followed by Assis. Rosell and Ronaldinho embraced, the warmth and friendship between them clear for all to see. 'Fantastic, fantastic,' repeated Laporta. There were hearty handshakes all round amid a palpable sense of mutual excitement and relief. Laporta, Rosell, Ronaldinho and Assis all hugged in a huddle: the new directors had got their symbolic star, and Ronaldinho had arrived at a club whose ambitions matched his own.

After posing for photos for the press, Laporta, Rosell, Ronaldinho, Assis, Deise and everyone else involved in the day's deal-making celebrated with dinner at the Botafumeiro restaurant in Barcelona's Gràcia district. The night ended with a toast: 'Visca el Barça! Visca Catalunya! Visca Brasil! – Long live Barça, Catalonia and Brazil'.

Ronaldinho passed his medical the following day and then, on the Monday, he was officially presented as a Barça player. The whole event was treated like a royal visit: TV3, the Catalan television station, presented live coverage and some 25,000 fans turned up at the stadium. It is a staggering figure and was unprecedented for what amounted to little more than Ronaldinho posing in the *blaugrana* (as the claret and blue uniform is known) and doing a few kick-ups.

And, speaking of the *blaugrana* shirt, the 3,000 of them that had been prepared with Ronaldinho's name printed on the back sold out immediately. There could be no more obvious signal that Barça had found the commercial star they so craved.

Barça had planned a pre-season tour of the US – in a delicious twist of fate, this included a fixture against Manchester United. For Ronaldinho to make his debut against the Red Devils would possibly have been an irony too far, and instead he first took to the field in a Barça shirt in a 2–2 draw with Juventus, played in Boston. Ronaldinho entered the fray at half-time as a substitute for Dutchman Marc Overmars with Barça two goals to the good. His very first touch was a taster of things to come: a sensational pass to put Dani in on goal. Juventus eventually scored twice in the last five minutes to take the game to penalties. The Catalans ran out 6–5 winners with Ronaldinho scoring his spot-kick, the fifth.

His next appearance was versus Milan in Washington, Ronaldinho's first in the Barça starting eleven, and he set up the first goal in a 2–0 victory. The Manchester United game followed: Barça scored first but the Mancunians ran out 4–1 winners.

The rest of the pre-season took place in the United Kingdom and included games against Leicester City and Manchester City: in the latter Ronaldinho was cheered by the home crowd every time he touched the ball; the Manchester City fans saw him as something of a hero having led their city rivals a merry dance all summer.

The final game of the trip took place in Londonderry, Northern Ireland. It was called the 'Match for Peace' and was presided over by Laporta in partnership with Nobel Peace Prize winner John Hume. Derry's team, of mixed religious ideology, was presented as a symbol of tolerance and Barça, as always on such occasions (representing Catalonia abroad), took their role in proceedings very seriously indeed. It was here that Barça first truly began to appreciate what Ronaldinho brought to the club: as well as his obvious footballing gifts – he scored the fifth in a 5–0 win – he was a natural ambassador, tirelessly dedicating much of his time to Derry's disabled supporters.

To round off the pre-season, Barça met Espanyol in the final of the Copa Catalunya. Barça won 1–0 with Quaresma, the young Portuguese winger, scoring from a Ronaldinho free-kick. It was Ronaldinho's first trophy for the Catalans but was not the happy occasion it should have been, as he was sent off near the end of the match for a second bookable offence.

The league, *La Liga*, got under way and was billed right from the off as Ronaldinho's Barça versus Beckham's Madrid. Barcelona managed a 1–0 away win at Athletic Bilbao, though the Basques were unlucky, Ronaldinho was anonymous and nobody took too much cheer from the performance. The *merengues* (the meringues, as Real Madrid are known), meanwhile, turned in a similar performance and also won, though Beckham bagged an opening-day goal.

The next game, a midweek contest against Sevilla at the Nou Camp, would be an altogether more memorable affair, not least due to the kickoff time.

A whole swathe of international fixtures were scheduled for the following weekend, decimating Barça's squad. Many players were obliged to join up with their respective national sides for the whole week – Barça would definitely be without the services of six first-teamers (their Dutch and Argentine contingents) – but some only had to be there by Wednesday, the day of Barça's league match with Sevilla. Barça asked Sevilla if they wouldn't mind switching the encounter to the Tuesday and Sevilla agreed, before fully comprehending that a Wednesday appointment would mean three other Barça internationals, including Ronaldinho, would also be absent.

Sevilla backtracked and insisted the Wednesday night engagement be honoured. Barça protested but the Spanish League sided with Sevilla: the fixture list said Wednesday and they were within their rights to refuse to budge.

Barça were left smarting. Quite apart from the fact that they would be severely disadvantaged by playing on the Wednesday, Sevilla's unco-operative attitude provoked fury. Then Barça struck upon a cunning ruse. If the game was to be played on Wednesday then Barça were still free to chose the timetable: by kicking off just after midnight on Tuesday it would be technically Wednesday but Ronaldinho and the gang could play, get a night's sleep and still join up with their national squads in time.

And so it was that on 3 September 2003, at 12.05 a.m., Barça versus Sevilla kicked off. The great unknown was how many fans would attend a match starting after the witching hour but 81,000 *culés*, as Barça fans are known, flocked to the Nou Camp. (*Culé* means bum and the nickname comes from Barça's early days when fans who couldn't afford to pay used to sit on a wall to watch their team and in so doing exposed their builder's bums to passers-by.) Rock bands performed before kickoff to better make a night of it and all spectators were given a free sandwich as part of a midnight-feast initiative.

Perhaps the whole absurd affair reminded Ronaldinho of the old days playing back home in Brazil. Whatever it was, he turned in a vintage display that night. All the confusion in the build-up to the game lent an extra edge to the contest and it was a fiery encounter from start to finish. Barça began well but José Reyes (latterly of Arsenal) scored a penalty after nine minutes and it remained 1–0 to Sevilla at the interval. The second half produced more of the same until Ronaldinho took charge. With the clock ticking up to 1.30 a.m., he gathered the ball deep in the midfield and burst forward, dribbling at pace. Beating two players as he cut from left to right, he then unleashed a rocket of a shot, which crashed into the back of the net via the crossbar in the top-left corner. The whole manipulation of the timetable had largely been for his benefit and in that moment of magic he had justified all the effort. He had immediately written himself into club history: no one would ever forget that night, that goal.

Ronaldinho impressed in his next home outing too, a 2–1 win over Albacete, and then again versus Osasuna when he scored the equaliser in a 1–1 draw. However, overall team performances left a lot to be desired. After a 1–0 loss at home to Valencia the knives were out, and Barça's lack of forward thrust was the principal point of grievance. Despite Ronaldinho's best efforts, the attacking trident comprising him, Dutchman Patrick Kluivert and Argentine Javier Saviola was getting nowhere other than in each other's way, and Barça had scored just five goals in six games. Rijkaard's system was seen to be too defensive, too 'Italian', and Barça had a proud tradition of attacking flair.

With pressure mounting on the new regime, Ronaldinho took a Uefa Cup fixture with Slovakian outfit FK Matador Púchov by the scruff of the neck and endeavoured to dispel the gloom single-handedly. He scored an early goal to lift the weight from their collective shoulders, allowing the team to settle and play freely. Ronaldinho ended with a hat-trick, his first for the club, in an 8–0 win.

Over the next few games, Ronaldinho's performances continued to dazzle: his change of pace, dribbling ability, passing vision and goal-scoring touch, as well as the delightful nuggets of skill he left as treats for the fans – against Murcia he improvised a pass using his back – kept everyone satisfied and revolt at bay, despite the team's mixed results. A torn muscle soon changed all this.

Without their Brazilian leader, Barça embarked on a run of defeats and accusations of 'Ronaldinho dependency' soon surfaced, just as they had done in both his Grêmio and PSG days.

The first loss came against Villareal but the next was even more painful for the *culés* to take – 5–1 by lowly Málaga. Some fans were calling for Rijkaard's head but Laporta made a point of supporting him. Coming, as it did, just prior to Barça's match at the Nou Camp with Real Madrid, alarm bells were ringing.

It is no secret that matches between FC Barcelona and Real Madrid, *el clásico* as it is predictably known, is about more than just football. Much as FC Barcelona developed connotations with Catalanism generally, so too did Real Madrid come to represent Castille. More widely, Real Madrid became Franco's team, the team of the dictatorship, and Barça, almost by default, the opposition. Each time the two sides clash, the tensions that led a country to civil war are revisited.

The corresponding fixture of the previous year had ended in utter disarray when the referee had been forced to lead the Madrid players off the pitch after Luis Figo had been prevented from taking a corner due to a barrage of missiles raining down on him from the stands. Figo had been branded a traitor by the Catalans when, as a Barça player, he accepted a big-money move to join their rivals a few years previously. Among the objects thrown his way was a roast suckling pig (though many Catalans believed the photo depicting the pig's head to be a fake: a case of photo manipulation by the Madrid press). Calm was eventually restored and the game restarted, but the shadow of a suspended two-match stadium ban still hung over the club.

Real Madrid arrived in town this time round as European champions, sitting pretty atop *La Liga*, with new signing Beckham performing superbly and exceeding everyone's expectations. Barça, in contrast, were suffering a crisis of poor form and missing their star player: Ronaldinho had failed to recover in time to play his first *clásico*. Barça had not lost to Real Madrid in the Nou Camp for twenty years, a record of which they were justifiably proud. Some *culés* feared their invincibility was about to come to an end.

They were right: Real Madrid won 2–1 and increased the gap between the two rivals to thirteen points as Barça slumped to eleventh in the table. Barça's morale had reached a new low. As the year drew to a close, an atmosphere of doomed resignation gripped the club: roll on 2004, was the consensus, for it couldn't possibly be as bad as 2003.

Before resolutions could be made there was the little matter of the city derby versus Espanyol, *el derbi*. While there does exist strong rivalry and political undercurrents to this fixture too, with Espanyol traditionally representing those from Barcelona loyal to the Spanish crown, the intensity of feeling is not the same as with Real Madrid and, coming immediately after the main event, it seemed something of an anticlimax. Except that Ronaldinho was fighting fit and ready to bring to the game a little rivalry of his own – sitting on the opponent's bench managing the Espanyol team would be his old nemesis, Luis Fernandez.

The pre-match build-up focused on their spat in Paris. Ronaldinho: 'I never had a problem with him, he had one with me.' Fernandez: 'I never had a problem with Ronaldinho, he had one with himself.' In the event, both men were eclipsed by the referee, who showed fifteen yellow cards and sent off six players, three from each team. Ronaldinho scored the first goal in what proved to be a 3–1 win but such details were largely lost in the farce of officialdom.

On a personal note, the New Year saw Ronaldinho become FC Barcelona *soci* number 111,545 but it brought little new cheer on the pitch: Barça went down 3–0 away at Racing Santander, leaving them stranded twelfth in the table, fifteen points off the lead. The transfer window provided the opportunity for new recruits and Rijkaard managed to secure the services of another Dutchman, midfield terrier Edgar Davids. While the extra bite was welcomed, most observers pointed to the misfiring frontline as the area most obviously in need of adjustment.

Davids entered the fray for Barça's home leg Copa del Rey quarterfinal against Real Zaragoza. Much was riding on the match: as well as providing Barça with their best chance of picking up some silverware that season, a money-spinning cup run would provide the new board with the means to balance the books.

An insipid team display brought a 1–0 loss and unrest in the stands: Laporta, the face of the new board, was subjected to his first handkerchief protest, when fans wave white hankies to show their disgust. Their project had never really got off the ground and many fans now questioned just how competent the new directors were.

An ugly 1–0 away win at Sevilla provided some relief, though failed to answer any of the bigger questions. Much was still riding on the away leg of the cup at Zaragoza. A 1–1 draw there was not enough and Barça crashed out. Ronaldinho seemed particularly miffed at the defeat: Rijkaard took him off when he was about to take a corner with a quarter of an hour to go and the Brazilian displayed his typical ire at being substituted, walking off the pitch right where he was and slowly kicking his feet around the perimeter back to the bench.

A 5–0 win over Albacete proved timely (and surprising, given that Ronaldinho was suspended) and was followed by a 2–1 victory at Osasuna in which Ronaldinho scored a delightful winner – controlling a loose ball in the area, he flicked it over his head with his second touch then spun around a defender to score with his third via a scissor-kick. Suddenly, the complexion of things had changed: Barça were producing exciting football and were back among the Champions League qualification placings.

Another game followed in which the best efforts of the players – Barça were 3–0 up with two goals from Ronaldinho before Deportivo La Coruña fought back to 3–2 – were eclipsed by the referee. Barça's Thiago Motta was sent off for two bookings despite each card being received in error: the first yellow followed a foul by Phillipe Cocu and a case of mistaken identity, and his second came after an infringement by Oleguer when the official confused the two players' numbers (23 and 32): a bemused Motta was ordered to an early bath.

Once again a surreal refereeing performance had hogged the headlines, but Barça had won and were on something of a roll. Victories over Mallorca, Murcia and Real Sociedad followed, the latter achieved through a spectacular free-kick (and equally spectacular celebration) from Ronaldinho in the 88th minute. It was their ninth league win in a row and had come on Ronaldinho's 24th birthday. The team commemorated the occasion with a cake for their Brazilian star.

To bring everyone back down to earth, Celtic arrived in town to edge Barça out of the Uefa Cup, and the setback seemed to halt Barça's momentum. A goalless draw at home to Villareal followed, bringing an end to their *La Liga* winning streak.

At Real Valladolid, Ronaldinho got himself sent off for refusing to wait to take a free-kick and then trying to wrestle the ball from the keeper's hands with his head, but his suspension was completed in time for the next date with Real Madrid.

In his first taste of the *clásico*, Ronaldinho proved decisive. A superb pass, scooped high over the Madrid defence, put Xavi in to score and send Barça home with a 2–1 win. Thousands of fans met the team at the airport on their return to Barcelona, such was the euphoria at Barça having avenged the home defeat suffered before Christmas. Barça were now just four points behind Real Madrid and five from Valencia with four games to play.

City rivals Espanyol were up next and dispatched with ease. Barça, having not lost in seventeen games (the second best run in the club's history), had propelled themselves into second place in the table. Just as fans began to contemplate the unthinkable – from twelfth in January to winning the league – a sloppy display away to Celta Vigo resulted in a 1–0 defeat. However, the last home game of the season brought a 1–0 win over Racing Santander, via a Ronaldinho penalty, and secured second place in *La Liga* and direct Champions League qualification.

Valencia won the title but it had been Ronaldinho's league right from that night-time strike against Sevilla. He finished with a tally of fifteen goals and was voted the league's player of the season. The pre-season hype had billed *La Liga* as a contest between its two highest profile new recruits, Ronaldinho and Beckham, and there had been one very clear winner. Both players started well individually but, while Ronaldinho and Barça went from strength to strength, Beckham and the rest of the *galácticos* self-destructed. Real Madrid boasted an eighteen-point advantage over Barça at the season's halfway stage and, towards its business end, were eight points clear of everyone, in the cup final and beating all-comers in Europe. They ended up trophyless and fourth in the table.

Ronaldinho's signing had been a huge success for FC Barcelona and its new board. He had, just as they hoped, made as big an impact off the field as he had on it. His style of play – the natural flamboyance, the outrageous skill – had brought excitement back to the Nou Camp. Yet he was also a tough and determined character. In that first season at Barça, he often almost single-handedly rescued the team from disaster or dragged them to reach new heights. This blend of flair and responsibility was exactly the image in which the new owners wished to shape the club. Although others went about their business quietly transforming the club behind the scenes, Ronaldinho had offered visual signs of hope when the team's form was initially poor and was the maestro as they went on their winning streak in the second half of the season. A football club's success is judged by results on the pitch. Therefore, thanks primarily to Ronaldinho's signing, the new project's first year could be given the thumbs-up.

All was not rosy off the pitch, however, and Ronaldinho was at the centre of a rift that would drag on through the following season and, in fact, never be fully resolved. Although the new regime had been founded on collective sacrifice and a philosophy of working for the good of the club, never for personal gain, issues of power and politics had inevitably reared their ugly head.

By spring 2004, minds began to focus on the season to follow and summer recruitment. Laporta and Rosell disagreed on how best to move forward. It was rumoured that they had grown increasingly suspicious of one another: Rosell saw Laporta becoming ever more dictatorial in the role of president; Laporta thought Rosell to be jealous and desperate for the top job himself. Matters came to a head as Rosell suggested a change in management in the close season, replacing Rijkaard with Luiz Felipe Scolari. Laporta wished to stick with Rijkaard.

Their debate stretched back several months. Rosell had wanted to sack the Dutchman back in late 2003, when results were appalling, but Laporta had insisted on giving him more time. The team was playing with no discernible shape and many observers, not just Rosell, were of the opinion that the coach didn't know what he was doing. Rosell had more reasons than most to harbour such suspicions. In his autobiography he tells how, at a dinner at Johan Cruyff's house in November 2003, Rijkaard had claimed the main problem with the team was Ronaldinho. Rijkaard admitted that he was very good technically but said he simply didn't know what to do with him. Barça kept losing, something was obviously fundamentally wrong and Rijkaard concluded it was Ronaldinho, that the team suffered as a whole due to his presence and the fact that he never contributed defensively.

That Rijkaard didn't know quite where to play Ronaldinho seemed obvious from the start: he put him on the right wing for his first home match in pre-season. He then tried him up front as the support striker before the Ronaldinho-Kluivert-Saviola trident was tried and failed. Yet, in fairness to Rijkaard, such tinkering did lead him to the winning solution and, although the trident itself didn't work, once Ronaldinho was deployed wide on the left his influence grew.

Initially, the three-pronged attack force formed part of a 4–2–1–3 formation and it was only once Davids arrived and a 4–3–3 line-up was adopted that results improved. Davids added that extra bite the team had been lacking and the formation provided better all-round balance, allowing players such as Xavi to raise their game and Barça to move onwards and upwards. Ronaldinho was consistently brilliant from start to finish, but only once the overall team structure improved could his efforts reap their rewards.

The 4–2–1–3 formation had come at the suggestion of Txiki Begiristain, the club's sporting director, and Cruyff himself. The system had been successful during Cruyff's time as manager, the era of the Dream Team, in which Txiki had played. For Rosell, the Cruyff influence and the shadow of the Dream Team were a major problem. Cruyff had not approved of Ronaldinho's signing in the first place and wasn't a man who liked being proved wrong. Rosell noted that seven months into the season, everyone was praising the Brazilian except Cruyff. The Dutchman wrote a popular newspaper column in *La Vanguardia* and the only times he ever even mentioned Ronaldinho was to highlight his weaknesses. He routinely accused him of immaturity, claiming his inexperience rendered him unable to use his talent effectively.

At season end, even Cruyff couldn't deny Ronaldinho's importance to the club. He finally admitted that his transfer had proved a success but said that his standard had been a surprise to everyone.

Even by December 2005, on the occasion of Ronaldinho picking up his second successive Fifa World Player of the Year award, Cruyff's compliments remained of the backhanded variety. 'Ronaldinho has quality and deserves it,' he stated, but was unable to resist adding, 'Barça is a team which lets him have the ball and show his quality. He doesn't have to tire himself with the work that some of the Madrid players have to do.' He could win more prizes, Cruyff agreed, 'but it depends upon how the team does'.

For Rosell, Cruyff's attitude was one of pure jealousy, typical of the former Dream Teamers. They saw their mythical status being diminished by the new star on the scene and so constantly sought to undermine him. In his book, Rosell points out a typical example that came at the Fifa 2004 awards. Former Dream Team hero Hristo Stoichkov was eligible to vote in his capacity as manager of Bulgaria, although he was also still actively involved at Barça. Instead of backing the Barcelona player, his nomination had gone to Andrei Shevchenko.

Such complaints are probably unfair: most of the Dream Team has nothing but praise for Ronaldinho. With Cruyff it is harder to judge: he is a complex character and his comments could be described as constructive criticism, but it is true that he reserves his constructive criticism for Ronaldinho (and Deco too) while the likes of Eto'o are spared.

Cruyff's influence in the new running of the club was one of Rosell's major gripes. Laporta, it was perceived, was at Cruyff's beck and call. Cruyff was close to Rijkaard and he remained as coach for the start of the 2004–05 campaign. Rosell and Laporta attempted to put a brave face on their disagreements but they wouldn't go away. As the new season got under way, a final and definitive split between them seemed inevitable.

In February 2005, Rosell made a business trip to Hong Kong. In his absence – or behind his back, as it seemed – Laporta invited Ronaldinho, Assis and Deise to a business lunch at his house in San Cugat, just outside Barcelona. Here, Laporta offered Ronaldinho a contract for life. Rosell had brought Ronaldinho to Barça and there were fears that, should his spat with Laporta force him to leave the club, he may take the Brazilian with him. By offering Ronaldinho a new deal in Rosell's absence, Laporta was, it seemed, seeking to separate Ronaldinho's connection to the club from his connection to Rosell. The president's explanation later, that he had arranged the meeting to give Ronaldinho a dog as a gift, only served to arouse suspicions further.

Although Rosell remained at the club until the end of the 2004–05 season, his role was hardly active from the turn of the year. He left in June 2005, citing a lack of central democracy and a belief that the initial project, the one he had joined and believed in, had been undermined by egotism. He was one of several directors who stepped down around the same time and speculation rumbled on that Rosell would present himself as a candidate for presidency at the next elections and split the administration. Rosell dismissed the suggestions as typical of the paranoid vanities he could no longer abide and in fact, in summer 2006 – when new elections were called – he proved true to his word (although the fact that a challenge right then would certainly have been suicidal may also have weighed).

From the moment that news of the fall-out between Laporta and Rosell was made public, Ronaldinho had acted diplomatically, refusing to take sides and saying nothing more than that he hoped the two men managed to resolve their differences. As the episode reached its logical conclusion, he declared himself sorry to see his friend go but made it clear that his future at the club was independent to Rosell's. He was happy at Barça and that contract for life appealed, no matter who was doing the offering.

RONALDINHO THE BRAND

Ahead of the 2006 World Cup, German consultancy firm BBDO proclaimed Ronaldinho the most valuable footballer in the world. Said to be worth a cool €47 million (£32 million), the Ronaldinho brand was ranked ahead of even David Beckham's, second at €44.9 million (£30.5 million).

In commercial terms, football has learned to administer itself more efficiently over the last decade and marketing executives have likewise pushed better to exploit the sport's selling power. As the beautiful game's signature spectacle, the World Cup produces an explosion of football-related advertising across the globe. In Brazil, the World Cup brings everyday life, from normal working hours to political decision-making, to a standstill. No product wishing to be taken seriously would miss out on the chance of a *verde-amarelo* tie-in. The various squad members of the *Seleção* endorse anything and everything.

Ahead of the 2002 World Cup, Ronaldo was the advertising industry's hottest property, but four years down the line his younger namesake had taken over as the marketer's dream. Ronaldinho's image was in demand. In Brazil alone, the number of products Ronaldinho was promoting reached double figures ahead of the tournament in Germany: Estrela games, Bubbaloo gum, Kibon ice-lollies, Gatorade isotonic drinks, Antarctica *guaraná* pop, Santander Banespa bank, Rexona deodrant, the Cartoon Network TV channel, Oi (cell-phone operator), Nike sportswear and Turma de Mônica comics.

Of course, the World Cup in Germany hardly went to plan from a Brazilian perspective and Ronaldinho failed to live up to his star billing. His advertising campaigns quickly became hollow and some Brazilians accused him of being a mercenary, of showing more dedication to cashing in on his celebrity than doing honour to the *canarinha*, but there was no serious suggestion that Ronaldinho's poor World Cup would impact upon his overall commercial popularity. For one thing, none of his potential market rivals (Rooney, Ibrahimovic, Messi, Robinho) were able to shine either. Those that did excel (Zidane, Cannavaro, Buffon) were either too old or playing in too unglamorous a position to challenge Ronaldinho's global marketing supremacy. On the domestic front, Brazil's was a squad-wide World Cup disaster: no player managed to raise his stock significantly and so nobody emerged to replace Ronaldinho as the nation's favourite.

Widely considered to be the best player on the planet, it is perhaps only natural that Ronaldinho should lead the way in endorsement terms too. What is striking, however, is that his physical appearance runs completely counter to the advertising standard. In Brazil, as elsewhere, the prototype publicity figure is white, tall, skinny and crop-haired; Ronaldinho is black, of average height, well built, with a long curly mane. Put bluntly, Ronaldinho is not your typical fashion model.

Obviously, he brings a whole different set of characteristics to a campaign. Researchers found that Ronaldinho had an almost unique quality in that he scored high in appealing to adults and children alike: he has the ball skills but the charm too. Another of his marketing attractions is that his behaviour off the pitch is almost exemplary. An advertising campaign can be ruined in one day should its figurehead be embroiled in some scandal or other, but Ronaldinho leads a quiet life out of the (non-sports) headlines and is unlikely to taint a product by doing something untoward.

The biggest problem with Ronaldinho from an advertising perspective is the sheer quantity of products he promotes. Saturation can mean that the public tires of seeing his mug and hence turns against the product in question. Overexposure and repetition can also make the target audience unreceptive: despite their diversity, the advertising campaigns of most of the products cited above featured Ronaldinho doing some kick-ups with a ball and grinning.

To some commentators, putting your name to so many different brands is a form of prostitution; they accuse Ronaldinho of selling his soul. Those who defend him would say that a footballer's career is short and he has every right to maximise the marketing potential of his sporting image. They also argue that Ronaldinho's endorsements are well chosen – he doesn't advertise beer, for example – and reflect his interests.

While one can imagine Ronaldinho playing one of Estrela's computer games and Gatorade does like to sell itself as a 'sports' drink, this argument falls down with many of the other products. His promotion of cars seems particularly out of step: he hates driving and was even once charged with possessing a fake driver's licence. In February 1999, aged eighteen,

Ronaldinho signed his first sponsorship deal. It was with Juvesa, a Fiat car dealer in Osório, a small town outside Porto Alegre, and he was presented with a Fiat Marea HLX to run around in. Out of the other young players at Grêmio, only Tinga had a motor, so it was something of an ambition fulfilled for Ronaldinho. Then, towards the end of the following year, his permit was exposed as a fake. As news of his transfer to Paris emerged, his diminishing popularity left him ripe for persecution and he was accused of never having passed his test and having bribed his way into obtaining a licence. These were slurs he strongly denied: his had been just one of a whole batch discovered to have been forgeries.

Nevertheless, the question lingers given his sponsorship deal with Hyundai. Along with Real Madrid goalkeeper Iker Casillas, Ronaldinho is the face of the Korean car manufacturer in Spain and yet Ronaldinho doesn't drive: he is chauffeured everywhere by his friend Tiago.

The brand with which he is perhaps most easily recognised is Nike and in this case he certainly does make good use of their products. He has been linked with the US sports brand since a boy in the Grêmio academy when an informal agreement saw Nike send him free kit to wear. By 2005, he had graduated to playing in a pair of boots designed especially for him, which were worth around £3,000 per pair, detailed as they were with 24-carat gold. Labelled the Gold Tiempo Legend, those sold on the High Street inevitably lacked the luxurious detail. A minor controversy, at least in Brazil, surrounded the advert made to promote them: Ronaldinho was filmed, documentary-style, training at the Nou Camp, casually kicking the ball from outside the penalty area onto the crossbar four times in a row; the image proved to be a digitally manipulated illusion and people questioned why someone with Ronaldinho's amazing ball skills had to resort to such fakery.

His first contract with Nike was signed when he was seventeen but their relationship really began to get serious once Ronaldinho had taken the 1999 Copa América by storm. Nike's man in Brazil, Sandro Rosell, improved the terms and tenure of the player's deal immediately after the tournament. (Edmundo, who had been overlooked, claimed that Ronaldinho had made the squad in the first place only because he was a Nike player.)

Back then, Ronaldinho was the only footballer from his state on a contract with a multinational company. He soon had another to his name when Pepsi signed him to front their advertising campaign in Brazil. One popular commercial featured him as a boy looking in the mirror and dreaming of growing up to become not a footballer but a referee.

Another well-liked advert was one for OMO soap powder in which his mother was supposed to take a cameo role: in fact Dona Miguelina stole the show during filming and became its chief protagonist. The shoot of an advert for Xacobeo (a pilgrimage festival in Galicia, northwest Spain) proved slightly more problematic: Ronaldinho was asked to kick a ball around the square in front of the ancient Santiago de Compostela cathedral; he got hold of one volley a little too well and ended up smashing one of the church windows. In the end, the damage was calculated at a mere one euro and twenty cents, which put the smile back on some very anxious looking faces.

Ronaldinho has also been turned into a cartoon. 'A Turma de Mônica' (Monica's Class) is a popular comic strip in Brazil and its creator, Mauricio de Sousa, has periodically introduced real-life figures into Mônica's animated world. In this way, Pelé became a cartoon figure called Pelezinho in the 1980s. Diego Maradona received similar treatment, although his two-dimensional persona, Dieguito, never made it into print.

'Ronaldinho Gaúcho', the cartoon, was launched as a spin-off to 'A Turma de Mônica' in Brazil before the 2006 World Cup in Germany, with a series of comic books and a sticker album. His stories revolve around Porto Alegre and are based on his actual youth, with Dona Miguelina, Assis, Deise and Diego all appearing as themselves (though artistic licence sees Deise transformed into a goalkeeper) along with Ronaldinho's faithful companions, Bala and Bola the dogs. Indeed, the cartoon figure Ronaldinho Gaúcho even has own advertising gig, promoting Perdigão fast-food products such as Chicken PopCorn.

All these commercial sidelines add up and Ronaldinho is believed to be the best-paid footballer on the planet. *France Football* conducts an annual study of players' earnings and in spring 2006 they revealed that Ronaldinho had knocked Beckham off the top spot for the first time in three years. In the 2005 survey, Ronaldinho had placed just eleventh on €8.2 million (£5.6 million), with the *madridistas* Beckham, Ronaldo and Zidane hogging the podium positions. Yet, just twelve months later, a combination of sporting achievement on his part, a lack of it from the *merengues* – none of whom were getting any younger – and a new contract at Barça put Ronaldinho head and shoulders above the others. His €23 million (£15.6 million) annual earnings break down as €8.5 million (£5.8 million) in wages and bonuses and just over €14 million (£9.5 million) from endorsements. Beckham was second and had to get by on a paltry €18 million (£12.2 million).

The BBDO survey came out soon afterwards and confirmed Ronaldinho's star commercial status. His top score of €47 million (£32 million) is a measure of his brand value taking into account average expected future income. Calculated using the BEVA system (Brand Evaluation for Accounting), such findings are used by the industry to analyse long-term advertising potential.

All this proved that if Ronaldinho had been working wonders on the pitch, Assis and Deise were doing likewise off it, maximising the marketing potential of their brother. Deise manages Ronaldinho's day-to-day activities (he refers to her as his *jefa*, the boss), while Assis is in charge of the bigger issues.

Assis returned from Switzerland more financially clued-up and began to explore private banking and wealth-management services. In this way, Ronaldinho's cash is now invested in portfolios of bonds, foreign currencies, stocks and other options. Assis speaks several languages, having enjoyed a globetrotting career, and is said to deal with everything personally. He drives a hard bargain and the role of businessman seems to suit him perfectly, though some people claim that success has gone to his head. Deise, meanwhile, is equally ruthless with regard to her brother's commitment schedule, vetting interviewees and turning down any requests considered inappropriate. All invitations to glitzy parties are simply ignored. Assis and Deise make a good team, ensuring Ronaldinho doesn't have to concern himself with the business side of things.

Yet Ronaldinho is no fool and understands the image he is expected to portray. He spends hours signing autographs because he is genuinely a giving person, but he is also aware that his popularity is built upon such gestures, that it is part of the job.

Early commentators at Grêmio noted his showman side, that with small and innocent-looking gestures – kissing the camera lens after scoring a goal, celebrating by punching the air in the manner of Pelé, pulling his shirt round back-to-front – Ronaldinho usually managed to make the spotlight fall upon him. Cynical observers suggested he was shamelessly working to raise his profile and boost his market value. A fairer assessment would acknowledge that, coming from a family as big as his, Ronaldinho had probably developed a few attention-grabbing tricks as a child and that, combined with his need to please, meant he often couldn't help but hog the stage. These days he is aware of how his commercial image is packaged but to suggest his every gesture is calculated to such an end would be unfair. His charisma is natural, not affected.

His now trademark hand gesture (a thumbs-up with the index finger released as one might suggest a telephone) is a case in point. The hand signal itself originated in Hawaii as a form of greeting and, Hawaii being synonymous with surfing, the gesture spread among the world's surfer fraternity. Hang Loose, a surfware brand in Brazil, adopted the symbol as a logo and it proved popular: Brazilians were soon repeating the gesture to each other, not least music band Grupo Molejo. At that time, there was a fad among footballers in Brazil for celebrating goals with dance routines taken from popular music videos. In this way Ronaldinho copied some

Molejo moves, including the 'Hang Loose'. People liked it and kept asking him to repeat it, which, eager to please, he did until he and the signal had become inseparable. These days, he can't pose for a photo without making the gesture.

Although Ronaldinho almost unintentionally ends up in the spotlight, the camera is not a natural friend. In 'Ronaldinho, la Sonrisa del Fútbol' (the smile of football), the film-makers perched him on a stool in a darkened studio for an interview. He seemed nervous and uncomfortable, both with the situation and having to talk about himself. 'I don't like being in front of cameras at all, especially when it's not natural,' Ronaldinho once told the *Guardian*. 'It's different when I'm playing, if they capture me celebrating and I'm not aware it doesn't worry me. But I really don't like a TV camera staring down at me.'

If the camera does capture him celebrating he often still does the 'Hang Loose' gesture but, in April 2006, after scoring against Real Madrid, he gained plaudits from the deaf community by raising his arms to the sky and turning his hands palm up, a movement which means 'applause' in sign language: he had visited a deaf girl earlier in the week and had promised to remember her.

As Juan José Castillo, Ronaldinho's Mr Fix-it at Barça, explains in *Amigo Ronaldinho*, a portrait of his friend: 'Ronaldinho has a big heart: with his friends, he is an extrovert and a joker. In unfamiliar company and situations he is more timid. He doesn't like appearing in public or performing publicity duties. However, meeting kids, going to visit a hospital, helping the needy: all these things please him and he is naturally generous and gives his all.'

When filming in Santiago de Compostela, Ronaldinho was introduced to a chronically ill thirteen-year-old boy and presented him with a football, which the boy kissed in delight. Ronaldinho was only too happy for such a diversion, preferring always to be himself and meet real people than pose as Ronaldinho the brand. The gesture is also typical of his ability to combine commercial obligations with a touch of charity. When Barça toured China he remained in the country an extra day after the rest of the team in order to visit a clinic for some 3,000 boys, an initiative arranged through Pepsi. He also regularly donates football shirts with personal messages for young victims of the Middle East conflict and fronted a similar project for Barça when the club sent kit to promote sport and peace in Somalia. This was conducted in collaboration with Nike and backed by Unicef and Unpos, the UN political office for Somalia.

Perhaps the best example of Ronaldinho using his high profile and marketing potential for a good cause came when he was named a UN Ambassador against Hunger in August 2005. The concept was that he could serve as a role model for those from a deprived background while at the same time raise awareness of their plight. The United Nations World Food Programme (WFP) thought him perfectly qualified to speak for them on such issues given that he is an example of someone who overcame poverty to conquer the world. 'I grew up with children from very poor families and I've seen the effect hunger can have,' Ronaldinho explained on accepting the post at a special ceremony in Barcelona. 'I was lucky: soccer rescued my family from poverty. Now I want to help the WFP rescue other kids who aren't so fortunate.' To this end, he made a Public Service Announcement film for the campaign, which was aired at the 2006 World Cup: Ronaldinho takes a football out of a fridge, boils it in a pan and then sits down to eat it; the subtitled message reads, 'Unfortunately not everyone can live off football.'

As a Grêmio player, Ronaldinho always represented the club on hospital visits. After one such trip he explained, 'If they can't get to the stadium to see me play, then it is only right that I go to see them.' It was also during his Grêmio days that Ronaldinho became a Unesco Athlete for Peace. Unesco, the United Nations Educational Scientific and Cultural Organisation, bestows the title upon sportsmen and women who can be considered examples to children around the world.

Ronaldinho has had an official role with Unicef, the United Nations Childrens Fund, since February 2006 when he and Edmílson (team-mate at Barça and the *Seleção*) became patrons of the organisation in Brazil. The Spanish division of Unicef, in collaboration with the Iberostar Foundation, was launching a health and education project for children in Mata de São José, an underprivileged part of Bahia in Brazil's poor northeast. Team-mates Sylvinho and Belletti were also involved in the scheme's launch.

Unicef also provided advisory assistance for the Social Futebol Clube project in Porto Alegre, of which Ronaldinho is chief patron. The scheme is a local government initiative in which former professional footballers from the region give coaching sessions, workshops, lectures and courses for needy children from the city's less prosperous districts. Football provides the focal point but the programme also incorporates health and social care. Ronaldinho attended the project's launch in June 2005 with his brother Assis.

FC Barcelona announced a five-year partnership with Unicef in July 2006, the aim being to work together for the benefit of orphaned children in vulnerable situations around the world. When the Laporta regime began at Barça, one proposal was to add a sponsor to the *blaugrana*. Barça (and Athletic Bilbao) had always been famous for their stance, increasingly rare in world football, that their club shirts were too sacred to be sullied for commercial purposes. However, with debts spiralling, the *socis* voted to allow Laporta and the board to break with tradition and seek a sponsor. In the event, the club's finances improved more quickly than had been expected and Barça were no longer compelled to take this measure of last resort. Yet in the process of considering who might be an appropriate shirt sponsor, the idea of carrying not a commercial message but a humanitarian one was raised. Barça consider themselves a symbol of human rights and the chance to promote a good cause seemed too novel and noble an opportunity to ignore. Given several of their players' links with the organisation, not least Ronaldinho, Unicef was chosen as the charity shirt 'sponsor' for the 2006–07 season.

Barça have also been quick to offer their facilities and services for high-profile charity games. After attending the ceremony in which he was honoured with the 2005 *Ballon d'Or* in Paris, Ronaldinho raced back to Catalonia the next day in time to play for Barcelona at the Nou Camp in a match versus an Israeli and Palestinian combined eleven. He landed in the city just hours before kickoff but was determined not to miss the peace initiative. The Nou Camp also played host to an exhibition game arranged to raise money for the victims of the Asian tsunami. Ronaldinho, in his capacity as Fifa Player of the Year, captained a world eleven against a European all-star team led by Andrei Shevchenko, then European Footballer of the Year. Some £5 million was raised via Fifa and Uefa donations, TV rights and gate receipts.

Ronaldinho rarely misses the opportunity to perform in a match for a good cause. He plays the Trianon Christmas charity match back in Rio Grande do Sul whenever he can. In 2004, having just been crowned Fifa World Player of the Year for the first time, he led a team called Amigos do Ronaldinho against Trianon. He managed to assemble a side featuring Brazilian internationals past and present such as Lúcio, Dunga, Júlio Baptista and Ricardo Oliveira, his brother Assis and Barça colleague Deco, guaranteeing a bumper crowd at Internacional's Biera-Rio. Ronaldinho was even applauded by the *colorados*. Ronaldinho also recalls the Trianon of 2000 fondly: he and his brother Assis played together in the same side for the first time.

All this charity is perhaps only natural for someone who considers himself to be a religious man. In an interview for the PSG website he explained, 'I am Catholic but not truly practising. I believe in God but I very rarely go to church. I carry him in my heart.' When he scores a goal, he finishes his celebrations by crossing himself and pointing with both hands to the sky, in thanks to God and in honour of his father, João, whom he likes to imagine looking down from heaven above.

Ronaldinho is religious in the same way as most of his fellow countrymen: holding a firm and unwavering belief in God by virtue of upbringing rather than any carefully considered religious conviction. There is a strong evangelical influence within Brazil as a country and likewise within the *Seleção* squad. The players' lockers are like mini shrines, covered in images and icons of virgins and saints. The Brazilian players always pray together in the dressing room before a match but Ronaldinho also likes to kneel in private prayer before he puts his shirt on. This is something he does with club sides too (he used to get funny looks from the French players at PSG but they soon got used to it). Once on the pitch, Ronaldinho mutters some further personal words of prayers immediately prior to kickoff then prays again in the dressing room afterwards. He says he doesn't ask God for special help, just to stay clear of injury and remain healthy.

Ronaldinho is arguably the best and most popular player of the best and most popular sport on the planet and, in a globalised commercial world, this inevitably makes him a wealthy megastar. Yet he is a man of wholesome values and he does endeavour to give a little back to the fans and the game which have given him everything. Few others in positions such as his are quite so generous of their time and image and for this he can be applauded.

MORE THAN JUST A CLUB – MORE THAN JUST A PLAYER

The European summer of 2004 provided the typical cocktail of national team commitments and transfer rumours for Ronaldinho. In the *canarinha*, he played for Brazil at the Nou Camp in a 5–2 victory over Catalonia but later ruled himself out of the Copa América in Peru with an injury.

Meanwhile, rumours circulated that two separate entities were prepared to meet Ronaldinho's €100 million (£68 million) *cláusula*, a buy-out clause fixed by Spanish league clubs to a player's contract, which must be paid in order to end employment early. One interested party was money-no-object Chelsea. In late May, Roman Abramovich even paid a visit to the Gaúcho's hotel room in Paris where he was with the Brazil squad ready to face France in Fifa's centenary match: Abramovich was clutching a Chelsea shirt with Ronaldinho's name on. The Russian billionaire asked Ronaldinho to pose for a photo in the shirt but the Brazilian wisely declined.

The other courtier was Lorenzo Sanz. A former Real Madrid president, he hoped to win back the role in that summer's elections by prising Ronaldinho away from Barça, a gesture certain to impress the voters.

Barça were adamant that Ronaldinho was going nowhere and the player seemed inclined to agree. However, it also seemed fair and prudent to improve his contract and a timely change in Spanish law meant the club were able to do this without spending an extra cent. New contracts for foreign executives, into which bracket Ronaldinho could be placed, would be granted special tax breaks. Barça were thus able to draw up a new deal in which the player effectively received a pay rise (he was believed to be on €4.5 million (£3 million) per year, rising steadily to €7 million (£4.7 million) by 2008 when the contract expired) although the club paid the same amount as before. They also made the most of the opportunity to ratchet up the buy-out clause to €150 million (£100 million), though this would drop annually to reach €80 million (£54 million) by deal-end.

Barça had also been busy adding to their roster that summer. Four Brazilians arrived, all of them naturalised Europeans: Belletti, Sylvinho, Edmílson and Deco (actually a full-blown Portuguese citizen). Barça had also signed Frenchman Ludovic Giuly from Monaco and Swede Henrik Larsson from Celtic. The final capture, the final piece of the jigsaw, was Samuel Eto'o, the Cameroon who had been playing in the Spanish league for Mallorca but who was part-owned by Real Madrid.

Ronaldinho was raring to go when Barça embarked upon their pre-season tour of Asia, not least because a fixture in Japan versus Júbilo Iwata allowed for reunions with a few old friends. Rodrigo Gral and Carlos Gavião, his old buddies from the Grêmio academy, were both on Júbilo's books so the occasion offered the opportunity for all to catch up with each other. Obviously keen to impress against his old pals, Ronaldinho was in an irrepressible mood as he inspired Barça to a 3–0 win, complete with all his individual flamboyant trimmings.

Back in Europe, Ronaldinho had to retire hurt from the final of the pre-season Copa Catalunya. Though he made two subsequent appearances in the *canarinha*, much to Barça's annoyance, Rijkaard proceeded with caution and brought him off early in the first few league games of the new campaign, a measure which met with the player's predictable disapproval.

Ronaldinho's first full ninety-minute outing helped Barça to a 4–1 victory over Real Zaragoza. This was possibly the first game in which the new-look Barça truly showed what it was capable of with a superb display, which included a double strike from Eto'o. Equally inspired conquests followed: 3–1 away at Mallorca and 3–0 at home to Shakhtar Donetsk, a game in which Ronaldinho scored his first Champions League goal via a penalty. Less convincing was a 1–0 win over Numancia, but it is often said the top teams have to grind out results when they play badly and that is what Barça had become: they sat atop the league for the first time in three years.

Barça were soon chalking up their eleventh win of the season – over city rivals Espanyol – before being brought down to earth with a frustrating 1–0 defeat away to Milan in the Champions League. Revenge was in the air for the return game against the Italians but Shevchenko opened the scoring for the Milanese. Eto'o equalised before half-time but, despite their pressure, Barça couldn't quite force the deserved winner. Couldn't, that is, until the last minute when Ronaldinho darted from right to left on the edge of the box before letting rip with an unstoppable shot into the top-left corner.

Ronaldinho went absolutely berserk. He had been playing well enough all season but hadn't quite been as imposing as the previous year. Undoubtedly this was because Barça had made some smart signings since then and Ronaldinho was no longer being asked to carry the team. No matter – he was accustomed to being the deciding factor and the passion with which he celebrated his winner suggested that there was more than a touch of relief in his proving, if only to himself, that Barça still relied upon him when the going got really tough.

There was another major reason to celebrate so thoroughly: it seems incredible but the goal was his first of any kind as a professional using his left foot.

Brazilian legend Falcão told *The Times* about teasing Ronaldinho about his weaker foot. 'I was once interviewing him on my radio show and I said to him, jokingly, "What about your left foot, when are you going to score with your left?" But Ronaldinho took it totally seriously.'

The two Gaúcho stars of football past and present met again, some time after Ronaldinho's goal with his swinger against Milan. 'He told me he had been looking frantically for my phone number. I asked why and he replied: "Did you see my goal against Milan with my left foot? I wanted to call you to say that I had finally done it." This is the beauty of Ronaldinho.'

Back in *La Liga*, Barça surprisingly lost away at Real Betis and this upset their stride ahead of the big one, Real Madrid at home.

It was to be the first time that Ronaldinho played against Ronaldo: in the previous season, one or the other had been injured. The general consensus was that, whichever of the two Ronnies was able to better impose themselves would decide the *clásico's* outcome.

It proved to be Ronaldinho's day and Barça turned Madrid over 3–0 in a commanding display of movement, control and purpose. The first goal was scored by Eto'o, who capitalised on hesitation in the Madrid defence from Roberto Carlos. The goal was seen to symbolise the opposing cycles the two clubs found themselves in: the hunger for victory of one, the twilight lethargy of the other. It was noted that even those Barça players who suffered an off day, on this occasion Larsson, still contributed in terms of work rate and aggression. By marrying these qualities of commitment to the touch of genius Ronaldinho supplied (he had set up the first, participated in the second and scored the third), Barça were looking irresistible.

A 1–1 draw with Celtic at home saw Barça go through to the next round of the Champions League, but the match was most notable for the giant mosaic of placards produced by the *culés* which read: 'Catalunya is not Spain'. This came in reference to the racist abuse several of England's black players had suffered in a friendly match against Spain played in Madrid the previous week.

Barça's next fixture was away at Getafe and the locals unveiled a banner proclaiming, 'Getafe sí es España' or 'Well, Getafe is Spain'. The atmosphere was tense and both Ronaldinho and Eto'o were subjected to racist chants from the home crowd. Ronaldinho rose above the politics and the bigotry to offer another of his sublime moments and put the wheels in motion for a beautifully worked Barça goal. The Brazilian's audacious back-heel to Xavi was a touch of genius, Xavi's skill in running with the ball and passing to Deco no less impressive, and Deco's powerful and precise finish was the icing on the cake. Barça won 2–0.

The end-of-year awards season soon came along and Ronaldinho was in the running for all the top prizes. He missed out on the *Ballon d'Or*, the Golden Ball organised by *France Football* magazine to honour the best performer in Europe, which went to Andrei Shevchenko. However, when Fifa announced their World Player of the Year, Ronaldinho's name was top of the list. The presentation took place at Zurich Opera House and Ronaldinho attended with his family – Dona Miguelina, Deise, Assis, Carla, Diego and Valdimar – and Barça representatives Rosell, Laporta, Txiki and Castillo.

Selected by the national team coaches and captains of all Fifa's affiliate countries, each voter gets to select a top three: a first place is worth five points, second three points and third just one. Ronaldinho topped the nominations with 620 points, Thierry Henry, with whom Ronaldinho spent much of the evening chatting, came second on 552 and Shevchenko took third with 253.

On acceptance, Ronaldinho dedicated the award to his departed father but also thanked Barcelona by saying the club had given more to him than he had to it. He then paraded the trophy in front of the Nou Camp faithful at the last fixture of the year, a 2–1 win over Levante.

The New Year got under way inauspiciously for the *culés* with a 3–0 loss to Villareal and an unconvincing win over Real Sociedad. Both Real Madrid and Valencia had begun the year brightly and started to eat away at Barça's lead at the top. Meanwhile, off the pitch, news of boardroom strife emerged with the Rosell and Laporta affair finally hitting the headlines.

An emphatic 3–0 home win over Racing proved timely. The goals were scored by Eto'o, Ronaldinho and Deco, the club's three best players issuing a statement of intent. Ronaldinho's goal was particularly breathtaking and involved a step-over and double feint before firing the ball into the corner of the net. This victory laid the platform for a productive run that included a 4–0 away win at Sevilla and triumphs over Zaragoza and Mallorca.

A double date with destiny followed. Since the draw had been made back in December 2004, everyone had been looking forward to Barcelona versus Chelsea in the Champions League second round: a clash between Europe's two form sides. The matches didn't disappoint.

José Mourinho had cut his teeth on the Barcelona bench under Bobby Robson and Louis van Gaal back in the late '90s and his achievements since then had put him in high regard in Catalonia. Chelsea arrived with a well-organised defensive wall and a determination to counterattack, tactics considered tantamount to gamesmanship by the *culés*, nurtured on their team's free-flowing style. A Belleti own goal played into the Londoners' hands but, once Didier Drogba was sent off by referee Anders Frisk, Barça found space and created more openings, eventually equalising through Maxi López and then taking the first-leg honours 2–1 thanks to an Eto'o strike. Ronaldinho had been a handful all night and was involved in the first goal but there would be more to come from him in this tie.

Mourinho's reputation was soon sinking like a stone in the Condal City. As if his overcautious tactics and the fact that he brought his team out late for the second half weren't enough, Mourinho accused Rijkaard of putting pressure on referee Frisk at half-time, resulting in the sending off. Rijkaard and Frisk and the Uefa assessor Graham Turner all denied the charge, though there had certainly been ugly incidents involving the two teams' backroom staff in the tunnel. Mourinho then failed to turn up for the post-match press conference and later berated the referee so much that some of Chelsea's so-called supporters felt inspired to issue Frisk with death threats.

The return leg would live long in the memory of all those who witnessed it. Chelsea raced to a 3–0 lead through goals from Eidur Gudjohnsen, Frank Lampard and Damien Duff and all looked lost for Barça. Ronaldinho had other ideas: he converted a penalty after a handball from Paulo Ferreira before poking an absolute gem into the corner to make it 3–2 on the night but 4–4 on aggregate, Barça with the advantage of the extra away goal. Ronaldinho released Eto'o for a strike that grazed the bar and Joe Cole hit the post at the other end. All this before half-time.

In the second period, Iniesta also found the woodwork for Barça but, with fifteen minutes to go, John Terry headed home what would prove to be the decisive goal for Chelsea. Barça argued, quite legitimately, that their goalkeeper Valdés had been impeded by Chelsea's Ricardo Carvalho. As the replay was shown on the giant screen, Ronaldinho implored referee Pierluigi Collina to look at it but he refused. Barça claimed the linesman had obviously seen the infringement as he had not run to the centre to signal a goal but the protests fell on deaf ears. Chelsea held on to win an epic tie and advance to the quarterfinals.

At the final whistle, Mourinho and his bench ran on to the pitch to celebrate. Emotions were running high and the Barça delegation took exception to what appeared to be the Chelsea camp rubbing defeat in their faces. Ronaldinho, as did Rijkaard and Eto'o, lost his usual cool and security guards rushed in to oversee what were angry altercations on the way to the tunnel.

Organised at the back once again, Chelsea had attacked this time with greater verve yet their goals had all come on the counter and Barça's policy of surging forward with wanton abandon had been exposed as overadventurous at best, plain naive at worst. Their error-strewn opening half-hour had played straight into the hands of Chelsea. Irritating as they found his antics, Barça were forced to recognise that Mourinho had set them a trap and they had jumped right in. Barça had been taught a lesson.

Most of the press reaction could be summed up with *Gazzetta dello Sport's* headline: 'Ronaldinho was great but Mourinho even more so'. Nevertheless, Ronaldinho's contribution will possibly have the longer shelf life. His second goal was a moment of such outrageous brilliance that it required endless television replays to show quite how he had contrived to score it. Surrounded by defenders on the edge of the box and with seemingly nowhere to pass to, let alone squeeze a shot through, he had toe-ended a bullet through the eye of a needle and into Petr Cech's bottom corner. The goal was eventually voted the best of that year's tournament, a judgement beyond question.

Ronaldinho would later describe his strike thus: 'When I see that goal it is as if someone pressed "pause" on the video and nobody could move except me. I thought I could try and dribble but I looked up at the goal and then I saw the gap, the angle was delicate but I tried with the toe. And it went in.'

Their Champions League dreams destroyed, Barça returned home determined to complete the job of winning *La Liga*. Hard-fought wins over Athletic Bilbao and Deportivo La Coruña followed, along with a dramatic draw with Betis via a very late Van Bronckhorst equaliser, but those errors committed against Chelsea returned to haunt Barça and at the most inopportune of moments. Haphazard defending ensured they went down 4–2 again, this time to Real Madrid at the Bernabéu. With this, the *merengues* had closed the gap with Barça to just six points. Ronaldinho had scored a late free-kick that seemed a mere consolation at the time but was a great deal more valuable. If Barça and Madrid finished the season level on points then their record against each other would be decisive: having won 3–0 against Madrid at home, Barça carried a 5–4 aggregate advantage; Ronaldinho's goal meant the gap was effectively seven points with seven to play.

The cushion was down to three points (effectively four) as Barça hosted Getafe: before Barça kicked off, Madrid had already played and triumphed in their game. Barça had not won for two matches, Puyol was suspended,

Eto'o injured, the fans nervous. They needn't have been – captain for the day, Ronaldinho was in a determined mood right from the first whistle. When the team most relies upon him, Ronaldinho usually produces his best and here was a situation when they didn't just need his ability but, in order to lift the doom and gloom, his personality too. Ronaldinho ran Getafe a merry dance, scoring the first goal via a free-kick then teeing Giuly up for the second. In between, he treated the crowd to all the tricks of his trade and clearly enjoyed himself thoroughly.

A similarly inspired display from Ronaldinho followed a few weeks later. For the fourth match in a row, Real Madrid had already played and won by the time Barça took to the field for their game, turning up the pressure on each occasion. This time Barça were away at Valencia, as tricky a fixture as they come. The *culés* were jittery but Ronaldinho showed no fear once again. Belletti fired a cross in from the right that was cleared as far as Ronaldinho some thirty yards out. He controlled the ball dead then fired it straight into the top-right corner. For sheer surprise factor it matched his strike at Stamford Bridge: seemingly playing to a tempo all of his own, Ronaldinho had found the time to effectively line up a free-kick without a wall. Barça went on to record a 2–0 victory.

The win meant Barça could conceivably seal the title in their next game, away at Levante. All the squad, the backroom staff, the board of directors and 10,000 *culés* travelled en masse to Valencia where Levante's modest stadium was to be found.

The game was hotly contested at first – both Ronaldinho and Deco were fortunate not to be sent off, Ronaldinho for what looked to be a head butt – and Levante took a first-half lead. However, Eto'o's equaliser on the hour brought a 1–1 draw providing Barça with a six point advantage over second-placed Real Madrid with two games to play. Madrid could in theory still close the gap but Ronaldinho's goal against them gave Barça the head-to-head edge and meant that the Catalans could celebrate early. (In fact, Madrid drew their next game and won their last while Barça drew both to end the season 4 points in front.)

Barça had won the league title for the first time in six years. At the final whistle, Ronaldinho jumped for joy. Only he and Motta remained on the field as their team-mates fled to the tunnel to avoid the pitch invasion. Surrounded by a scrum of pressmen, security and stray supporters, Ronaldinho was also the last to leave: heading towards the dressing room he appeared to have a change of heart and instead charged back to salute the fans one last time. The whole entourage were to fly straight back to Barcelona after the game and Ronaldinho and Motta had spent so much time celebrating that they didn't even have time for a shower – the pair of them led the party on the plane still dressed in their match kit. The cava flowed all the way home until they touched down at Barcelona airport around 4 a.m. to be met by a tumultuous reception of waiting fans. Festivities that night were as long as they were deserved.

A parade was organised for the very next day and three open-top buses left the Nou Camp at six in the evening. All the Barça footballers wore a red T-shirt that said *Campions* (Catalan for champions) and Ronaldinho could be seen at the front of the bus with a Brazilian flag draped over his shoulder. Some one million people lined the streets to cheer them by.

They arrived back at the Nou Camp as night fell. The players were introduced one by one and Ronaldinho was last up and appeared wearing a giant glove puppet of his trademark 'Hang Loose' gesture. He then led the team in a conga lap of honour. Various players took to the mic to offer a few dedications. Ronaldinho thanked almost everyone he could think of before initiating a prayer in the centre circle. In contrast, Samuel Eto'o shouted into the microphone: '*Madrid, cabrón, saluda al campeón* – 'Madrid, bastards, salute the champions.' In deep trouble afterwards, Eto'o claimed that it was a chant he had picked up off the fans without grasping the full meaning. Those familiar with how he had been treated by the team from the Spanish capital suspected otherwise.

At around 11 p.m., the final rendition of the Barça anthem rang out, by which time some of the players had been partying for a full twenty-four hours.

Barça had been crowned champions for the first time in six years, the seventeenth title of their history. There are many different ways to come out on top and, had Barça ground their way to a scrappy, lucky or even unmerited league win, none of their followers would have complained: the important thing was to get back to winning ways.

However, the title had been won in a style of which all involved with the club could be proud, and this made the victory all the more satisfying. Barça have high standards both in terms of achievement and style and the new team did honour to the club, playing an offensive football popularly identified as 'the Barça way'. They were a young and determined bunch that played vibrant yet pragmatic football and the sense of unity within the squad was obvious for all to see – another element that made their victory all the more refreshing.

Ronaldinho remained the maestro although he was not solely responsible for the success. In his first season, his performances had perhaps been more outstanding in their impact but he was no longer the lone ranger, burdened with the obligation to carry the team on his own. That season, Deco and Eto'o had both been at least as important. This was a good thing for all concerned and Ronaldinho recognised as much in one of many interviews conducted after the league win. 'The first season was more complicated as I had to prove myself in a Barça shirt. This year I didn't have to kill a lion every day. Other quality players arrived with the will to show things too.'

He added, with evident pride, 'We played our way and we won the league but the key to winning it was that, when someone wasn't on form, someone else took over; if someone failed to score, another colleague did instead. Luckily, we had a very balanced and consistent team. We all get on well and that makes the work easier.'

He was also full of praise for the coach. 'Rijkaard understands me and lets me play how I like to. I can go to the right, to the left, forward or further back. When we have the ball, I have total freedom to create, find gaps, seek out my colleagues.'

Ronaldinho evidently had few regrets about having chosen to join Barcelona. At the end of his first season he told reporters, 'The atmosphere, the young ambitious directors, the way the game is played – everything makes me feel like I'm at the door to great adventures.' How right he was.

If playing conditions suited him, so too did the city. In an interview with the *Observer* he explained that off-the-pitch considerations had influenced his decision of where to move. 'The most important thing for me was to be happy, and not just me but my family as well. I put everything in the balance, my style of play and my family, and I thought that this would be the place where I would be happiest and to which I would adapt most quickly.'

In Paris, of course, his nocturnal antics made as many headlines as his football. In Barcelona, the wild-man image had been put to bed. 'Now I am a man. I have changed club, changed life. I am more mature on the pitch and off it,' he declared to pressmen who broached the subject. He had arrived in Paris aged just 21, 'an age when you sometimes don't realise all the demands of the job', he said. 'Now I understand, I have matured, I am more professional. I've grown up.' This didn't mean he had turned into a hermit: he still enjoyed a good night out. 'It is in my Brazilian culture and I am not going to change,' was his justification. 'But I choose my moments and enjoy myself when I won't be reproached like at PSG.' He cites cultural differences as well. 'In Barcelona people are Latin too, they understand my attitude. They don't worry about my lifestyle. They look at how I play on the pitch and trust me (off it).'

It is true that the Catalan press don't pry into his personal affairs in the way, say, that the Madrid media does with its local stars, but the sense of respect is mutual. As a Barcelona player, it is impossible not to realise that you are representing something greater than a mere football team: *Més que un club* – More than just a club – as the tag line goes. Ronaldinho is not overtly political but he is sensitive to the Catalan identity at Barça. He is said to be attempting to learn Catalan, at least a new word every day. While this is only natural for the keen linguist he is – he even endeavoured to pick up some Turkish to communicate with Rüstü Reçber – it also demonstrates an appreciation of his surroundings. He speaks Spanish, albeit with a fairly heavy Portuguese influence, and this is enough for him to get by, but he is conscious that at least trying to grasp the Catalan language is a significant gesture.

As regards the *clásico* games against Real Madrid, he is aware of their wider resonance. 'Because of the difference which exists between Catalonia and Spain, you live the (Barça v Real Madrid) game a bit differently,' he admitted to *Avui*, a Catalan-language daily. 'I don't like to talk about politics in any sense at all but I am conscious of the rivalry, external to the football, between Catalonia and Spain. When the two most powerful clubs from each side clash, the rivalry manifests itself emotionally.'

Ronaldinho spent his first few months in Barcelona cooped up in Hotel Arts, one of the two towers on the seafront that originally formed the Olympic Village. The Ronaldinho clan now live in Castelldefels, a beach town just outside Barcelona. It is a district popular with footballers – Motta, Van Bronkhorst, Valdés and Larsson are among Ronaldinho's neighbours – but most live on the seafront itself while Ronaldinho resides up on the mountain.

His living arrangements obviously suit him down to the ground, as he told the makers of *Ronaldinho, la Sonrisa del Fútbol* when he invited their cameras into his home. 'I am just fifteen/twenty minutes from the stadium and yet it is calm. I am up on the mountain but it is only five minutes to the beach. I can't imagine myself living in Barcelona itself.'

The house itself is as luxurious as one might imagine, with a large garden, outdoor swimming pool and barbecue area, and spacious lounge, dining and kitchen areas inside. A huge television can naturally be found in the sitting room where it fights for attention with the equally grand (and somewhat tasteless) *Hello*-style framed photograph of Ronaldinho and Dona Miguelina above the mantelpiece. The garage has a table-tennis area and a lift up to the house proper to save the athlete having to waste energy in negotiating stairs.

The film-footage showed him lazing around his home, watching television, eating his lunch, drinking a coffee, playing with his dogs. Whatever he was doing, he always had a ball at his feet or in his arms, clung to like a comfort blanket.

Security is tight. Ronaldinho never goes anywhere alone, never carries any money on him and is driven around by Tiago in a sports version Hummer, the armoured four-by-four used by the US army in Iraq. This may seem excessive, but in November 2003 team-mate Saviola was held up in his car on the motorway en route to training: one car stopped in front of him, another behind and they forced him to hand over his wallet and other belongings; the consensus was that it could have been much worse. Ronaldinho's house is also well protected, though, compared to Brazil, precautions are relaxed. Ronaldinho's nephew, Diego, apparently loves coming to visit because in Castelldefels he can ride his bike in the street, a liberty he sadly can't take back home in Porto Alegre.

His family's safety became a major issue back in Ronaldinho's Grêmio days. While helping the *tricolor* to a 3–0 home win over Caxias, thieves broke into his house in Guarujá. Although they ultimately fled empty-handed – Ronaldinho evidently scaring them when he returned home from the match – the incident served as a warning that a young wealthy footballer and his family were obvious targets and security was stepped up at their home.

A few years later, a spate of kidnappings in Brazil involved the mothers of famous footballers. The most high-profile case was that of Robinho's mum, who spent forty days in captivity until the then Santos star coughed up the ransom. Measures to protect Dona Miguelina were stepped up and now she never leaves the house alone either.

Diego is considered equally vulnerable and there were even suggestions that the youngster might move to live in Barcelona. This did, however, have as much to do with his football ability as his safety: an elegant midfielder at Grêmio juniors, Barça are said to be monitoring his progress. In time-honoured fashion, Ronaldinho claims his nephew will end up a better player than he is himself. However, Assis and Carla prefer their boy to live with them in Porto Alegre, at least for the foreseeable future.

Nevertheless, the house at Castelldefels is still a constant buzz of family and friends. Deise lives with her brother and continues to look after all his affairs; Tiago drives Ronaldinho around and generally remains his friend's right-hand man; cousin Valdimar moved out of the house to live with his girlfriend but still acts as Ronaldinho's personal trainer, occasionaly conducting early-morning exercise on the beach. Dona Miguelina is a regular visitor, as is Assis. When the cameras paid him a visit it was spring 2006, a fortnight after Ronaldinho's birthday, so several friends from Porto Alegre were also around, including Samba Tri. Ronaldinho had paid for them to come out and celebrate with him and threw a three-week holiday into the bargain. There were some eighteen of them for lunch that day – though above average, this was not unusual.

His inner circle continues to rally round him and ensures he can concentrate his efforts on being the best footballer in the world. As Ronaldinho himself says, 'My only concern is playing. Everything else my family looks after. In my house everyone has a job and my job in our house is to play football.'

According to Juan José Castillo's description of them in 'Amigo Ronaldinho', the player's days tend to be fairly stress-free. He gets up around nine and is made an orange juice by his sister or cousin. Tiago drives him to the ground, he trains, takes a long shower and has a massage. He might give an interview or two before being driven home, where he has lunch and then retires for a siesta. In the afternoon, he usually trains a little more.

The routine can get tedious and means that sometimes he likes to escape the world of the professional sportsman. 'I love to forget about football,' he told the *Guardian*. 'Not football as such but just the obligation to eat at the same time every day, sleep at the same time every day. Every day's the same.' The only real change to the programme comes before match days when his diet is even more strictly dictated to him and he has to go to bed earlier.

This last part is perhaps not such a hardship. Ronaldinho is said to love to sleep and can nod off under almost any conditions. On boarding an aeroplane he is almost immediately out for the count. After waking on a normal work day, he is a slow starter, certainly no morning person, and usually doesn't get going until he is running around in training. Then the laughing and the joking begin.

Ronaldinho and his compatriot Thiago Motta are known as the pranksters at Barcelona. Their practical jokes tend to be of the rare kind found amusing only by footballers: cutting sleeves of suits, hiding car keys or mobile phones, pushing the unprepared into swimming pools. All the fun of the fair.

Motta is Ronaldinho's best friend at Barça and they used to room together until Motta got injured. Along with Edmílson, Belletti, Deco and Sylvinho, they form a close-knit Brazilian core at the club. They socialise a great deal together, often gathering at Ronaldinho's for the ubiquitous Playstation football tournaments.

Another member of Ronaldinho's Brazilian community is Eduardo Costa, who plays for city rivals Espanyol. He and Ronaldinho were team-mates back at Grêmio and were both in France at the same time too, Costa at Bordeaux. Ronaldinho also used to socialise with Anderson Varejão, a Brazilian basketball player now playing in the NBA. Barça also have a successful basketball team and Ronaldinho's first year in the *blaugrana* coincided with Varejão's last. A basketball fan, Ronaldinho regularly went to watch the matches when his friend played.

That Ronaldinho has a close group of Brazilian friends in the city and, more importantly, in the Barça dressing room, undoubtedly helps him feel more at home and ward away the *saudades* (the 'longings').

However, they are all very conscious of not becoming too cliquey a group. A good example of their sensitivity to this matter was when Brazilian magazine *Placar* requested a photograph of Ronaldinho gathered with his

Brazilian Barça team-mates. Ronaldinho said he would consider it but, after consulting with his colleagues, informed *Placar* that they didn't think it was appropriate: they were Barcelona players who happened to be from Brazil, not Brazilian players at Barcelona. Around the same time, Real Madrid and their band of *Brazucas* were busily causing offence with a goal celebration that imitated a cockroach. Quite apart from how silly it was (they lay on the ground and wiggled their legs in the air) their non-Brazilian team-mates looked on disapprovingly, clearly not privy to the pre-rehearsed routine. Real Madrid were a team divided, Barça united.

As well as his compatriots, Ronaldinho is said to get on particularly well with Puyol, Xavi and Márquez. Attempts from outsiders to create a dressing-room war of egos between Ronaldinho and Eto'o ultimately came to nothing because of the affection and respect both players felt for each other. When it was time for Larsson to leave the club, Ronaldinho said he was losing a friend first, a colleague second.

He may be the star of the Barça team, the main man in the eyes of fans and media, but he remains humble and appreciative of his colleagues. Although he is the one who collects most of the individual awards, he goes to great pains to acknowledge the importance of his team-mates. His speech on collecting the 2005 *Ballon d'Or* was typical: 'When things go well for the team individual prizes follow. It is an honour for me to bring the names of Barça and the *Seleção* to these heights.'

On winning the Fifa prize he was asked what it felt like to be the best footballer in the world. 'I don't even feel I'm the best at Barça. I know I'm important to the team, but the best? No, not really. I do what I can and others do what I can't.' Whenever Ronaldinho scores a goal, he immediately points to and then runs towards whoever set him up to make sure they share the plaudits.

This modesty, false or otherwise (and it does seem genuine), is of paramount importance because it helps to form the great sense of unity so evident at Barça. In a dressing room of superstars, if the most high-profile player of them all carries himself with humility, it follows that the others will be more likely to do the same. Comparisons with Beckham and Real Madrid's team of underachieving *galácticos* have to be made: on paper the *merengues* were as good as anyone but on the pitch individuals played to their own agenda. Barça were a collection of stars but played as a team.

Ronaldinho has also made the welfare of the younger players his responsibility and is the senior figure who dedicates the most time to them. He still recalls what it meant to him as a young player when established stars took time to offer him advice and help him integrate. He believes that a relaxed and jokey atmosphere best puts the youngsters at ease, and to this end is always teasing them while at the same time asking after their families and generally treating them as one of the gang.

He has made particular efforts to mentor Lionel Messi. In his first year at the club, Ronaldinho heard a lot about the star of the academy. Recognising many similarities to himself when a boy – South American, slightly frail of stature, the biggest promise of his generation – he asked to meet him and then, when some of the juniors came to train with the first team, he called Messi over to sit with him. From then on, Ronaldinho adopted him like a little brother. He incorporated him into the group of Brazilians and Sylvinho and Deco have also been particularly generous with the Argentine.

When Messi finally made his debut, it was appropriate that he came on for Ronaldinho. The Brazilian hugged him and gave him some private words of encouragement.

The importance of Ronaldinho's aura, his grace and charisma, cannot be overstated: it has been absolutely fundamental to Barça's transformation. He not only gets on well with all the players, coaches and backroom staff, but also everyone who works at the club from the cleaners to the guides in the Nou Camp museum. He always has time for everyone and greets most people by name. Such small details should not be underestimated: if the star player treats you as an equal then you feel more a part of the whole organisation and are happier in your work. Ronaldinho has managed to lift the mood of the entire club.

Before him, compatriot Rivaldo worked similar miracles to Ronaldinho on the pitch. Yet Rivaldo was a tormented soul whose melancholy infected the club and set the emotional tone. Ronaldinho's character is just as contagious, but his is a positive, cheerful disposition. He transmits an enthusiastic optimism and this rubs off on everyone, especially the other players. As they get changed before a match, he likes there to be music and samba blasting from the stereo right up until kickoff. This is not the way at most clubs. When team-mates, players who possibly appreciate that their role is not as fundamental as Ronaldinho's, see how the supposed best player in the world copes with the pressure, their own personal burdens can suddenly seem less daunting. With Ronaldinho looking relaxed yet confident, cheerful yet focused, they begin to feel the same way themselves. The record-breaking winning streaks Barça have enjoyed during Ronaldinho's time at the club have undoubtedly been a product of the self-belief he emanates.

Ronaldinho, along with Deco and Puyol, is one of the most dominating characters in the dressing room. Puyol is the captain and motivator, Deco the advisor and tactician, Ronaldinho the calming influence. Before going on to the pitch – and the Gaúcho always likes to be the last one out –

Ronaldinho goes round each player individually, embraces them and gives a few words of encouragement in their ear. He repeats the routine on the pitch at final whistle.

When asked by the *Guardian* if pre-match nerves affect him, Ronaldinho replied, 'No, never. I'm more attentive than nervous – knowing who you're playing against, their characteristics – those things occupy me more.'

Here is the key to another reason for Ronaldinho's success. His play may seem to be all invention and instinct but few players prepare, consider and visualise how they are going to play like Ronaldinho. 'What I try to do is to calculate, know the characteristics of my team-mates, how they like to receive the ball, at what speed they like it, if they need it at their feet or a little in front,' he explained. 'After putting all that together you can begin to mount something. As Samuel Eto'o is faster than most defences I have to deliver him the ball in this fashion, but it's something that's practised time and time again at training. In the end it comes naturally.'

Larsson too gives an indication of what he is like to play with. 'I know that whenever I play and he's playing I only have to make the runs,' he says. 'There's not many he misses. He always sees you. You always have to be on the move when Ronaldinho has the ball. Even when you don't expect to receive it, you might.'

CHAMPIONS OF EUROPE

After the 2004–05 season, while most of the Barça squad enjoyed a well-earned rest, Ronaldinho had other duties to fulfil: he was named as Brazil captain for the Confederations Cup in Germany. There was also the little matter of the by-now ritual close-season contract renegotiation. Chelsea had been heard sniffing around once more, supposedly prepared to buy out Ronaldinho's €120 million (£82 million) *cláusula*. Barça, wishing to put an end to the speculation once and for all, proposed extending Ronaldinho's contract to the end of his playing career and even beyond, with some kind of role at the club promised to him for when he hung up his boots: 'a contract for life' as it was being called.

The wheeling and dealing dragged on for most of the summer with the player's image rights the first sticking point. It then emerged that Barça wished to include some kind of criteria into the contract that would measure Ronaldinho's playing contribution in the latter years of the deal, offering them some form of a guarantee.

In the end, a two-year extension was agreed, taking them to June 2010, with an option attached for four further years. While the *cláusula* of the previous agreement began at €150 million (£100 million) but stepped down annually to end up at €80 million (£54 million), the new package set his buy-out at a fixed €125 million (£85 million).

Ronaldinho and Márquez, who had been involved in the Confederations Cup as captain of Mexico, were excused the first stage of Barça's pre-season in Denmark, yet both were back in time for the club's trip to China. Given the success of the previous season, Barça hardly felt the need to tinker with the squad and Dutchman Marc Van Bommel and Basque Santi Ezquerro were the only additions.

However, Barça made a sluggish start to the new season. They won the Spanish Super Cup versus Real Betis at a canter and began their Champions

League campaign with élan, registering a 2–0 away win at Werder Bremen, including a Ronaldinho penalty, but their league performances were poor and yielded just five points from the first four games. Deco and Xavi had looked off-colour while Ronaldinho was a shadow of his former self, hugging the left touchline and seeming indifferent as to whether the ball came his way or not.

For the away fixture in *La Liga* at Real Betis, Ronaldinho and Deco found their names were not on the squad list. Rijkaard claimed to be resting them and, with a Champions League game to come later in the week, who was to argue? For most observers, though, the pair had been dropped. Ronaldinho had been poor in the previous two games and there were worries that off-field matters (he had only learned he had become a father in August) had caused him to lose his focus. Deco's omission was perhaps the more surprising, but the fact they had been omitted together and neither of them even made the bench was most alarming.

The tactic paid off spectacularly: Eto'o rose to the challenge of leading the team and inspired a 4–1 victory. Reinstated for the Champions League a few days later, Ronaldinho and Deco were then unstoppable as Barça put Udinese to the sword with a 4–1 win, Ronaldinho scoring a hat-trick, and Deco the other. Ronaldinho's 'rest' had clearly roused him and he left the pitch with the match ball tucked under his arm and topless (the Udinese manager, Serse Cosmi, had asked Ronaldinho for his shirt after the match: his son was a big fan).

Rijkaard was suddenly being hailed as a motivational genius and commentators marvelled at how confident he had grown in the role of coach after such a timid start. When asked by Canal Plus what he made of it all, Ronaldinho simply replied, 'The *mister* knows what he is doing.' (Spanish league managers are still known as *misters*, a legacy of a long-forgotten era when the most knowledgeable people in the game were Englishmen.)

Yet Barça still couldn't quite get up to full speed: draws with Zaragoza, Depor and Panathanaikos in the Champions League were all cases of Barça not getting what they deserved out of a game. A 2–0 win at Málaga followed but this victory owed much to a theatrical tumble from Ronaldinho, which earned the team a penalty he promptly converted. This was a far cry from the stylish manner in which Barça had picked up their points the previous season.

Perhaps anxious to wipe the image of his gamesmanship from everyone's memory, Ronaldinho was at his flamboyant best as Real Sociedad visited the Nou Camp. Exhilarating yet ruthless, he scored twice from free-kicks and laid another on a plate for Van Bommel in a 5–0 thrashing. The scoreline seemed to suit Barça and they repeated the trick against

Panathanaikos at home to secure their place in the second round of the Champions League.

By now, *el clásico* had come round again and although just one point separated Barça and Real – the Catalans were second in the table, Real third – the two clubs were on very different trajectories. Barça had run into a bit of form while Madrid were struggling with injuries and playing badly. Be that as it may, Ronaldinho was keen to lower expectations before the match. 'You don't win the league against Real Madrid. It is a game worth three points just like any other,' he deadpanned, unable to imagine what was about to follow.

In purely practical terms, Barça took the points with a 3–0 victory. However, the authority with which they did so caused incalculable damage to the morale of the team from the capital: Madrid would not recover to challenge Barça that season.

The *merengues* were second best in every department but Barça's forwards, Eto'o, Messi and especially Ronaldinho, were most obviously operating on another level. Eto'o opened the scoring after fifteen minutes and then in the second-half, just when Madrid entertained fantasies of having weathered the storm, Ronaldinho scored twice. Both goals involved the Brazilian gathering the ball deep on the left flank and embarking on a slalom dribble that left a couple of Madrid defenders for dead before cutting into the box to fire an unstoppable shot past Casillas.

The second time he did it, something quite remarkable happened: sections of the home crowd got to their feet and started to clap. A Barça player was being applauded by Real Madrid's fans.

This gesture wasn't quite unprecedented: two Barça players of the past had also provided moments of such skill that they had transcended team loyalties and inspired the *madridistas* to offer their recognition. Details of those two previous occasions only served to show the company Ronaldinho now kept: in February 1974, Johan Cruyff led Barça to a 5–0 win in the Bernabéu and had his efforts applauded; in June 1983, an audacious League Cup-winning dribbled goal from Diego Maradona roused the Madrid fans to magnanimous displays of appreciation. Ronaldinho had earned his place among the greats.

Ronaldinho appreciated the significance of the gesture. 'I'll never forget it. It was perfect. There are few moments in a player's career like that,' he said after the game.

Seeing their own fans clapping the opposition was the final act of humiliation for the Real Madrid players. Few people could remember such an emphatic victory from either side in the *clásico* and it was easy to read more into it than a mere league win. Real Madrid had followed a recruitment strategy led by marketing priorities rather than footballing ones, assembling a team of superstars that failed to gel into an all-star team. Barça, meanwhile, had signed talent first and let the results build their brand. Nobody, least of all the Madrid fans, was in any doubt about whose approach deserved to be applauded.

Barça captain Puyol was in respectful mood as he dismissed talk of a thrashing. 'The better team must prove itself over many games not just one. We came here confident but humble and ready to work hard for ninety minutes.' There had been little evidence of humility and hard work at the Bernabéu for quite some time. Ronaldinho was clapped by the Madrid fans for the goals he had just scored but also for his attitude and the attitude of a team carved in his image. The *galáctico* project was being rejected.

Indeed, Real Madrid's then manager, Vanderlei Luxemburgo, would never recover his reputation after that night and was dismissed shortly after. Recalling how the player's poor performances for Brazil at the Olympics had contributed to the coach's sacking as national team manager, witty observers suggested it was the second time Ronaldinho had cost Luxemburgo his job. President Pérez, meanwhile, lasted a few months longer but had resigned by February 2006.

The momentum that win in the *clásico* generated enabled Barça to go on a winning run to the year-end. By the last game of a successful 2005, a 2–0 home win over Celta Vigo, Ronaldinho had more prizes to parade: he had been named the Fifa World Player of the Year for the second successive season and had also picked up the *Ballon d'Or*.

For the Fifa award, he had earned 956 points in the voting (Frank Lampard had come second with 306, Eto'o third with 190) while for the *Ballon d'Or*, the Golden Ball Europe-wide prize organised by *France Football*, he had gathered 225 nominations (Lampard was second again with 148, Steven Gerrard third with 142). Generous as ever, he thanked his club and national-team colleagues as well as his family and God in his acceptance speeches for both awards. All this meant that, in 2005, Ronaldinho had been voted the best by journalists, managers, fans and players: the *Ballon d'Or* judging is conducted among pressmen; managers decide Fifa's award; he won both the *World Soccer* and *Onze* Player of the Year prizes, voted for by the readers of the respective and respected magazines; and he came top in a poll for FIFPRO, an organisation of 38,000 professional footballers.

Eto'o had come third in the Fifa prize but had not figured in the Golden Ball placings. The snub had riled him, it was claimed, and Eto'o felt undervalued and was fed up of living in Ronaldinho's shadow. In an interview with *France Football*, Eto'o was quoted as saying, 'I wasn't among the top three yet I have earned the same merits as the others. I'm not saying

I'm the best but, since I arrived at Barça, name one player who has done more than Samuel Eto'o? I've scored more goals than anyone.'

Barça's harmony on and off the pitch had been seen as an example for others to follow. For those observers who had become accustomed to the faultless success story emanating from the Nou Camp, tales of inner conflicts were too tasty to ignore. For their rivals, dressing-room unrest offered a last hope of derailing the Barça juggernaut. Much media stirring of the supposed jealousies ensued.

However, Eto'o, Ronaldinho and the rest of the *culé* clan proved too canny to react. Rijkaard's assistant, Henk ten Caat, took Eto'o and Ronaldinho to one side and made them see what people were trying to do: turn the players against each other and create trouble where there was none. Meanwhile, the pro-Barça press pointed out that Eto'o had also said, in the very same *France Football* interview, that 'Ronnie I love dearly and he is like my brother', and, on prize-winning, 'if he is happy, I am too and vice versa'.

Eto'o's name remained in the headlines as 2006 got under way, first because he scored the winner away at Espanyol, then because he had to leave the club to join Cameroon in the African Nations Cup. He finished as top scorer in the tournament and was reported as saying that if only he was called Eto'odinho then his talents would be much the better recognised. Again the troublemakers circled and Eto'o was forced to explain that he was making a point generally about how African and Brazilian footballers were perceived and not specifically comparing himself with Ronaldinho.

Barça fans worried how their team would cope with Eto'o's absence, as he had been averaging a goal per game. Yet Barça did cope and, after beating Alavés 2–0 at home, had completed eighteen consecutive victories: thirteen in *La Liga*, three in the Champions League and two in the Copa del Rey, a club record. They had also gone 24 games undefeated and stood a great chance of beating the club record of 27, set by that Cruyff team of 1974.

However, defeat came in the next match, a 4–2 cup reverse at Zaragoza. The second leg brought further misery: Ronaldinho was controversially dismissed just after half-time and was so upset with the decision that tears came to his eyes. Inconsolable, he had to be escorted from the field by Rijkaard. Ronaldinho had closed Zaragoza's Cani down in the centre circle and raised his boot to block a potential pass. To the referee it looked like he had gone into the tackle studs first, but it was a harsh dismissal. His suspension meant he would miss the home match with Atlético Madrid, where a win would bring a fifteenth successive league victory, an all-time record. It wasn't to be: Atlético won 3–1 and the run was over.

Attention now turned to Europe and the showdown football fans everywhere had been waiting for. Chelsea and Barça had been paired once again in the second round of the Champions League: the *blaugrana* were being offered a chance to avenge the defeat of the previous year.

The usual shenanigans from Mourinho served to spice up the hype but it was a more street-smart Barça who arrived in London this time round. When they arrived to train on the Stamford Bridge pitch they saw the ground staff watering the turf, despite the day's rain. A heavy surface could only hamper Barça's more free-flowing style but the Barça camp refused to be riled and allowed themselves a wry smile instead. Ronaldinho pretended to surf in the wash.

In the match itself, Chelsea invited Barça to attack them but the Catalans were cautious and a fascinating contest remained deadlocked and evenly balanced until 36 minutes in. The impressive Messi then flicked the ball past Asier Del Horno in the corner. The Basque's hot-headed lunge would have hacked Messi down had the Argentine not managed to jump above the studs, but he was clattered to the ground all the same and Del Horno was given his marching orders.

After a smart cut-back from Oleguer, Ronaldinho had a shot saved well from Cech on the half-hour. Then in the second half a Lampard free-kick forced an own goal from Motta and gave Chelsea a surprise lead. A similar incident saw John Terry put through his own net, a Ronaldinho free-kick flicking off the Chelsea captain's head, and it then became a question of whether Chelsea could hold on. They couldn't: a Márquez cross was met by a rampaging Eto'o header and Barça won 2–1.

Mourinho, of course, ranted and raved about the injustice of it all: Messi had made a meal of the challenge, he claimed, conveniently overlooking Del Horno's own play-acting. But Barça had grown tired of his act and kept their counsel. Mourinho's comments were designed to protect the confidence of his players, to prevent them from realising they were actually mortal, and deserved to be recognised as spin and nothing else. If Mourinho had become delusional enough to believe his own hype then that was his problem; such was the attitude of Rijkaard and the rest of the Barça brigade for the return leg.

Barcelona played a controlled game: Chelsea tried to tempt them into overcommitting going forward but the Catalans refused to take the bait. Barça stroked the ball around and gave the impression they were looking to attack, but really they were defending their first-leg lead by keeping the ball away from their opponents. The match seemed destined for deadlock until Ronaldinho burst into life. He dribbled through Carvalho and Lampard, pushed Terry aside and slammed in a shot to the bottom corner. The move was full of skill but, in bouncing off Terry's challenge, Ronaldinho betrayed one of his best-kept secrets: his game may be all about outrageous skill but he is as strong as anyone when he needs to be.

A late Lampard penalty levelled the scoreline but it was a consolation prize for the Londoners as they were knocked out. The sides had been evenly matched but Chelsea had no answer to Ronaldinho: when two very good teams clash then the difference between winning and losing is always going to be marginal; the unknown quality (or quality of the unknown) of Ronaldinho can tip the balance. Mourinho's chicanery had defeated Barça the previous season but they had learned their lesson and now looked on his supposed mind games (he brought his team out three minutes late after half-time again, having been fined for the same thing the previous year) with bemusement. Barça were through and would play Benfica in the quarterfinals.

Meanwhile, Barça's league campaign continued to tick over, although a game away at Zaragoza brought controversy. Eto'o was subjected to a torrent of racial abuse from the home crowd and the striker resolved to abandon the pitch. Ronaldinho was one of several players from both teams who, along with Rijkaard and the referee, successfully persuaded Eto'o to play on. They argued that leaving the field would be a victory for the bigots, but Ronaldinho was among many Barça players who later said that, had Eto'o carried out his threat, they would have followed him to the dressing room in solidarity. When play restarted, Barça won a penalty from the subsequent corner, which Ronaldinho converted before running to embrace the Cameroon. Barça went on to register a 2–0 victory and Ronaldinho dedicated his goal jointly to Eto'o and João, Ronaldinho's son, who was celebrating his first birthday.

For Ronaldinho's own birthday the following month, Getafe visited the Nou Camp and, though the Brazilian couldn't mark the occasion with a goal, Barça did win 3–1. The *culé* faithful paid a special tribute to their idol: with ten minutes to go, a chorus of 'Happy birthday to you' echoed down from the stands and brought a smile even bigger than usual to Ronaldinho's face.

Rijkaard rested Ronaldinho against Málaga in order to have the Brazilian fresh for the first leg of the Benfica tie. Ronaldinho did indeed look perky against the Portuguese side, but Barça couldn't convert their obvious superiority into goals and took a 0–0 draw back to Catalonia. Barça hit the post twice and spurned several other chances but were ultimately thankful that the referee interpreted Motta's handball in the penalty area as unintentional. Everything would come down to the second leg but, in the meantime, there was the little matter of the season's second *clásico*, this one in the Nou Camp.

Roberto Carlos did his best to ensure it would be Barça's day by giving away an early penalty, which Ronaldinho dispatched, and getting himself sent off. Yet Barça couldn't find another way past Casillas, who was in an inspired mood, and Ronaldinho couldn't recapture the form he had shown in the Bernabéu earlier in the season. Ronaldo equalised before half-time and 1–1 it remained. The result was a slight anticlimax if no disaster, but it did mean that, despite a flood of chances, Barça had only scored once in three matches and that from the penalty spot. There were nervous suggestions that their cutting edge had been lost.

At home to Benfica, Barça faced another keeper in sensational form. Marcelo Moretto saved a penalty from Ronaldinho in the fourth minute and made a string of fine saves to make the match a lot tenser than it should have been. Barça eventually ran out 2–0 winners but were really made to suffer. Ronaldinho made amends for his missed spot-kick when he dispatched an Eto'o cross in the nineteenth minute, his wild celebrations betraying his relief. Yet Barça were unable to add to their lead, meaning a strike for Benfica would prove critical and take the Lisbon outfit through on the away goal. Eto'o finally made the victory safe with a score in the dying minutes.

The semifinal would be against AC Milan in what many commentators were hailing as a clash of the heavyweights, a final in itself. Comparisons with the Chelsea game were inevitable given there was little to chose between the two teams on paper: that 'little' was Ronaldinho and the pre-match media attention fell upon the Brazilian. Reports emerged that Milan coach Carlo Ancelotti had decorated the players' room at the club's training ground with pictures of Ronaldinho to try to motivate and focus his players. There were suggestions of special plans and tactics to stop him.

The atmosphere in the San Siro was incredible. Ronaldinho and his Barça colleagues had been there the previous month to play a friendly for Dimitri Albertini's testimonial and Ronaldinho had been cheered by the locals on that occasion. It was an altogether more partisan crowd this time around and Ronaldinho could be seen before the game affording a few moments to himself, looking up to the stands, taking it all in: these were the sort of occasions he lived for. The game itself lived up to its billing and was a tense if fascinating contest: two teams on top of their games trying to outwit one another. They looked to be cancelling each other out until, just ahead of the hour mark, one inspired moment from Ronaldinho opened the door. An exquisite chipped pass found Giuly making an angled run and the French forward's finish was worthy of the Brazilian's delivery. It proved the only goal of the game.

Ronaldinho had been quiet generally, well marked and monitored. Renato Gattuso was always quick to aid Ronaldinho's shadow, Jaap Stam, whenever the ball went the Brazilian's way. Yet Ronaldinho made the few moments when he did find space count. Before the goal, he left Gattuso for dead with a marvellous dribble, helping Barça begin to gain the psychological initiative. A similar moment of trickery occurred before his assist and later he wriggled free and flashed a shot against the post. On this occasion, the Milanese felt Ronaldinho should have put the ball out of play instead of running on and shooting, as Gattuso had collapsed to the ground 'injured', so the Brazilian left the field to a chorus of boos. The Italian press, however, were deeply impressed. *Il Corriera della Sera* summed up the general verdict with its headline: 'In half a metre of space, with half a second of time, Ronaldinho put Barça half way to the final'.

The return leg at the Nou Camp proved equally balanced and evenly contested. Barça had the upper hand but couldn't come up with a goal and in the end were grateful that a Shevchenko strike was ruled out for a foul few people saw. Stam played Ronaldinho even tighter but in the latter stages Milan threw caution to the wind and brought on Rui Costa to chase the goal they needed. Rijkaard made his own tactical switch: Larsson entered the fray to harry on the right and Eto'o switched to do the same on the left with Ronaldinho moved inside, straight down the middle. Thus Milan's full-backs were pinned back while Ronaldinho's potential for mischief at the core of their back line meant the Italian midfield couldn't afford to completely abandon their defensive duties.

The game ended 0–0 and Barça were in the Champions League final for the first time since 1994. Ronaldinho was the last of the players to leave the pitch, running around twirling a shirt over his head and sporting an ear-to-ear grin. Barça hadn't been brilliant and had even ridden their luck but they deserved to be in the final. They would play Arsenal in Paris and try to win the continent's top prize for only the second time in the club's history.

Although the Champions League had become Barça's priority, *La Liga* form continued to be good, this despite Ronaldinho missing four games through rest and recuperation after he picked up a knock versus Benfica. He was back for a home fixture with Cádiz and scored the only goal of a 1–0 win.

The next league appointment, the third last of the campaign, was at Celta Vigo. On the same day, Valencia, Barça's nearest challengers, were playing Mallorca and needed to win to keep their title hopes alive. The game in Vigo kicked off an hour after Valencia's and, as Barça came off the field at half-time, they learned that Mallorca had won 2–1. Barça were already champions. The Barça camp restrained themselves until they reached the privacy of the dressing room where a mini celebration ensued. There was no bubbly – they still had 45 minutes to play – but the players sprayed bottles of water around in traditional fashion. When they went out for the second half, the Celta fans clapped the champions on to the pitch and several of their players shook hands with their opposite numbers: Celta's Brazilian Fernando Baiano was the first to congratulate Ronaldinho.

Somehow keeping their focus, Eto'o scored ten minutes later to ensure that Barça would be crowned champions in style. Ronaldinho was withdrawn shortly thereafter, a reminder from Rijkaard to the team that the season's job was only half done – the Champions League awaited. For once, Ronaldinho put up no protest but instead, along with Motta, his usual partner in crime, dedicated himself to building the party feeling from the bench. At full-time, the two of them charged on to the pitch to jump on Larsson and other players soon joined the pile-on. The cava then flowed in the dressing room but they couldn't afford to truly indulge as the local airport closed soon and they had a plane home to catch. On the coach to the airport there was more cava and takeaway pizza, while the flight itself was full of further merriment, Ronaldinho displaying all the excitement of a little boy as, sat alongside Motta and Deco, they made music with anything to hand. When they arrived back at Barcelona airport, thousands of fans were there to greet them.

A few days later and Barça were at home to city rivals Espanyol, an appropriate time for players and supporters to celebrate the title together. The day went perfectly to plan: Barça did the occasion justice and recorded a comfortable 2–0 victory, Ronaldinho bagging the second, while not overexerting themselves ahead of the Champions League final. Rijkaard felt it a little inappropriate (with the main prize still to play for) but the players insisted upon a victory parade and the next day a trio of open-top buses made their way through the Barcelona streets and some 1.2 million people came along to cheer them by. One of the local papers had given out large yellow placards in the shape of Ronaldinho's 'Hang Loose' sign, which many fans waved by the roadside. Ronaldinho spent most of the journey at the front of the players' bus singing and making use of the various props fans threw his way: a tambourine, a Brazil flag, a jester's hat, an Afro wig.

Paris, Arsenal and a date with destiny were soon upon Ronaldinho and the rest of the team. Barça had only previously won Europe's premier tournament once, at Wembley in 1992, something of an underachievement given the club's size and stature.

The final, at least in Catalonia, was being billed as the fun-loving Ronaldinho versus the seriously determined Henry. The players did their best to dismiss such hype and reminded everyone that it was a team game, quite apart from the fact that such caricatures were far too simplistic. Below the surface, the two stars' temperaments were very similar. Nevertheless, everyone realised that the influence of both would be vital. The two players were friends and occasionally spoke to one another by phone, though that week Ronaldinho said contact had been reduced to the odd text.

Ronaldinho had some new kit made by Nike especially for the final. His usual white and gold boots would be detailed with embroidery reading

'Barça v Arsenal, Paris, 17 May 2006' on the outstep and the names of his siblings 'Roberto' and 'Deise' on the instep. A new pair of shin-pads, designed by Ronaldinho himself, featured the messages *Paixão* (Passion) on one and *Alegria* (Happiness) on the other. Before kickoff, Ronaldinho made a quick phone call to his mother in the stand before performing his customary solitary and ball-orientated warm-up (while the rest of the players perform a co-ordinated team routine, Ronaldinho is free to prepare just as he sees fit and never so much as jogs two paces without touching the ball). Back in the changing room, he performed his equally traditional one-on-one huddle with each team-mate before bringing up the rear as they entered the playing arena.

The match itself was full of drama. Arsenal started the brightest and should possibly have scored through Henry early on. Ronaldinho began in an unusual role, playing straight down the middle with Eto'o occupying the Brazilian's usual stomping ground towards the left touchline. Although it had been used fleetingly before, notably in the first leg of the Super Cup versus Betis when Ronaldinho was only half-fit and again at the end of the second leg of the Milan tie when Barça were merely holding on, the tactic remained unfamiliar and seemed wasteful of both Ronaldinho's and Eto'o's best talents. Only when they reverted to their usual roles, just before half-time, did they look more comfortable: straightaway Ronaldinho fed Eto'o, who swivelled and shot against the post.

However, it has to be acknowledged that the strategy did prove critical to the game. The idea was that Ronaldinho could get hold of the ball in the middle of the pitch and use his vision to feed the speedy Eto'o and Giuly making angled runs from the flanks. With one such delightful pass, Ronaldinho put Eto'o in clean on goal. As the Cameroon rounded Arsenal's keeper, Jens Lehmann, he was crudely brought down outside the penalty area by the German. The ball ran for Giuly to roll into the now open net but, fatefully, the referee had already whistled for the foul. The goal was disallowed, the goalkeeper sent off and Barça awarded a free-kick. Everyone, from both the Arsenal and Barcelona camps to the millions of neutral fans watching the game globally, would have preferred the goal to have stood and Arsenal remain at full strength. Yet the referee, Terje Hauge of Norway, applied the letter of the law instead of a liberal dose of common sense and the match make-up was altered irrevocably. Sharper observers noted that Hauge had also been the official who gave Del Horno his marching orders for Chelsea. Both decisions could be argued against, but neither was actually wrong.

A Barça onslaught was expected but, far from rolling over, Arsenal drew strength in adversity and even went ahead. After a blatant dive from Emmanuel Eboué, himself already on a booking and so risking another sending off had the referee not been fooled, the Londoners were awarded a free-kick. Henry whipped it in for Sol Campbell to meet with a powerful header to give Arsenal the lead. The Gunners then battled and defended their lead with incredible will and tenacity: there looked no way through for Barça. Indeed, Arsenal had the next clear scoring chance when Henry was put clean through by Alexander Hleb, but the Frenchman spurned the opportunity.

Ultimately, a substitution swung the game back in Barça's favour: Larsson's entrance would prove to be decisive. With a quarter of an hour to go, the Swede laid a ball into the path of the galloping Eto'o to fire home the equaliser (Arsenal would later claim offside which, though technically correct, was so marginal as to make any serious gripe ridiculous) and then provided a similar assist for full-back Belletti to bang in the winner with just nine minutes left on the clock.

Arsenal would bemoan the officiating – one of the original linesmen had to be replaced after being photographed in a Barça shirt before the game – but, though Hauge did have a poor night, he was bad for both teams. If either side truly had cause for complaint it was Barça; they scored a goal that was disallowed when advantage should have been played, then conceded one from a free-kick that never was.

Ronaldinho, like Barça generally, was not at his best. Such matches are unlike all the other games in the tournament. They are one-offs and just have to be won, whatever it takes; courage and determination become components as key as skill and application. Indeed, if Arsenal had held on to win, their achievement would have been recalled as one of bloody-mined resolve. Equally, Barça's triumph was one of strength of character. They kept going, kept believing, kept striving and were ultimately rewarded for their faith. Ronaldinho's match could be described in much the same way. Things weren't coming off for him and the position he was being played in didn't suit him but he never stopped looking for the ball, even after a few horrible miscues. He tried to assume the role of responsibility when the going got tough and those rare moments of fallibility were perhaps the most obvious indications that he was simply trying too hard.

He was usually double-marked, partly because Rijkaard had stuck him in between the two central defenders, but even after Larsson's introduction, which allowed Ronaldinho to drop into space deeper and see more of the ball, Arsenal were quick to commit a tandem taskforce. And this was ultimately his winning contribution: he may not have been directly involved in the goals but his presence and constant movement helped create the spaces, helped tire the opponents' legs. In this respect, his killer pass that reduced Arsenal to ten men perhaps did definitively determine the game. As for his overall contribution to their Champions League victory, he had been utterly decisive in several games, most notably versus Chelsea and Milan, and finished as his team's top scorer in the competition, second overall behind Shevchenko: Ronaldinho bagged seven, the Ukrainian nine.

Always before a final, Ronaldinho tries to play down his own importance and tells everyone that, as long as his team wins, he doesn't care whether he scores or contributes himself. The way in which he celebrated Eto'o's equaliser and Belletti's winner, particularly the goal from his Brazilian colleague and friend, showed this to be completely true. He had even foretold Belletti's goal, telling the full-back before the game that he would score that day. At full-time, Ronaldinho celebrated with Belletti by giving him a big kiss. Captain Puyol lifted the cup itself, but Ronaldinho was right by his side, his face flushed with exhilaration.

FC Barcelona had hired the function room of a hotel in Bois de Boulogne for the official celebration, where there were around a thousand guests. Ronaldinho spent most of the evening tirelessly posing for photos and signing autographs. Dancing went on to 4 a.m. while the likes of Rijkaard remained chatting until 6 a.m., but Ronaldinho headed off much earlier: with Motta, Messi, Rodri and Rubén in tow, he proceeded to the Montecristo on the Champs-Élysées, his favourite haunt during his PSG days. Back then, he had got to know the owners well and had celebrated his *Ballon d'Or* presentation there the previous December. They had promised to keep a VIP area saved for him if Barça won the Champions League and so the players partied there until Ronaldinho's presence caused too much of a commotion and they decided to move on to the Galerie Les Arcades nearby. Márquez, Maxi López and Giuly were already there. At some point, Ronaldinho rendezvoused with his then new flame, Alexandra Parresant, before heading to the team hotel in the early hours.

Back in Barcelona, the official celebration began with an open-top parade through the streets of the Condal City. A *Trio Elétrico*, the giant carnival truck used in Brazil for such celebrations, wound its way through the streets showing off the cup. The players were all wearing T-shirts which proclaimed: '*Més que un club, Campions de Lliga i d'Europa*' – 'More than just a club, League and European Champions'. Ronaldinho, as per usual, stationed himself at the front of the truck next to the drums. He and Belletti kept the beat going throughout, pausing only to lift the trophy and offer it to the fans.

Once the caravan arrived at the Nou Camp, the players witnessed a theatre and firework spectacle performed by Catalan circus troop Els Comediants before the presentations got under way. All the players were to take to the microphone but after Rijkaard and the three club captains – Puyol, Xavi and Ronaldinho – had said their piece a sound fault cut the speeches short.

'I just want to celebrate with you all. Enjoy the party and thank you for the support you have given us this season,' said Ronaldinho. 'We are living the moment I always dreamed about since the day I arrived in Barcelona.'

WORLD CUP 2006

Qualification for the 2006 World Cup proved a lot more straightforward for Brazil than it had in 2002. After eventually seeing his team crowned champions in that tournament, Luiz Felipe Scolari moved on to new challenges, becoming the manager of Portugal (and flirting with England), and Carlos Alberto Parreira was given the responsibility of steering the *Seleção* through the qualifiers for Germany. Appointing Parreira meant banking on experience: he had guided Brazil to victory in the 1994 World Cup, *o tetra*, their fourth.

The *Seleção* only lost twice in finishing top of the South American qualifying group, with Ronaldinho playing twelve of the eighteen qualifying games. His stand-out performances came in bagging the goal in a 1–0 win over Ecuador and scoring the first two of a 4–1 victory versus Paraguay in Porto Alegre. Despite his solid contribution, he never quite hit his Barcelona heights for Brazil and there were those who still complained that '*joga mais no Barça do que na Seleção*', that he gave much more for Barça than for the *Seleção*.

Brazil were the reigning champions and it was the first time the reigning champions had been forced to qualify: previously, the cup-holders had automatically taken their place at the finals. Yet qualification had gone well and so the new rules seemed like a good thing: the team had been allowed time to gel and would not arrive to defend the trophy rusty of competitive football, as used to be the case.

In fact, there was seemingly nothing to stop Brazil from retaining their title. The core of the team that had won in Japan was still present and still playing for Europe's top clubs, so there was no shortage of experience or know-how where winning a World Cup was concerned. The manager had also been there and done it all before. What's more, in the four years that had elapsed since victory in Japan, Ronaldinho, who had played no more than a supporting role there, had developed into the two-times World Player of the Year. He had just won the Champions League with Barcelona and had been in unstoppable form all season. Brazil were logically the overwhelming pre-tournament favourites. What could possibly stop them?

A few killjoys in the Brazilian press pointed out that the favourites never win, and that, in terms of talent, the 2006 vintage might compare favourably with that of 1982 – Zico, Sócrates, Falcão et al. – but look what happened to them, they were dumped out at the quarterfinal stage. Other commentators noted that it was extremely rare for a non-European country to win in Europe (only Brazil had ever managed it, in Sweden in 1958) while the cynics suggested that, as Brazil had won wearing Nike last time round, an Adidas team was sure to win in Germany as part of a corrupt capitalist conspiracy. More analytical critics pointed out that the two fullbacks, Cafu and Roberto Carlos, were getting on a bit (35 and 33 respectively) and that goalkeeper Dida's form had been indifferent.

Such talk was generally the media doing its duty, going through the motions of considering all the angles and possible outcomes. Most Brazilians strongly believed that Brazil would win their sixth World Cup, *a hexa*.

Switzerland was decided upon as the *Seleção's* pre-tournament warm-up base, an excellent choice as far as Ronaldinho was concerned given that he was familiar with the country from his visits when his brother used to play there. The small town of Weggis was picked out as a calm and tranquil resting place for the team to start its preparations, but calm and tranquil it would not remain. Having a usual population of 3,000, over 130,000 people descended upon the community to get a glimpse of the boys from Brazil. Getting a glimpse was no chance encounter either: 5,000 spectator tickets – at €14 (£9.50) a pop – were put on sale to watch training sessions and every day they sold out – the circus was in town and nobody wanted to miss the show. Many of the players even obliged with their own acrobatic tricks: Ronaldinho performed a forward-roll with the ball stuck to his foot. At the end of one session, he rested on a training mat: a female fan jumped the barriers, ran from the spectator area on to the pitch and threw herself on top of him, telling the player how much she loved him. There were smiles and jokes all round until she was led away by security.

In this climate, it was difficult to see how much serious preparation was getting done. Brazil did win two friendly games, 8–0 versus Swiss club Lucerne and 4–0 against New Zealand, neither featuring a Ronaldinho strike, but Parreira complained about the training arrangements and said it was hard for the players to concentrate in such an environment. He complained briefly until, presumably, his employers at the CBF told him to keep his counsel and not spoil their money-making scheme.

As the team left the hotel on their final day in Weggis, the hysteria of the assembled crowd seemed more in tune with groupies following a rock band than fans cheering a football team. Ronaldinho was the lead singer, easily the favourite of the masses. Yet he was eclipsed by Ronaldo in terms of being the most desirable, if absent, bedfellow. The Park Hotel Weggis had set up an online auction offering punters the chance to bid to sleep in the beds of several Brazilian players on the night after their departure. Ronaldinho's room had been attracting the big money all week but Ronaldo proved that, though he had perhaps lost some of the old magic on the pitch, he retained his international playboy charm off it and he pipped the young pretender at the post. The winning bid to sleep in Ronaldo's bed was for 1,010 Swiss francs (£435) while Ronaldinho only managed to attract a top offer of 850CHF (£365). The other vacated rooms available were Kaká's, Adriano's and Roberto Carlos', but they went for small change in comparison.

Once in Germany, Brazil were stationed in Koenigstein, a pretty little town in the countryside near Frankfurt. Parreira had requested that players travel without family and friends but, although there were none at the team hotel, most of the Brazilian squad had relatives or partners in Germany staying close by, Ronaldinho included. At the hotel, the players' favourite leisure pursuit was the trusty Playstation, with competitions in constant progress. Émerson proved the man to beat: always playing as Arsenal, he had defeated all-comers until Ronaldinho finally got the upper hand, the score being 2–1 appropriately enough, although Ronaldinho played as Valencia rather than Barça.

Parreira met the relative peace and quiet at training in Koenigstein with relief. Only 800 spectators were permitted each day, though they did have to perform a one-off open session to 25,000 in nearby Offenbach. In Weggis, Ronaldinho had trained slightly differently to the other players, having had a particularly long season, and in Koenigstein he had frequent strategic conversations with the coach about how and where he would play. The aim was to make sure Ronaldinho took the field with the same enthusiasm as he did for his club and put those cries of 'joga mais no Barça do que na Seleção' to rest once and for all. Ronaldinho also practised a lot of free-kicks with the new World Cup ball, the Adidas Teamgeist, and noted its extra curve.

Parreira had announced his starting eleven several months before the tournament started, but there was some speculation that Ronaldo wasn't fit. He seemed to be carrying a few too many extra pounds and Lula, the Brazilian president, even asked Parreira (in a teleconference between arguably Brazil's two most powerful figures) whether all this talk of the Real Madrid man being overweight was true. Yet as the teams lined up for the opening match against Croatia, Ronaldo took his place alongside Adriano up front with Ronaldinho and Kaká tucked in just behind: the so-called magic square.

The *Seleção* started brightly but faded and Croatia were soon matching them. Brazil were looking all at sea but on the stroke of half-time, Kaká shot from the edge of the box into the top corner and the South Americans were ahead. Brazil were uninspiring in the second half too, and Croatia carved out a few half-chances to equalise. Only once Robinho entered the fray did play improve, but 1–0 it remained.

Brazil had won their opening game again, something they had managed at every World Cup since 1982, and had set a new national record of eight consecutive victories in the tournament to boot. However, it had been a more laboured triumph than had been expected and so the inquest back home began. A lack of movement was cited as Brazil's principal weakness. Ronaldo's lumbering certainly vindicated those fatness rumours, Adriano was just as ponderous and Ronaldinho and Kaká had lacked fluidity also; the magic square was far too rigid. The game largely passed Ronaldinho by: he followed in a Roberto Carlos free-kick with a shot that was saved, hit a free-kick into the wall himself and had a header parried in the second half, but that was about it. He did nothing wrong per se, indeed showed the nice odd touch, but more had been expected.

Ronaldinho was one of several players who sneaked away from the stadium without facing the media. He eventually said on his online blog, tellingly: 'We did everything Professor Parreira asked of us.' As the Brazilian press continued to analyse just why Brazil had failed to play their usual beautiful game, the *Joga Bonito* of the Nike advertisement campaign, the coach's tactics came under increasing scrutiny. Ronaldinho was being asked to play in the classic *meia* position, a midfield role, and seemed to have been overburdened with defensive duties. The word 'bait' was bandied about: he was to attract the defensive attention and pull markers in his direction, thus opening spaces for others. It was a sound enough tactic but did seem dreadfully wasteful of the talents of the best player in the world.

Ronaldinho was in resigned if philosophical mood as he spoke to the press at the team hotel after training. 'It's different (to at Barça) but I've played it before at Grêmio and PSG,' he stated. 'I will come from the middle and take the game to the side and if two or three come to mark me, it opens space for team-mates. At Barça I play further forward, with more freedom.' He also went on to say that Parreira had spoken with him a great deal about his responsibilities when the opposition had the ball, something he didn't have to bother with at Barça.

The press conference itself proved chaotic. So many people wished to attend that it had to be split into two sections, the first for Brazilian media, the second for foreigners. At the end of the second session, in which Ronaldinho answered questions in Portuguese, Spanish and French, several people surged towards where he was seated to try and get his autograph or take a photo. A table was unsettled resulting in cups smashing to the floor, bottles of water and microphones being toppled and a portable camera light falling on Ronaldinho. The player kept his cool but had to be escorted from the room.

For those who fondly recalled Scolari's fable of the deaf lion at the 2002 World Cup, Parreira had a *Jungle Book* parable of his own for the *Seleção*'s clash with Australia. 'The game reminds me of the story of the crocodile and the bear,' he explained to the gathered press throng. 'Who would win a fight between them? It depends. If the fight were in water, the crocodile would win. If it were on terra firma then it would be the bear. The same can be said of this match.' The suggestion seemed to be that whoever imposed their own style on the game, the samba-skilled Brazilians or the physical Socceroos, would triumph.

In the end, Brazil won 2–0 but what exactly this meant was unclear: they had lacked bite and for long spells had been unbearable to watch. After an uneventful first period, Ronaldinho fed Ronaldo who laid it off to Adriano to fire home early in the second half. The weight of expectation lifted, most observers expected Brazil to turn on the style, but instead they stopped looking for the ball and sat back, seemingly content to counterattack. Australia strove in vain for an equaliser and conceded again in the last minute as Brazil's substitute Fred pounced for a tap-in.

Ronaldinho disappointed once more. Australia were mean in defence and both Ronaldinho and Kaká were man-marked as soon as they set foot in their opponents' half. The Gaúcho provided one good dribble, jinking past two defenders before being easily dispossessed by the third, but the lasting impression was of him preparing to take on Craig Moore one-on-one but treading on the ball instead.

Afterwards, Ronaldinho admitted to a sense of frustration. 'We get annoyed too. Teams that play against us put many men behind the ball but we just have to be patient and wait for the right moment to strike,' he said, before adding, 'My role is to help my colleagues with the midfield marking. So long as the forwards are scoring I don't mind.' His smile lacked its usual sparkle and observers weren't so sure.

There had been much talk during the World Cup about the relative importance of substance and style, and Brazil had won. They were through to the next round and would very likely top the group. In fact, the performance could even be described as a slight improvement from their first outing. Yet nobody was being fooled: Brazil had been poor again and were certainly not in World Cup-winning form. General movement had again been lame and the magic square was proving to be something of a stumbling block. The *Seleção* had been subjected to sporadic boos from their own fans in the stadium and the media were heavily critical back home too.

Part of the problem was a lack of respect, naivety even, on Brazil's part. Australia might not be a country of great footballing pedigree but they had made giant strides in recent times and boasted a squad almost entirely based in Europe. They also had an astute coach in Dutchman Guus Hiddink – as well as forming a very organised defence, Hiddink packed the midfield and had his charges attack via the flanks, thus restricting much of Brazil's potential movement – and would prove themselves no pushovers by qualifying for the next round and going the distance with Italy. No matter, in Brazil they were unknown and seen as an easy touch, so the unconvincing victory was deemed something of a failure.

Japan were a much more serious proposition from a Brazilian perspective. This was not because of any in-depth knowledge of the J League or even a tremendous Japanese record against the *verde-amarelo*, it was purely and simply because they were managed by Zico. However, with qualification already assured, Parreira decided to rest a few of his first-teamers. Cafu, Roberto Carlos, Émerson, Zé Roberto and Adriano all dropped to the bench and Brazil produced their best performance so far and notched up a 4–1 win. Japan actually took the lead after half an hour, the first goal Brazil had conceded at a World Cup since Michael Owen's strike back in Japan itself, but Brazil reacted with goals from Ronaldo, Juninho, Gilberto and then Ronaldo again.

With Adriano absent from the attack, the magic square had been disbanded. Ronaldo led the line alone and found more space while Ronaldinho, Kaká and Robinho floated behind him, interchanging position and taking turns to support the big man up front. It all meant Ronaldinho was more involved and often operating closer to the danger zone. A good one-two move with Ronaldo resulted in the Real Madrid player shooting wide, but Ronaldinho's cross to Cicinho was headed back for Ronaldo's first goal and a delightful pass from the Gaúcho's boot put Gilberto in for the third. Job done, Ronaldinho made way for Ricardinho with twenty minutes to go.

There had been a marked improvement in Brazil's play but the sceptics pointed out that Japan had been chasing a victory: they needed to win by a two-goal margin to progress to the next round and played a much more open game than had Croatia and Australia. Brazil may have attacked with greater verve but Japan had also defended loosely.

Brazil would face Ghana in the second round and the *Seleção* anticipated a physical match dominated by tight marking. Yet Brazil had never before lost to an African side at the World Cup, in fact never even conceded a goal, and so the players were full of confidence when they arrived at the Dortmund stadium to a self-produced cacophony of drumbeats.

Parreira recalled those players rested from the previous match and began with the same starting eleven as in the first two group games, meaning the magic square was back intact. Ronaldinho remained the only member of the quartet yet to have scored. Poor positional play from Ghana's centre-halfs allowed Ronaldo to sneak in on goal after five minutes and open the scoring. As had become a familiar routine, Brazil then sat back and allowed their opponents to dominate possession, and the Black Stars would have equalised but for a fine save from Dida. Moments later, just before half-time, Brazil counterattacked and benefited from a dubious offside interpretation on behalf of the linesman to score through Adriano. The second half followed a similar pattern but Ghana lacked a cutting edge going forward – Michael Essien, their best player, was suspended – and eventually tired. Brazil scored a late third as Zé Roberto burst clear and even had several chances to add a fourth at the death.

Brazil had won 3–0 and their exemplary record against African teams was intact. Indeed, it had been a day for records: Ronaldo scored his fifteenth World Cup goal to surpass Gerd Müller as the competition's all-time top scorer; Adriano scored the *Seleção*'s two-hundredth tournament goal, Brazil being the first team to reach such a milestone; Cafu made his nineteenth World Cup appearance, a national record, and in doing so won his sixteenth game, a world record.

Yet such landmarks masked another woeful performance. Brazil had won at a canter and had been extremely efficient, ruthlessly making Ghana pay for their defensive disorganisation, but they had not imposed themselves and had benefited from some very favourable officiating. Ghana's coach, Serbian Ratomir Dujkovic, was sent off at half-time for approaching the referee and would later complain that Brazil were not only unbeatable but untouchable. He had a valid point. Every first-half Ghanaian challenge resulted in a foul, most in a booking, and it became only a matter of time until they would be reduced to ten men: after 36 minutes of the second half, this duly occurred, Gyan Asamoah getting his marching orders. Against a tired and resigned ten men, Brazil notched up an extra goal and left a good lasting impression with a flurry of late chances, but before all that their fans had booed them, so wanting was their play.

As for Ronaldinho, he had been lacklustre once more. In the first minute he fed Ronaldo only for a flag to be raised in error and he also put Roberto Carlos in for a shot later on. Generally though, the game passed him by.

When Adriano made way for Juninho on 61 minutes, Ronaldinho was pushed further forward on the left. With Kaká doing likewise on the right and Ronaldo alone down the middle, it was Barcelona's formation. Still Ronaldinho failed to make an impression and his body language told of a player frustrated and unsure of himself.

He did lay off one neat flick to Kaká, which the Milan man was unable to gather, and he produced the odd neat pass or mini-dribble, but in drawing attention to such moments commentators were merely highlighting how few and far between they had been. Everyone wanted to see Ronaldinho on top of his game and it was tempting to elevate the importance of tiny contributions, to try to see what one wanted to see. Yet the statistics didn't lie: Ronaldinho touched the ball just 42 times against Ghana, down from his 66 average in the group games. Although he had clearly not been hiding, with Fifa counting him the third player overall in touches of the ball in the tournament, he kept things simple, rarely trying anything other than a short pass. As an indication of his unwillingness to dribble, he had been fouled just six times in four games, while Kaká had provoked fifteen. Of Brazil's ten goals, Ronaldinho had been involved in just two and had scored none himself. In fact, a whole calendar year had passed since Ronaldinho had last scored a goal in the *canarinha*, versus Argentina on 29 June 2005.

Ronaldinho said he wasn't concerned, that a goal would come, and stuck to his line about playing a different role. 'I have to pass one, two, three, four players and even then I'm still far from goal,' he insisted. But he had been presented with thirty minutes of complete freedom against a wounded opponent in Ghana and still failed to shine. 'I alternated good moments with bad moments,' he confessed, adding, 'When I lose important balls, of course I'm disappointed.'

Parreira was critical of Ronaldinho and Kaká, saying they both gave the ball away too easily. 'We are making a fundamental confusion which happens in any sport,' said the coach. 'We are confusing speed with haste.'

There was no suggestion of it either from media or fans, but any other player experiencing such a slump as Ronaldinho's would have been facing the axe for the next game against France. Ricardinho had come on in the 37th minute versus Ghana, given one assist and set up three other direct shots, but there was no serious campaign for him to replace Ronaldinho. Instead, a new formation was called for and when Parreira did make changes, with Gilberto Silva in for Émerson and Juninho for Adriano, they were the alterations the public had demanded back in Brazil. Though the line-up had never been tested before, the new formation placed Ronaldinho up front with Ronaldo and it was hoped the extra space and proximity to goal might finally bring the best out of him.

For the first ten minutes, Brazil looked sprightly, guarded possession and camped out in France's half. Yet soon, Zinadine Zidane began to impose himself, France were winning the midfield battle and Brazil looked static again. The score remained goalless at half-time but, ten minutes after the break, Zidane swung a free-kick in from the right and Thierry Henry sauntered in unmarked at the back post to side-foot home. Brazil tried to react but France were canny, experienced opponents and allowed them possession only in areas where they could cause no harm. Zidane was running the show, keeping the ball circulating, and Ronaldinho, Ronaldo and Kaká continued their struggles to get involved. Adriano came on for Juninho and the magic quartet was reunited, charged with rescuing the game and with it Brazil's World Cup challenge – in the end, their efforts amounted to the square root of nothing.

With just two minutes left on the clock, Ronaldinho was presented with a free-kick on the edge of the box. This was his chance to make an impression, to stamp his authority on the tournament and kick-start his World Cup. He struck the ball well enough but it fizzed just over.

France held on to win 1–0 and extend their reputation as Brazil's bogey team, if such a magisterial side can be called such a thing: *Les Bleus* had now beaten the *verde-amarelos* three out of the four times they had met at the World Cup and in doing so had become the only team to have knocked Brazil out three times – in 1986, 1998 and 2006. It was the first time Brazil had not reached the World Cup final since 1990 and their first defeat in the tournament since France had beaten them in the final in 1998.

At the end of the match, Henry, who had been taken off late on, rose from the bench and ran over to find Ronaldinho, his friend and respected adversary. The roles had been reversed not so long ago in Paris at the Champions League final, but now it was Henry whispering words of consolation into the Brazilian's ear. They embraced firmly, swapped shirts and then embraced again, this time bare-chested. Henry seemed to be saying that he understood, that it wasn't Ronaldinho's fault but that of those who had failed to let him play his way.

When Brazil doesn't win a World Cup, some excuse or conspiracy theory usually emerges as an explanation. In 1998, Ronaldo's mysterious fit is thought by some to have come as a result of poisoning, while Argentina supposedly spiked water bottles with tranquilisers before offering them to Brazilian players in 1990. This time around, one obvious explanation was much more straightforward: France and Brazil of 2006 were two evenly matched teams and it took an individual, a maestro, to tip the balance between them. Zidane rose to the occasion and played that role – Ronaldinho, who was supposed to be Brazil's man for such occasions, did not. What was less straightforward was why Ronaldinho had shrunken so?

At full-time, he was in no mood for explanations. 'We would have all liked to have done something better to help Brazil. Now is not the time to look for our faults.' But faults would be looked for and the inquest began right away. In terms of tactics, why they had lost to France was no real mystery: switching Ronaldinho's position had failed and resulted only in there being a gaping void between the Brazilian midfield and forward line. With no link-up between the two, France had imposed themselves and made sure Zidane saw plenty of the ball, allowing him to run the show.

Yet this was only half the story: the Brazilian team had been booed once again by their own fans and that boiled down to criticism of their effort levels rather than positional play. Losing was part of the game and had to be dealt with, but what the followers of the *canarinha* objected to was that their team had not gone down fighting. Where there should have been blood, sweat and tears for the honour of the shirt, there seemed only apathy and resignation. Brazil may have had the best players on paper but Germany was a tournament in which the will to win and the shame of defeat were equally as important.

Brazil had arrived in Germany as massive favourites to lift the trophy and acted as if doing so was nothing less than their divine right. Ghana's coach, Dujkovic, talked of Brazil being untouchable in the sense that the referees seemed to be in awe of their reputation, but it was an observation that could be applied to their overall conduct. They carried themselves with a sense of superiority that was bewildering, certainly never justified, and strutted around the pitch like aristocrats, confident that their star status provided them a right of passage through the tournament that didn't have to be earned. This air of supremacy was enough to intimidate opponents of modest ambition (and even officials) but not France, whose players had no notion of an inferiority complex.

This whole concept of operating on a higher plane also manifested itself in their less-than-serious approach, as if Brazil were so good they didn't have to train and prepare as much as everyone else. The tone was set in Switzerland where there seemed an obvious lack of dedication to hard work. Photographs in the Swiss tabloid *Blick* showed several of the players, including Ronaldinho, partying in a hotel. They had been given the evening off after playing a friendly against Lucerne, and everyone needs to wind down once in a while, but hitting the tiles just a few weeks before the World Cup finals is possibly not the behaviour of serious athletes.

Ronaldinho's relationship with French catwalk model Alexandra Parresant began to make headlines during the tournament too and it was said that they were regularly hooking up for a bit of nooky. After the Japan game, the players were given the evening off and all of them except Ronaldinho headed straight out. He claimed that he was tired and began his evening playing video games with members of the hotel staff in the absence of any team-mates, but he was reportedly seen out on the town later that night with his girl, quaffing champagne with other players.

Before the tournament, Ronaldinho told the *Independent* that at the World Cup in 2002, 'I frequently dreamed about football. Football occupied my brain for 24 hours a day during the entire tournament.' In Germany, it was unclear if he was even getting enough sleep, let alone dreaming of football.

Be that as it may, the *Seleção* squad certainly enjoyed the odd social night out before the 2002 World Cup and it didn't seem to do them any harm then – besides, nobody could seriously begrudge Ronaldinho the joys of being young and in love. Such matters only gain attention when results on the pitch are poor and a player's social life becomes the scapegoat. When Ronaldinho the footballer is on song, much praise is heaped on his sense of fun and *joie de vivre*, so it is perhaps unfair to be critical of the same qualities when his form suffers a dip.

Brazil had been poor individually but more so as a unit. Perhaps it was just the natural end of a winning cycle. Much of that Brazilian generation's success had been based on the penetration offered by full-backs Cafu and Roberto Carlos: both players had been in the team for years, so opponents had possibly just figured out how to stop their forward raids. Even more importantly, their bursting down the flanks no longer carried that element of surprise. In fact, in Brazil, attacking with the full-backs had become a cornerstone of any team's offensive tactics rather than an extra dimension. This meant increasingly that the role of the *meia* or wide midfielder had evolved into providing cover for the rampaging full-backs rather than instigating the attack themselves. When Ronaldinho was being asked to act as a decoy and open up spaces for colleagues, the idea was for him to leave the coast clear for Roberto Carlos. All well and good, except for the fact that opponents had learned to neutralise the threat by providing the full-back with added defensive commitments by attacking the spaces he left behind, not to mention that Roberto Carlos was well past his best.

Increasingly, Brazil had come to rely on the counterattack as the only way they could burst forward down the flanks and catch opponents unprepared. However, the World Cup has become a more level playing field over the years and countries are no longer content with simply taking part. Teams that may have been considered minnows in the past now have realistic ambitions of gaining at least a draw from any game and to this end pack many men behind the ball and commit few when going forward. The counterattack is just not a reliable option.

As Ronaldinho himself noted: 'It is hard to play against a team with eight behind the ball, it means fifteen people in a space of fifty metres.' He tried to provide the killer pass but frequently there was simply no way though. Ronaldinho kept on probing but more often than not he would receive the ball, look up and, faced with congested chaos ahead, be forced to abandon anything ambitious and play it short and simple. When he did try to force a decisive pass, it would usually be intercepted and he would be castigated for giving the ball away cheaply.

Of course, Barcelona often face negative opponents too, but Barça spread out and stretch themselves to try to create space. For Barça, Ronaldinho plays further up the field and wide on the left. Naturally, when he gets the ball and looks up there are fewer obstacles ahead and he is able to use his skill and vision to feed the runs of the forwards, assuming there are any, which wasn't always the case for Brazil. If no such pass is on, he can try to dribble, safe in the knowledge that, if it doesn't come off and he loses the ball, there is a long distance and several colleagues between him and his own goal. Meanwhile, his defender faces the opposite dilemma: deep in his own half, he knows that a mistimed challenge could prove critical, either in letting the attacker through on goal or conceding a dangerous free-kick, so trying a tackle becomes a risky business. If Ronaldinho's dribble then proves even half-successful, which in such circumstances is more than likely, he will be far enough up the field to try a shot on goal or commit another defender and thus free up a colleague for a decisive pass.

Parreira always was a conservative tactician – his 1994 World Cup winning team were no exponents of the beautiful game – and in Germany he wasn't alone. Several coaches said with evident pride that they were happy to win ugly, deluding themselves into thinking this somehow made them full of wisdom: they smugly mocked those naive fools who still thought you could play attractive football and win. Yet Parreira missed a trick in confusing conservative football with efficient football: in fact, the most efficient way for Brazil to play would have been in a free-flowing manner. If he was obsessed with defensive cover then he should have realised that the best form of defence is attack. If freedom of movement and irresponsibility brings out the best in your best attacking players, the best attacking players in the world no less, then the most prudent style of football is a style that makes the most of the skill set you have at your disposal.

For most Brazilians, the fault for the 2006 failure lay with the coach. Parreira, it was claimed, with evident nostalgia for the passionate touchline antics of Scolari, was too cold to motivate this group of players and also failed to supply them with the winning formula. Ronaldinho was finally deployed up front against France but he rarely received the ball and by then it was probably too late anyway: his confidence had been wrecked.

Back in Weggis, the warning signs had been there: Ronaldinho laughed and joked around but looked more timid than his usual self. At Barça, he is the main man and enjoys a freedom to be and play as he wishes, but Brazil was not his team and he knew it. Cafu, Roberto Carlos and Ronaldo were the senior figures and, although Ronaldinho was a popular and influential member of the gang, he knew he lagged behind the old guard in the pecking order.

In several matches, Ronaldinho could be seen beckoning for the ball with hand signals. For Barcelona, such demands would always be met but not so for the *Seleção*. In the final minutes of the Ghana game, Cafu burst in on goal and should have squared the ball to Ronaldinho to roll into the open net, but instead elected to take the shot himself and missed. Ronaldinho was furious – Cafu offered a shrugged and not overly regretful apology.

At Barça, Ronaldinho is excused defensive duties but for Brazil he was expected to knuckle down to the benefit of others. Quite apart from the tactical side of the debate, forcing Ronaldinho to do the dirty work undermines his sense of importance to the team. Ronaldinho is a player who performs best when he knows he is the main man. He revels in, practically craves, attention and needs to feel wanted. Against France, he took to the field wearing a black headband with 'R' emblazened at the front. A cry for recognition?

The team was not arranged to play to his strengths yet everyone still expected him to shine as its best player. After each match he tried to explain his role to the media, tried to explain that it was unrealistic to expect him to be running teams ragged. The paradox of bowing to the coach's wishes and moving in other players' shadows, while being criticised elsewhere for not dazzling the watching world with his typical flamboyance, naturally deflated him. He never complained, never obviously sulked, but to expect him to carry his usual cheerfulness was asking too much. Both Cafu and Parreira stated that they wanted him to play with his usual sense of joy, but happiness is not something that can be switched on and off. Ronaldinho could smile and lead the music on the coach trips to the stadium, but he couldn't pretend to himself that he was genuinely his usual cheery self.

Being his usual cheery self is fundamental to Ronaldinho's game. He needs to feel completely at ease with his surrounds to perform at his best. Barça create that environment perfectly: he is considered the leader in the Barça dressing room and his team-mates are prepared to sacrifice themselves for him; the coaching staff know how best to maximise his talent and set Barça's style to suit him; the board banked on him as the spearhead of their new regime; the fans adore, trust and respect him. All these factors mean he can play his own way, he feels perfectly comfortable to try anything without fear of failure.

In Germany, Ronaldinho was poor: he didn't dribble, didn't threaten the goal, mishit passes and at no point assumed the responsibility of leading the team. Brazilians had come to expect more, so he let them down and in doing so added fuel to the fire of the '*joga mais no Barça do que na Seleção*' debate. In fact, a 7.25m tall statue of Ronaldinho was even set alight by disgruntled fans in Chapecó, Santa Catarina, his friend Rodrigo Gral's home town. The sculpture had been made from paper, resin and fibreglass and installed on the main road of the city in Ronaldinho's honour, but was subjected to an arson attack two nights after Brazil crashed out. '*Fogo Bonito*' (Beautiful fire) declared Argentine sports daily *Olé* with evident glee. Artist Kattielly Lanzini replaced the footballer with a model of a chicken's head in protest at the vandals' cowardly action, without considering that a cockerel chicken is the very symbol of the French football team.

For some commentators, Ronaldinho was simply too exhausted, both mentally and physically, after his long and successful season with Barcelona. Others suggested that the *canarinha* weighed on his shoulders, recalling the Olympic fiasco and pointing out that he had never really turned it on for Brazil. Yet comparisons between Ronaldinho's Barça form and his form for the *Seleção* are unfair and not really valid: it is not comparing like with like. Barça were prepared to structure their whole club to suit him, Brazil were not. For Brazil he had to reinvent himself, but perhaps the back-to-back World Player of the Year shouldn't have had to.

Yet all is not lost. Ronaldinho won the World Cup aged 22 and flopped in Germany aged 26. He certainly has another tournament in him and with the passing of the old guard the team will surely be formed around him. Parreira departed the scene soon after Brazil's 2006 exit to be replaced by Dunga, whom Ronaldinho knows extremely well.

In the European summer of 2005, in the absence of Cafu, Roberto Carlos and Ronaldo, Ronaldinho captained Brazil at the Confederations Cup in Germany. The *Seleção* played some breathtaking football to win the competition in style. Film cameras captured the Brazilian dressing room before the final against Argentina. Ronaldinho had all the players and coaches in a giant huddle and gave a rousing and passionate speech. He clearly had everyone's attention and the players nodded in acceptance and appreciation of what he was saying. It ended, 'Everyone respects Brazil but we have to go on earning that respect. We give everything from first minute to last. We'll do a Hail Mary then get out there and give it our all.' They swept Argentina aside 4–1 with Ronaldinho at the hub of everything, scoring the third goal.

'It was almost the perfect tournament,' he would say later. 'I was captain of my country and you could tell that the players had a great unity and spirit. That grew and grew with every game.' That was his team and perhaps the one which should have gone to Germany the following summer too. It didn't, but its possible reassembling bodes well for the World Cup in South Africa in 2010 and for Ronaldinho and his quest to 'win it all again.'

BIBLIOGRAPHY

Notes

Although there has never been a comprehensive biography of Ronaldinho widely published before, three books launched in Catalonia are worthy of a mention. *La Magia de un Crack* was a short authorised biography sold as a promotion via the *Sport* news daily; *Estimat Ronaldinho* was a partly fictional work based on *La Magia de un Crack* and aimed at children; *Amigo Ronaldinho* was an album produced by Ronaldinho's personal assistant at Barcelona and sold through the *El Mundo Deportivo* sports paper. All were useful as references and provided some insight into different parts of his life.

Felipão – A alma do Penta and *Benvingut al Món Real* were both extremely helpful with regard to the 2002 World Cup chapter, the former including Scolari's diary. The latter was also invaluable for the early Barça chapters.

All newspapers listed were useful but especially *Correio do Povo* and *Zero Hora* for Grêmio coverage and early Brazil reporting; *L'Équipe* for PSG; *Jornal do Brasil* for the 2002 World Cup; *El Mundo Deportivo* and *El Mundo* for Barça; *Folha de São Paulo* and *Lance!* for the 2006 World Cup.

Books

Alex Bellos, *Futebol – The Brazilian Way of Life*, Bloomsbury, 2002
Jimmy Burns, *Barça – a People's Passion*, Bloomsbury, 1999
Juan José Castillo, *Amigo Ronaldinho*, Mundo Deportivo, 2005
Toni Frieros, *Ronaldinho, la Magia de un Crack*, Sport, 2004
Jordi Sierra i Fabra, *Estimat Ronaldinho*, Editorial Empúries, 2004

Ruy Carlos Ostermann, *Felipão – A alma do Penta*, Zero Hora Editora Jornalística, 2002

Sandro Rosell, *Benvingut al Món Real*, Ediciones Destino, 2006

Specific press/online articles in chronological order

'O duro país dos Ronaldinhos', Alfredo Ogawa, *Placar*, No. 1154, August 1999

'20 Perguntas para Ronaldinho Gaúcho', Dalila Magarian, *Playboy*, April 2000

'Aquele Abraço', Jáder de Rocha, *Placar*, No. 1198, September 2001,

'Entrevista Ronaldinho Gaúcho', Ruth de Aquino, *Playboy*, November 2002

'A Lei Pelé e a modernização conservadora no futebol brasileiro', Francisco Xavier Freire Rodrigues, cidadedofutebol.uol.com.br

'The golden child', Michael Kessler, the *Guardian*, 7 March 2005

'Homage from Catalonia', Justin Webster, the *Observer*, 5 June 2005

'La Saudade n'est plus ce qu'elle était...', Valérie Paillé & Rico Rizzitelli, and

'Ronaldinho – Corps Impatient', Franck Annese & Alexandre Gonzalez, *So Foot*, No. 24, July/August 2005

'Eles querem o seu milhão', Erik Farina, *Amanha*, August 2005

'A lei do jogo', Maurício Cardoso interviews Carlos Miguel Aidar, *Consultor Juridico*, 16 October 2005

'Irmão contra hermano', Arnaldo Ribeiro & Elias Perugino, *Placar*, No. 1290, January 2006

'O melhor guri do mundo', Luiz Antônio Prósperi, *Jornal da Tarde*, Grupo Estado, 5 April 2006

'Morte do pai transforma família em time para lidar come prestigio', Rodrigo Bertoletto, *UOL*, May 2006

'Pão, circo e grana', Paula Pacheco, *Carta Capital*, No. 391, 3 May 2006

'Ronaldinho's respect for his team-mates is the key to his success', Tim Vickery, BBC Online, 15 May 2006

'Visions of a star in the making; Bare earth where genius flourished; Perfectionist who can outshine the greatest', Owen Slot, *The Times*, 16 May 2006

'Ronaldinho the boy genius growns into a full-scale marvel', Richard Williams, the *Guardian*, 17 May 2006

'A Winning Smile', Andy Mitten, the *Independent*, June 2006

'El mundo a sus pies/The World at His Feet', Andy Mitten, *24-K*, Issue 003, 2006

Newspapers

Brazil: *Zero Hora, Correio do Povo, Sports News* (of Porto Alegre), *Olá*

Botânico, Jornal do Comércio, Jornal do Brasil, O Globo, Folha de São Paulo, Estado de São Paulo, O Dia, Diario Catarinense, Lance!
France: *L'Équipe, Le Parisien, Le Figaro*
Spain/Catalonia: *El Mundo Deportivo, Sport, El Mundo, El País, Marca, As*
UK: *The Times, Guardian, Independent, Sun*

Magazines

Brazil: *Placar, Goool, Época, IstoÉ, Veja, Playboy*
France: *France Football, So Foot*
Spain: *24K*
UK: *FourFourTwo*

Films

Barca: the Inside Story, directed by Daniel Hernández & Justin Webster, JWP/ALEAE TV production for BBC
Ronaldinho, la Sonrisa del Fútbol, directed by Juan Carlos Crespo & Víctor Catalán, co-produced by Sogecable and BSM
L'Afecte (Efecte) Ronaldinho, directed by Joan R. Anguera & Lluís Canut, TV3

Websites

www.fifa.com
www.uefa.com
www.conmebol.com
www.fgf.terra.com.br
www.portoalegre.rs.gov.br/prefeituradePortoAlegre
www.sambafoot.com
'Que fim levou' at www.miltonneves.uol.com.br
Ronaldinho's blog at www. worldcup-br.spaces.live.com
Archive at www.psg.fr

CAREER CHRONOLOGY

Born: 21 March 1980, Porto Alegre, Rio Grande do Sul, Brazil

Grêmio

1987: Joins the Grêmio Escolinha

Honours with Grêmio Juniors:
1995 and '96 Junior state champions
1995, '96 and '97 Romeu Jacques Santiago tournament winners
1996 Brazil Under-16 national champions

For Grêmio senior side:
Official professional debut: 18 January 1998, Grêmio v Ortopé, Canela, RS
Last appearance: 31 January 2001, America MG v Grêmio

Honours:
1999 Copa Sul winners
1999 Gaúcho State Champions

Statistics:
1998: 48 games, 7 goals
1999: 47 games, 21 goals
2000: 42 games, 38 goals
2001: 3 games, 2 goals

Paris Saint-Germain

Official debut: 4 August 2001, Auxerre v PSG
Last appearance: 31 May 2003, Auxerre v PSG, French Cup final

Statistics: League and Europe
2001–02 season: 34 games, 11 goals
2002–03: 31 games, 9 goals

FC Barcelona

Debut: 27 July 2003, Barcelona v Juventus, Boston

Honours:
2003 Copa Catalunya winners
2004 Copa Catalunya winners
2004–05 La Liga champions
2005 Super Copa winners
2005–06 La Liga champions
2005–06 Champions League winners

Statistics: League and Europe
2003–04 season: 39 games, 19 goals
2004–05: 42 games, 13 goals
2005–06: 41 games, 24 goals

Brazil

Seleção debut: 7 March 1995, Under-15 International, Scotland v Brazil, Hampden Park, Glasgow, Scotland

Junior Honours:
1997 Under-17 South America champions
1997 Under-17 World Cup winners

Seleção senior debut: 26 June 1999, Brazil v Latvia, Curitiba, Brazil

Honours:
1999 Copa América champions
2000 South America Pre-Olympic Tournament winners
2002 World Cup winners

2005 Confederations Cup winners

Statistics:
Played 72 games (3 non-official), 29 goals (2 non-official)

Individual Honours

1999 Gaúcho State Championship top scorer
1999 Confederations Cup Player of the Tournament
1999 Confederations Cup top scorer
2000 *Placar* Silver Ball
2002 Oscar du Foot
2004 EFE La Liga South American Player of the Season
2004 Fifa World Player of the Year
2005 Fifa World Player of the Year
2005 European Player of the Year (*Ballon d'Or*)

All data accurate at 31 July 2006. Grêmio statistics from the Grêmio memorial archive; PSG from *L'Équipe*; FC Barcelona from *El Mundo*; Brazil from *Folha de São Paulo*.

INDEX